Parallel Curriculum Units for
Science
Grades 6–12

Jann H. Leppien | Jeanne H. Purcell
EDITORS

CORWIN
A SAGE Company

D1224261

CORWIN
A SAGE Company

FOR INFORMATION:

Corwin
A SAGE Company
2455 Teller Road
Thousand Oaks, California 91320
(800) 233-9936
Fax: (800) 417-2466
www.corwin.com

SAGE Ltd.
1 Oliver's Yard
55 City Road
London EC1Y 1SP
United Kingdom

SAGE Pvt. Ltd.
B 1/I 1 Mohan Cooperative Industrial Area
Mathura Road, New Delhi 110 044
India

SAGE Asia-Pacific Pte. Ltd.
33 Pekin Street #02-01
Far East Square
Singapore 048763

Acquisitions Editor: Jessica Allan
Associate Editor: Allison Scott
Editorial Assistant: Lisa Whitney
Production Editor: Veronica Stapleton
Copy Editor: Amy Rosenstein
Typesetter: C&M Digitals (P) Ltd.
Proofreader: Dennis W. Webb
Indexer: Molly Hall
Cover Designer: Rose Storey
Permissions Editor: Karen Ehrmann

Printed in the United States of America

Library of Congress Cataloging-in-Publication Data

Parallel curriculum units for science, grades 6-12 / editors, Jann H. Leppien, Jeanne H. Purcell.

p. cm.
Includes bibliographical references and index.

ISBN 978-1-4129-6542-2 (pbk. : alk. paper)

1. Science—Study and teaching (Middle school)
2. Science—Study and teaching (Secondary) I. Leppien, Jann H. II. Purcell, Jeanne H. III. Title.

LB1585.P365 2011 372.35'044—dc22 2010051775

This book is printed on acid-free paper.

11 12 13 14 15 10 9 8 7 6 5 4 3 2 1

Parallel Curriculum Units for Science

Grades 6–12

Contents

About the Editors   vii

About the Contributors   ix

Introduction   1

1. **Genetics: Our Past, Present, and Future:**
   A Middle School Unit for Grades 6–8   11
   Lindsey Asbury
   Introduction to the Unit   11
   Background to the Unit   11
   Content Framework   12
   Unit Components and Rationale   14
   Unit Sequence, Description, and Teacher Reflection   15
       Lesson 1.1: Preassessment and Unit Introduction
          (Dominant and Recessive Genes)   15
       Lesson 1.2: Punnett Squares and Predicting Heredity   19
       Lesson 1.3: DNA   24
       Lesson 1.4: DNA Extraction Lab   27
       Lesson 1.5: DNA Fingerprinting and Crime Lab Investigations   30
       Lesson 1.6: Genetics and European History   33
       Lesson 1.7: Genetics in Practice   36
   Unit 1 Appendixes   41

2. **The Exxon Valdez Oil Spill: What's At Stake?**
   The Convergence of Science and Society, Grade 6   63
   Julie Martinek
   Introduction to the Unit   63
   Background to the Unit   64
   Content Framework   65
   Unit Assessments   69
   Unit Sequence, Description, and Teacher Reflection   69
       Lesson 2.1: Pretest: The Cause-and-Effect Relationship
          Within a System   69
       Lesson 2.2: Introduction to the Exxon Valdez Problem   72
       Lesson 2.3: Setting Up the Stakeholders' Research Activities   76
       Lesson 2.4: Prioritizing the Sites and Constructing
          a Persuasive Argument/Essay   82
   Unit 2 Appendixes   89

3. **Systems: An Integrated Approach to Science and English Instruction, Grades 9–10**   107

Kristina J. Doubet, PhD

Introduction to the Unit   107
Background to the Unit   109
Content Framework   109
Lesson/Unit Assessments   112
Lesson Sequence and Teacher Reflection   114
    Lesson 3.1: An Introduction to Systems   114
    Lesson 3.2 (English): *The Pearl*, Part 1 (Chapters 1–3)   122
    Lesson 3.3 (Science): Introducing Cell Structure   129
    Lesson 3.4 (English): *The Pearl*, Part 2 (Chapters 4–6)   134
    Lesson 3.5 (Science): Movement in Cells   140
Unit 3 Appendixes   147

4. **The Periodic Table: Getting to Know and Appreciate the Elements and Their Families, Grade 10**   173

Fie Budzinsky

Background to the Unit   173
Content Framework   174
Overview of Key Lesson Ideas/Purposes   177
    Lesson 4.1: The Elements: Getting to Know You   178
    Lesson 4.2: The Elements: Up Close and Personal   182
    Lesson 4.3: We Are Family!   186
    Lesson 4.4: The Elements in Action   194
    Lesson 4.5: Breaking News   200
Unit 4 Appendixes   207

Online Resources Included

Additional materials and resources related to
Parallel Curriculum Units for Science, Grades 6–12
can be found at www.corwin.com/sciencecurriculum

About the Editors

Jann H. Leppien is an associate professor at the University of Great Falls in Great Falls, Montana, where she teaches course work in curriculum and instruction, gifted education, assessment and learning, educational research, and methods in social sciences. In addition, she teaches curriculum courses and thinking-skills courses online and in the Three Summers Program at the University of Connecticut. Before joining the faculty at the University of Great Falls, she worked as a research assistant for the National Research Center on the Gifted and Talented (NRC/GT). She has been a classroom teacher, enrichment specialist, and coordinator of a gifted education program in Montana. She is the coauthor of *The Multiple Menu Model: A Practical Guide for Developing Differentiated Curriculum* and *The Parallel Curriculum: A Design to Develop High Potential and Challenge High-Ability Students.* She conducts workshops for teachers in the areas of differentiated instruction, curriculum design and assessment, thinking skills, and program development.

Jeanne H. Purcell provides leadership for Advanced Placement and gifted and talented education at the Connecticut State Department of Education. Prior to her work at the State Department of Education, she was an administrator for Rocky Hill Public Schools, where she was a K–8 curriculum coordinator and conducted a 3-year staff development initiative on curriculum differentiation; a program specialist with NRC/GT, where she worked collaboratively with other researchers on national issues related to the achievement of high-achieving young people; and a staff developer to school districts across the United States and Canada. She was an English teacher, Grades 7–12, for 18 years in Connecticut school districts. She is the author of five books and has published many articles that have appeared in *Educational Leadership, Educational and Psychological Measurement, National Association of Secondary School Principals' Bulletin, Our Children: The National PTA Magazine, Gifted Child Quarterly, Parenting for High Potential,* and the *Journal for the Education of the Gifted.* Her special interests include curriculum and instruction, with a particular interest in differentiation for all learners.

About the Contributors

Lindsey Asbury is Gifted and Talented teacher in Fayetteville, Arkansas, where she currently teaches eighth and ninth graders. She earned her undergraduate degree from Southern Nazarene University in 2004 and completed her master's degree in Special Education with an emphasis in Gifted Education at the University of Arkansas, Fayetteville in May of 2009. She loves teaching and learning as well as traveling around the world. Before becoming a gifted and talented teacher, she taught eighth-grade math and science for 4 years.

Fie Budzinsky received her chemistry degree in 1971 from the University of Connecticut. She earned her master's degree in chemical oceanography. She taught chemistry for 24 years and earned a Sixth Year degree in Administration during that time. Later she received her PhD from the University of Connecticut in curriculum and instruction. Currently, she is the Director of Curriculum, Instruction and Technology for Portland Public Schools in Connecticut. Teaching is still her passion, and she spends as much time as possible working with teachers in two areas—the use of technology to enhance educational opportunities and the differentiation of instruction to address the diverse learning needs of students.

Kristina J. Doubet, PhD, is an Assistant Professor of Middle and Secondary Education at James Madison University in Harrisonburg, Virginia. With more than 10 years of experience teaching at the middle and secondary levels, she now prepares future middle and high school teachers for careers in the classroom. Kristina completed her MEd and PhD in Curriculum and Instruction at the University of Virginia, where she studied the impact of differentiated instruction on student performance in elementary, middle, and high school classrooms. Her current research, consultancies, and publications also focus on differentiated instruction as well as on assessment and curriculum design. Kristina works regularly with practicing teachers from all grade levels as a staff developer for schools and districts implementing differentiated instruction.

Julie Martinek is a sixth-grade teacher and in her fifth year at Sky Vista Middle School in Cherry Creek School District, Aurora, Colorado. She is the chair of the science department for Grades 6–8. She has a bachelor's degree in Evolutionary Biology and currently is completing her master's degree in educational leadership. Prior to teaching, she worked for the Girl Scouts of the Mile Hi Council in Denver, Colorado, as a program development coordinator to organize and facilitate residential camps. Her interests include outdoor activities, philosophy, photography, music, and conducting research in arctic ecology with the Inuit tribes in Alaska.

Introduction

A BRIEF HISTORY OF THE PARALLEL CURRICULUM MODEL

When *The Parallel Curriculum: A Design to Develop High Potential and Challenge High-Ability Learners* (Tomlinson, Kaplan, Renzulli, et al., 2002)[1] was published, the six of us who authored the work knew we had found ideas in the model to be interesting, challenging, and worthy of a great deal more thought and articulation. Since the original book's publication more than 6 years ago, we have spent a great deal of time talking among ourselves and with other practitioners about the Parallel Curriculum Model (PCM). These colleagues were as passionate as we were about the nature of high-quality curriculum and the increasing need for such learning experiences for all students. Our colleagues offered us invaluable viewpoints, opinions, suggestions, and probing questions. We surely benefitted in countless ways from their expertise and insights.

Our conversations led to the publication of two new books about PCM in 2006. *The Parallel Curriculum in the Classroom, Book 1: Essays for Application Across the Content Areas, K–12* featured articles that we hope clarified and expanded upon selected aspects of the model. We continue to hope that it helps educators think more deeply about important facets of the model and some of its nonnegotiable components.

The Parallel Curriculum in the Classroom, Book 2: Units for Application Across the Content Areas, K–12 invited readers to consider eight curriculum units that were designed using PCM. As we compiled the units, we sought to answer the question, "What is necessary in the design process of any Parallel Curriculum unit?"

We did not consider these units as off-the-shelf selections that a teacher might pick up and teach. Rather, we viewed the eight units as professional development tools helpful to any educator who wanted to reflect on one way of creating thoughtful curriculum.

Over the last 2 years, we continued to engage in conversations about the nature of curriculum models and how they can be used to create rigorous learning opportunities for students. As before, these conversations ultimately led us to two additional projects. The first was to create an updated version of the original publication. This second edition of PCM was completed in spring 2008 and is called *The Parallel Curriculum: A Design to Develop Learner Potential and Challenge Advanced Learners*

---

[1]Tomlinson, C. A., Kaplan, S. N., Renzulli, J. S., Purcell, J. H., Leppien, J. H., & Burns, D. E. (2002). *The parallel curriculum: A design to develop high potential and challenge high-ability learners.* Thousand Oaks, CA: Corwin.

(Tomlinson et al., 2008)[2]. The second edition of PCM extends our understanding of how this framework for curriculum development can be used to create, revise, or adapt curriculum to the needs of all students. In addition, it explores the concept of Ascending Intellectual Demand for all learners in today's heterogeneous classrooms.

The second project was the creation of a series of curriculum units, based on PCM, that could be used by practitioners. To address the varying needs of teachers across the K–12 grade span—as well as different content areas—we decided to create a series of five publications. The first publication is dedicated to the elementary grades, K–5. It features lessons and curriculum units that have been designed to address the needs of primary and elementary learners.

The last four publications span the secondary grades, 6–12. Each of the four publications focuses on a different content area: English/Language Arts, Social Studies/History, Science, and Mathematics. It is our hope that the lessons in each not only underscore important and discipline-specific content, but also illuminate the four parallels in unique and enduring ways.

We could not have completed these tasks without the invaluable assistance of two new team members. Cindy Strickland contributed to both publications in 2006, and she also created *The Parallel Curriculum, Second Edition: A Multimedia Kit for Professional Development*. Marcia Imbeau is also a long-time user and trainer in PCM. She contributed her editing talents to the K–5 book in this series.

THE PARALLEL CURRICULUM MODEL: A BRIEF OVERVIEW

A wonderfully illuminating fable exists about seven blind men who encountered an elephant. Because each man felt a different part of the beast, none was able to figure out the true nature of the gigantic creature.

Did you ever stop to think that students' perceptions about their learning experiences might be as limited as the perceptions the blind men had about the nature of the elephant? Perhaps, like the blind men, students learn only bits and pieces of the curriculum over time, never seeing, let alone understanding, the larger whole that is mankind's accumulated knowledge.

What if we were able to design curriculum in a multifaceted way to ensure that all learners understand the following: (1) the nature of knowledge; (2) the connections that link humankind's knowledge; (3) the methodology of the practitioner who creates knowledge; and (4) the fit between the learner's values and goals and those that characterize practicing professionals? How would classrooms be different if the focus of curriculum was *qualitatively differentiated curriculum* that prompts learners not only to accumulate information, but also to experience the power of knowledge and their potential role within it?

PCM suggests that all learners should have the opportunity to experience the elephant and benefit from *seeing the whole*. Moreover, as students become more

---

[2]Tomlinson, C. A., Kaplan, S. N., Renzulli, J. S., Purcell, J. H., Leppien, J. H. Burns, D. E., Strickland, C. A., & Imbeau, M. B. (2008). *The parallel curriculum: A design to develop learner potential and challenge advanced learners.* Thousand Oaks, CA: Corwin.

expert in their understanding of all the facets of knowledge, the curriculum should support students' developing expertise through ascending levels of intellectual demand. This overview of PCM will provide readers with a very brief summary of the model and an opportunity to see how the sum of the model's component parts can be used to create qualitatively differentiated curriculum for *all* students.

THE PARALLEL CURRICULUM: A UNIQUE CURRICULUM MODEL

What is a curriculum model? Why are there so many models to choose from? A curriculum model is a format for curriculum design developed to meet unique needs, contexts, goals, and purposes. To address specific goals and purposes, curriculum developers design or reconfigure one or more curriculum components (see Figure 0.1) to create their models. PCM is unique because it is a set of four interrelated, yet parallel, designs for organizing curriculum: Core, Connections, Practice, and Identity.

Figure 0.1 Key Curriculum Components

Curriculum Component	Definition
Content	The knowledge, essential understandings, and skills students are to acquire
Assessment	Tools used to determine the extent to which students have acquired the content
Introduction	A precursor or foreword to a lesson or unit
Teaching Methods	Methods teachers use to introduce, explain, model, guide, or assess learning
Learning Activities	Cognitive experiences that help students acquire, rehearse, store, transfer, and apply new knowledge and skills
Grouping Strategies	The arrangement of students
Resources	Materials that support learning and teaching
Products	Performances or work samples that constitute evidence of student learning
Extension Activities	Enrichment experiences that emerge from representative topics and students' interests
Differentiation Based on Learner Need, Including Ascending Levels of Intellectual Demand	Curriculum modifications that attend to students' need for escalating levels of knowledge, skills, and understanding
Lesson and Unit Closure	Reflection on the lesson to ensure that the point of the learning experience was achieved or a connection to the unit's learning goal was made

THE FOUR CURRICULUM PARALLELS

Let's look at these parallel designs through the eyes of Lydia Janis, a Grade 5 teacher who develops expertise in using the four parallels over several years. We will focus on one curriculum unit, Lydia's Civil War unit, to illuminate how it changes, or transforms, to accommodate the goals and purposes of each parallel. For the sake of our discussion, we treat each parallel as a separate unit. In reality, teachers use the parallels fluidly to address students' talent development needs. At the end of this summary, we will speak directly to when and how these parallels are used. Readers wishing for a more detailed analysis of Lydia's work are referred to Chapters 4 through 7 in both editions of *The Parallel Curriculum Model*.

The Core Curriculum

Lydia Janis sat at her kitchen table and looked over her textbook objectives for the Civil War unit as well as her state frameworks. She was troubled. She realized that the textbook objectives were low level; they simply called for students to identify and describe facts, such as "Describe how the Civil War began," and "Identify the differences between the North and South." Her frameworks, conversely, required different kinds of knowledge and understandings: "Explain reasons for conflicts and the ways conflicts have been resolved in history," and "Understand causal factors and appreciate change over time."

Lydia realized that the content embedded in her frameworks—concepts and principles—lay at the heart of history as a discipline. These key understandings were vastly more powerful, enduring, and essential to the discipline than the facts in the textbook objectives. She decided to keep her textbook and use it as a resource, however. After all, the information was right there on her shelf, she was familiar with the contents, and the topics covered were fairly well aligned with her state frameworks. But Lydia decided to replace the more simplistic objectives found in the text with the objectives found in the state frameworks.

Lydia realized that the change in *content* would necessitate changes in other curriculum components. Her *assessments* would need to match the content. Her assessment tools would need to measure—both pre and post—students' conceptual understanding in addition to basic facts about the time period. Her *introduction* would need to be retooled to prepare students for the various roles they would assume during the unit as analyzers of documents, data, maps, and events, and to lead them to the powerful understandings she had targeted.

Lydia's *teaching methods* would no longer be strictly didactic, such as lecture and direct instruction, but more inductive to support students as they constructed their own understanding of the time period. Her *learning activities* invited students to think about and draw conclusions about maps, documents, and related data. She supplemented the textbook with other *resources*, such as primary source documents, college textbooks, and the video series *The Civil War*. She imagined that she would have students who wanted to pursue *extension activities*. She gathered a few books about the Underground Railroad, Abraham Lincoln, and strategic battles. Finally, because she knew already that her students were at different stages in their ability to understand materials and content, she gathered print materials that varied in complexity from song lyrics and easy-to-decipher documents to several "dense" primary source documents so that *all* students could work at *ascending levels of intellectual demand*.

Lydia also altered the *products* that students created. In a variety of *grouping* arrangements, they completed document-analysis worksheets, ongoing concept maps, and time lines to chronicle their deepening understandings about conflict and the causal relationships of events that led up to the Civil War.

Lydia reflected on her work. She had made significant changes to her teaching and student learning, and she was confident in her improvements. She felt the power of the Core Curriculum as a foundational curriculum.

The Curriculum of Connections

Later in Lydia's career, she became aware of initiatives for interdisciplinary teaching. She was puzzled by some of the units that were labeled "interdisciplinary." A unit on Mexico, completed recently by fourth graders, came to mind. Students learned and performed the "Mexican Hat Dance," held a fiesta during which they broke a piñata and ate tacos, viewed a display of Mexican money, and drew maps of the migration route of monarch butterflies. "Yikes," she thought to herself, "this unit is an illusion. It *looks* integrated, but it lacks a powerful theme to tie the activities together!"

Lydia sat looking at the Core Curriculum unit on the Civil War that she had created a few years ago. She thought about the concept that earlier had focused her work: conflict. It reminded her that history repeats itself across people, time periods, and cultures: the Vietnam War, women's suffrage, the Civil Rights movement, and the civil war in Bosnia. This principle, "history repeats itself," held so much power. She realized that she could use the macroconcept, conflict, and the generalization, "history repeats itself," as the content centerpiece to help students build authentic and powerful *bridges* between their understanding of the American Civil War and other times, events, cultures, and people.

Lydia made preliminary plans for her Curriculum of Connections unit. She prepared some assessment prompts, with accompanying rubrics, to assess students' understanding of conflict and the idea that "history repeats itself." She developed a preassessment and essential questions for the introduction to clarify the focus for this unit: "What is a war? Do all conflicts have a resolution? Does history repeat itself?" She knew that her teaching strategies would need to help students make their own *bridges* for the connections among the American Civil war and other events and time periods. She decided to emphasize synectics, metaphoric thinking, Socratic questioning, problem-based learning, and debriefing. Her learning activities emphasized analytic thinking skills to help students in the comparisons and contrasts they needed to make and to encourage analogy making. Her supplemental resources were more varied and covered more events, cultures, and time periods than the resources she had used in her old Core unit, and the materials that she developed to scaffold student thinking included many more graphic organizers, such as Venn diagrams and reader-response questions. She was pleased when she realized that the products, grouping strategies, and extension activities would remain similar to those she had used in the Core Curriculum.

For students needing support with this unit, she developed more detailed graphic organizers; for those needing increasing levels of ascending intellectual demand, she thought of several unfamiliar contexts to which students could apply their new learning, such as the Irish conflict and additional revolutionaries such as Nelson Mandela and Elizabeth Cady Stanton. She tucked away these ideas for later use.

Lydia reflected on the modifications she had made. "This unit will benefit all my students, especially my abstract thinkers, students who value the 'big picture,' and my scholars," she thought. "It holds so much promise . . . much different than the 'Mexican Hat Dance' unit," she mused.

The Curriculum of Practice

That summer, Lydia realized she could polish the same unit even more. Even though she had seen her students engaged and learning deeply about the Civil War, she began thinking more about how talent develops, specifically how students become acquainted with and skillful in the use of methodologies. "Now that students have the important ideas within and across disciplines, they need to learn how to act like a practitioner," she thought to herself.

So began Lydia's journey through the Curriculum of Practice. She sought out her state and national frameworks to identify the standards related to the role of the historian. To address them, she decided to invite students to read historical novels set during the mid-1800s and record the characters' feelings, analyze images, and identify perspectives as well as note how they changed throughout the story. Second, she would deepen students' understandings of these historical perspectives by asking them to read related primary source documents and find evidence to support the characters' feelings and attitudes.

For students to complete these tasks, she decided to focus her teaching on the skills of the historian: the steps of historical research, taking notes, determining bias, and analyzing point of view, to name a few. She decided to demonstrate or model these skills for students and then use more indirect teaching methods, such as Socratic questioning, to help students construct their own analyses of primary source material. To help students focus on the methodology of the field, she decided to invite a local museum curator to take part in the introduction of the unit.

Lydia subsequently decided to scaffold students' work with a learning contract. The learning contract required specific learning activities and also asked students to complete several short-term products as well as a culminating project, their historical research. Lydia provided them with a rubric to guide and assess their final work. Lydia knew her grouping formats needed to be fluid to honor students' interests and to acknowledge that there were times when students needed to work alone or in pairs. This fluidity would be especially important if students elected to complete extension activities around self-selected research questions.

To accommodate students with sophisticated knowledge about the historical research process, Lydia prepared a list of more complex research topics that required ascending levels of intellectual demand, such as inviting advancing students to conduct oral histories on a topic of their choice.

Lydia reviewed the lessons that now reflected the Curriculum of Practice. "Wow," she thought. "So far, I have three ways to optimize learning." Lydia compared and contrasted the three sets of revisions to the Civil War unit: Core, Connections, and Practice. "Each approach is unique and powerful," she thought. And she understood why teaching artful curriculum was a satisfying, career-long journey. "What will I discover next?" she wondered.

The Curriculum of Identity

It was a student who set Lydia on her next journey through the PCM. His name was Jacob, and she was amazed at his knowledge of American history. She envisioned this boy as a history professor, immersed in his own research about historical topics and mentoring others as they investigated questions not yet answered.

She spent time thinking about how she could morph her curriculum once more. The content for any Identity unit has a triple focus: her already rich Core curriculum; the ideas, attitudes, beliefs, dispositions, and life outlooks of a professional; and the learning profile of each student, including his or her interests, learning style preferences, values, and goals. Her task, she thought, would be to increase students' awareness about the degree of *fit* between their own emerging sense of self and the profile of practitioners in the field.

Lydia developed a survey of her students' abilities, interests, grouping preferences, goals, and cocurricular activities. Next, she sketched out the stages that students might go through as they went from an early awareness of and interest in history to self-actualization *through* the discipline. "This tool will help me identify where each student currently is on this continuum so I can support his or her progress," she thought.

Now familiar with the many teaching strategies available, Lydia selected visualization as an important method because students would have to move back and forth between their past self, current self, and future self. She also knew that she would use problem-based learning, simulations, and coaching to help students come to understand their place in the Civil War unit as they acted as historians, authors of historical fiction, or war correspondents.

She envisioned her students in varied grouping formats as they spent time with learning activities that required self-analysis and reflection, prediction, and goal setting, among others. Ideas for products came easily to Lydia: completed learning profiles, prompts that asked students to reflect upon and note patterns in their changing profiles, and prompts that invited students to reflect upon the fit between themselves and those of the guest speakers (i.e., a local historian and journalist), who would take part in the introduction to the unit.

Lydia anticipated several extension activities including explorations about notable leaders from the 1860s, as well as less well-known figures, such as the girls who dressed and fought as soldiers during the Civil War. As she gathered resources to support this unit and its potential extensions, she made sure that her collection featured a variety of introspective materials that would help students understand the beliefs, values, goals, achievements, and sacrifices made by practitioners and enable students' comparisons between their own emerging beliefs and attitudes and those of the professionals.

Lydia reflected on her continuing journey with the Parallel Curriculum Model. Her journey elicited a clarity that comes only with time and persistence. She now understood deeply the model's power and promise. It held the power to awaken and support a teacher's passion and focused creativity. Equally important, it held such promise for uncovering and supporting the gifts and talents of all students.

Lydia imagined each of her students as a diamond (see Figure 0.2). The model's four parallels—Core, Connections, Practice, and Identity—served as unique polishing tools to reveal the brilliance in each young person. The Core fostered deep understanding in a discipline, while Connections elicited the metaphoric thinking required to span the breadth of man's knowledge. Practice advanced the methodologic skills required to contribute in a field, and Identity cultivated the attitudes, values, and life outlook that are prerequisites to self-actualization in a field.

The Four Parallels: When and How

We began this discussion by talking about seven blind men, their limited perceptions about an elephant, and their ultimate realization that "Knowing in part may make a fine tale, but wisdom comes from seeing the whole." Lydia's work with each

Figure 0.2 Lydia's View of the PCM

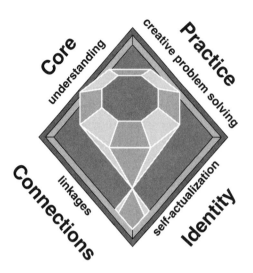

Reprinted from *Teaching for High Potential* (Vol. IV, No. 1, April 2002), published by the National Association for Gifted Children, Washington, DC. www.nagc.org

of the parallels illustrates how different curriculum components can be modified to help students gain an understanding and appreciation for the whole of a particular discipline.

An infinite number of ways exist to draw upon the parallels. They can be used to *revise* or *design* tasks, lessons, or units. With a revised or designed unit in hand, a teacher can move back and forth across one, some, or all parallels in a single unit. Equally attractive, a teacher might use just one parallel to extend a Core unit.

Various individuals within a school can use the parallels differently. A classroom teacher can use the parallels separately for different purposes, or teachers can work collectively—within grade levels, across grade levels and subjects—to use the parallels to support the learning for all, some, or a few students. Furthermore, classroom teachers can use the parallels to modify learning opportunities for students who need something beyond the grade-level curriculum.

What is the driving force behind decisions about when and how to use the parallels? Decisions stem from teacher expertise, the learning goals, and, most important, the students themselves. We draw upon the parallels to make curriculum more meaningful, emotive, powerful, engaging, and more likely to advance energetically the abilities and talents of students.

The PCM holds the power to help students and teachers *see the whole* of what they are learning. It is our hope that curriculum based upon this model will optimize student learning and enhance the likelihood that all students will lead productive and fulfilling lives. We invite practitioners to read more about this model and join us on a professional journey that we believe will yield the joy and wisdom that come from seeing the whole. The possibilities are limitless.

THE FORMAT

The curriculum books that are part of our latest initiative share four features that will provide common threads to readers as they transition among the publications. First, each unit contains a section called *Background to the Unit,* which provides readers with a snapshot of the lessons or unit. If a series of lessons is provided—instead of a whole unit of study—the author may suggest ways to incorporate the subset of lessons into a larger unit. The author may also identify the parallel(s) he or she has elected to emphasize and his or her rationale for highlighting the Core Curriculum, the Curriculum of Connections, the Curriculum of Practice, and the Curriculum of Identity. The author may share his or her experiences regarding the best time to teach the unit, such as the beginning of the year or well into the last half of the year. Finally, the author may share what students are expected to know before the unit is taught as well as resources that would support the teaching and learning activities.

The second common element is the *Content Framework.* One of the nonnegotiables of PCM units is that they lead students explicitly to a conceptual understanding of the topics and disciplines on which they are based. Thus, each set of lessons or unit contains a list of concepts, skills, and principles that drive the teaching and learning activities. We also included the national standards addressed in each unit and lesson.

Unit Assessments is the third common element. Within this section, authors have the opportunity to describe the assessments that are included within their lessons. Some authors, especially those who supplied an entire unit of study, included preassessments that align with a performance-based postassessment. All authors have included formative assessments. Naturally, scoring rubrics are included with these assessments. In many cases, authors describe the nature of students' misconception that surface when these performance measures are used as well as some tips on how to address students' mistaken beliefs.

The final common element is the *two-column format* for organizing the lessons. In the left-hand column, authors sequence the instruction in a step-by-step manner. In the right-hand column, readers will hear the author's voice as he or she thinks out loud about the introduction, teaching and learning activities, and closure. Authors provide many different kinds of information in the right-hand column, including, for example, the following: teaching tips, information about student misconceptions, and suggestions on how to differentiate for above-grade-level or below-grade-level students.

OUR INVITATION . . .

We invite you to peruse and implement these curriculum lessons and units. We believe the use of these lessons will be enhanced to the extent that you:

- **Study PCM.** Read the original book as well as other companion volumes, including *The Parallel Curriculum in the Classroom, Book 1: Essays for Application Across the Content Areas, K–1, The Parallel Curriculum in the Classroom, Book 2: Units for Application Across the Content Areas, K–12,* and *The Parallel Curriculum, Second Edition: A Multimedia Kit for Professional Development.* By studying the model in depth, teachers and administrators will have a clear sense of its goals and purposes.

- **Join us on our continuing journey to refine these curriculum units.** We know better than to suggest that these units are scripts for total success in the classroom. They are, at best, our most thoughtful thinking to date. They are solid evidence that we need to persevere. In small collaborative and reflective teams of practitioners, we invite you to field test these units and make your own refinements.
- **Raise questions about curriculum materials.** Provocative, compelling, and pioneering questions about the quality of curriculum material—and their incumbent learning opportunities—are absolutely essential. Persistent and thoughtful questioning will lead us to the development of strenuous learning opportunities that will contribute to our students' lifelong success in the 21st century.
- **Compare the units with material developed using other curriculum models.** Through such comparisons, we are better able to make decisions about the use of the model and its related curriculum materials for addressing the unique needs of diverse learners.

THE SCIENCE BOOK, GRADES 6–12

This volume contains four units and sets of lessons. The first is a Grades 6–8 science unit, *Genetics: Our Past, Present, and Future.* Lindsey Asbury designed this seven-lesson unit to introduce her students to classical genetic concepts, including the structure and function of DNA, Punnett squares and predicting heredity, and dominant and recessive genes while also providing an opportunity for them to examine the cross-disciplinary relationships—how one field may influence the findings in another field of study.

Julie Martinek created the second unit, *The Exxon Valdez Oil Spill: What's At Stake? The Convergence of Science and Society.* It is designed for students in Grade 6 and focuses on how personal, stakeholder, and scientific perspectives shape the decision-making process as they explore the Exxon oil spill disaster. Across the lessons in this unit, Julie provides opportunities for her students to explore how society and science often find themselves in conflict with one another based on the various perspectives each possess.

Kristina Doubet created the third unit, *Systems: An Integrated Approach to Science and English Instruction,* for students in Grades 9–10. The series of four integrated lessons focuses on the Curriculum of Connections, and students are provided with multiple learning opportunities to understand both disciplines through the macroconcept of *systems.* The English instruction is based on the dynamic interaction among Kino, his family, and society in John Steinbeck's *The Pearl.* The complement for this dynamic literary interaction in the science field is the cell and its various structures.

The final unit, by Fie Budzinsky, *The Periodic Table: Getting to Know and Appreciate the Elements and Their Families,* was created for high school sophomores. The five lessons are different from the traditional lessons about the periodic table because these lessons are highly interactive and constructivist. Students are required to explore the principles and concepts in multiple ways: lab explorations, kinesthetic activities, research that requires a deep understanding about the multiple influences that shape scientific understandings, and creative writing. This Core Curriculum unit—if fully implemented—requires about twenty 45-minute periods to complete.

Genetics: Our Past, Present, and Future

A Middle School Unit for Grades 6–8

Lindsey Asbury

INTRODUCTION TO THE UNIT

As a student, I always enjoyed looking at topics in depth and learning about how one field of study connects to another. As I developed this unit, I designed lessons that help students explore how the field of genetics relates to other disciplinary fields. Students are asked to examine not only the core ideas of genetics but also the cross-disciplinary relationships—how one field may influence the findings in another field of study. Without helping students to make these connections, I believe that learning becomes isolated and is more than likely forgotten by the students. While conducting the research for this unit, I learned so much about the field of genetics and all of the implications that genetics has in our everyday lives, from the food we eat, to the sports we watch and participate in, to the connections it has to our family and our sense of well-being. Understanding how genetics plays a role in our past, present, and future helps us to better understand ourselves and those around us.

BACKGROUND TO THE UNIT

This unit focuses on the key concepts of form and function, expression, image, chance, order, and cycles through the window of genetics. It provides students with opportunities to learn the basic concepts of genetics that lead to understanding about heredity, DNA, and genetic diseases. This unit contains three parallels. In the Core Curriculum parallel, students are introduced to classical genetics concepts, including the structure and function of DNA, Punnett squares and predicting heredity, and dominant and recessive genes. The Curriculum of Connections parallel uses the same concepts to connect genetics with forensics and crime fighting as well as history and the royal families of Europe. In the Curriculum of Practice parallel, students get to extract DNA from peas and also conduct in-depth research to understand the work and practices conducted by genetic scientists.

CONTENT FRAMEWORK

Organizing Concepts

Macroconcepts

M1   Form and Function

M2   Expression

M3   Image

M4   Chance

M5   Order

M6   Cycles

M7   Controversy

M8   Change

Principles

P1   Genetics is the science of genes, heredity, and the variation of organisms.

P2   Heredity involves probability and predicting the likelihood of a certain genotype to occur.

P3   Science as a discipline crosses over, affects, and is affected by other disciplinary fields of study, including history, literature, and mathematics.

P4   Outward expression of a characteristic or trait depends on the individual's genes and specific genotype.

P5   An individual's genes play a part in an individual's identity but do not control everything.

Skills

S1   **Answer questions through scientific investigations.** Students should develop the ability to refine and refocus broad and ill-defined questions. An important aspect of this ability consists of students' ability to clarify questions and inquiries and direct them toward objects and phenomena that can be described, explained, or predicted by scientific investigations. Students should develop the ability to identify their questions with scientific ideas, concepts, and quantitative relationships that guide investigation.

S2   **Design and conduct a scientific investigation.** Students should develop general abilities, such as systematic observation, making accurate measurements, and identifying and controlling variables. They should also develop the ability to clarify their ideas that are influencing and guiding the inquiry and to understand how those ideas compare with current scientific knowledge. Students can learn to formulate questions, design investigations, execute investigations, interpret data, use evidence to generate explanations, propose alternative explanations, and critique explanations and procedures.

S3   **Use appropriate tools and techniques to gather, analyze, and interpret data.** The use of tools and techniques, including mathematics, will be guided by the question asked and the investigations students design. The use of computers for the collection, summary, and display of evidence is part of this standard. Students should be able to access, gather, store, retrieve, and organize data, using hardware and software designed for these purposes.

S4   **Develop descriptions, explanations, predictions, and models using evidence.** Students should base their explanation on what they observed, and as they develop cognitive skills, they should be able to differentiate explanation from description—providing causes for effects and establishing relationships based on evidence and logical argument. This standard requires a subject matter knowledge base so the students can effectively conduct investigations, because developing explanations establishes connections between the content of science and the contexts within which students develop new knowledge.

S5   **Think critically and logically to make the relationships between evidence and explanations.** Thinking critically about evidence includes deciding what evidence should be used and accounting for anomalous data. Specifically, students should be able to review data from a simple experiment, summarize the data, and form a logical argument about the cause-and-effect relationships in the experiment. Students should begin to state some explanations in terms of the relationship between two or more variables.

Standards

Life Science Content Standard C (Grades 5–8)

SD1   Every organism requires a set of instructions for specifying its traits. Heredity is the passage of these instructions from one generation to another.

SD2   Hereditary information is contained in genes, located in the chromosomes of each cell. Each gene carries a single unit of information. An inherited trait of an individual can be determined by one or by many genes, and a single gene can influence more than one trait. A human cell contains many thousands of different genes.

SD3   The characteristics of an organism can be described in terms of a combination of traits. Some traits are inherited and others result from interactions with the environment.

SD4   Disease is a breakdown in structures or functions of an organism. Some diseases are the result of intrinsic failures of the system. Others are the result of damage by infection by other organisms.

Life Science Content Standard C (Grades 9–12)

SD5   In all organisms, the instructions for specifying the characteristics of the organism are carried in DNA, a large polymer formed from subunits of four kinds (A, G, C, and T). The chemical and structural properties of DNA explain how the genetic information that underlies heredity is both encoded in genes (as a string of molecular "letters") and replicated (by a templating mechanism). Each DNA molecule in a cell forms a single chromosome.

UNIT COMPONENTS AND RATIONALE

Curriculum Component	*Description*
Content	The understanding of basic and complex components of genetics leads students to a better understanding of themselves and the world in which they live. They examine past discoveries in this field as well as what is currently being researched. They are also encouraged to predict the future implications of the findings in the field of genetics.
Assessments	Preassessments are designed to assess students' prior knowledge. By preassessing, the teacher can know strengths and weaknesses the individual student possesses. Teachers can use this information to add or to modify curricular tasks based on student need. If the preassessment shows students know and understand the concept a teacher plans to teach, changes can be made to the curriculum to eliminate sections of content students already know. If the preassessment shows students have no knowledge in a given area, a teacher can plan to provide all the necessary scaffolding and support to help students achieve success. A variety of assessments, both informal and formal, are obtained through the use of lab experiments, research investigations, case studies, virtual lab activities, and journal entries.
Introductory Activities	Every lesson begins with an introductory activity or questions the students are asked. This is meant to engage the students and provide motivation by sharing what they already know about the content being presented.
Teaching Strategies	The following teaching strategies are used throughout the unit: lecture, direct instruction, strategy-based instruction, assisted instruction in the content areas, graphic organizers, coaching, concept attainment, demonstrations/modeling, Socratic questioning, visualization, role-playing, cooperative learning, case study, simulation, and inquiry-based instruction.

Curriculum Component	Description
Learning Activities	Several different types of learning activities are used throughout the unit. These are designed to help the students learn deeply about critical concepts and acquire understanding of essential principles. Students complete experiments and demonstrations that require them to draw conclusions about the effects of genetics in their daily lives and the world around them.
Products	All products are selected to illustrate students' acquisition of the concepts, principles, and skills learned throughout the unit.
Modifications for All Learners	Ascending Intellectual Demand (AID) is designed specifically for students who need more intense cognitive tasks because they have greater prior knowledge than their peers. AID prompts are written throughout the unit for students who require more challenging tasks.

UNIT SEQUENCE, DESCRIPTION, AND TEACHER REFLECTION

Lesson 1.1: Preassessment and Unit Introduction (Dominant and Recessive Genes)

Time allocation: 1 class session

Concepts

These concepts are overarching and can be associated with many different topics. By focusing on these "Big Ideas" students can gain understanding about more than just the individual topic being studied. Use these ideas to help shape the questions that you pose during class discussions.

M1	Form and Function	M5	Order
M2	Expression	M6	Cycles
M3	Image		

Form and Function   Structures in nature and science have a specific form because of their function. Phenomena have certain forms for a reason. DNA's form for example is a double helix or twisted ladder. Its form allows more information to be coded in a small amount of space.

Expression   Expression plays a role in everything we see and do. Dealing with genetics, genes express certain characteristics based on an individual's genotype. Phenotype is what is actually expressed.

(Continued)

(Continued)

Image	How we see and are seen by the world around us greatly affects our image. Genetics shapes our image. Our genetic makeup determines what we are, but it is our responsibility to determine who we are.
Order	Without order nothing makes sense. By learning about genetics, students can see on a micro and macro level the organization and order of the world of genetics and the world around them.
Cycles	Everything goes through cycles, whether it is the Earth cycling or revolving around the sun approximately every 365 days or the human race creating new generations, or history repeating itself. By learning and studying cycles in relationship with genetics, students can see how genes are passed on from generation to generation.

Principles

P1	Genetics is the science of genes, heredity, and the variation of organisms.
P4	Outward expression of a characteristic or trait depends on the individual's genes and specific genotype.
P5	An individual's genes play a part in an individual's identity but do not control everything about the individual.

Skills

S1	Questions that can be answered through scientific investigations.
S3	Use appropriate tools and techniques to gather, analyze, and interpret data.

Standards

SD1	Every organism requires a set of instructions for specifying its traits. Heredity is the passage of these instructions from one generation to another.
SD3	The characteristics of an organism can be described in terms of a combination of traits. Some traits are inherited, and others result from interactions with the environment.

Guiding Questions

1. What does genetics have to do with me?

2. Do I have any dominant traits? Recessive traits?

3. What things can I inherit?

4. What do dominant and recessive traits have to do with genetics and heredity?

Unit Sequence—Core Curriculum	Teacher Reflections
Preassessment	
Begin the unit by writing the word "Genetics" on the board. Have students brainstorm words and ideas that they know about genetics and organize them into a concept map or web. Students will connect the concepts to one another by writing what relationship exists between each of the concepts.	Students probably will have heard of genes and other general topics related to the study of genetics but will probably not have an understanding of how the individual topics fit together and relate to each other. These concept maps inform me as to which students have some prior knowledge of the field of genetics and will help me to determine who may benefit from AID experiences that I create. If students have trouble with brainstorming topics related to genetics, try to guide their thinking, but do not provide them with answers. Remember, this preassessment is about assessing what students already know. It is possible that some students have no prior knowledge of genetics, while others will be able to tell you what DNA stands for before you even teach them the concept of DNA.
Preparation	
After the pretest, provide each student with a copy of the **Dominant and Recessive Characteristics** and **Genetic Traits and Me** worksheets (see Appendix 1A) that list common dominant and recessive traits that are easily testable. The second worksheet is for students to record their information.	The student worksheets should be prepared prior to instruction. The worksheet provides all students with the same information, and students who struggle with recording information will be provided with the scaffolding that is necessary for their academic success.
Teaching Strategies and Learning Experiences	
Introductory Activity Pose the following question to students, "If you were asked to describe yourself to a stranger so she could recognize you at a school event, what would you say? What traits make you unique and different from others?" Next introduce students to the concepts of form and function, image, and expression. Write two words on the board, "Dominant" and "Recessive." As a class, brainstorm how these concepts associate with the words dominant and recessive. Tell students that today they are going to discover if they express any dominant or recessive traits. Pass out the **Dominant and Recessive Characteristics** worksheet (see Appendix 1A), which lists traits, and have them identify which trait they express. After they complete the sheet,	Understanding dominant and recessive traits provides the conceptual foundation for understanding heredity and how genes are passed down from one generation to the next. Starting instruction with an understanding of dominant and recessive traits enables the teacher to use these words throughout the remainder of the unit and to be assured that the students understand their meaning. Also, an understanding of dominant and recessive traits leads to predicting heredity and using Punnett squares taught in an upcoming lesson. Genetics studies how living organisms inherit many of the features of their ancestors—for example, children usually look and act like other people in their family. Genetics tries to identify which features are inherited and work

(Continued)

Unit Sequence—Core Curriculum	Teacher Reflections
have students identify which traits they express are dominant and which traits they express are recessive (Appendix 1A). Tell students that all people express traits that they have inherited from their parents. Have the students write down the word "inherit" and give them the definition. Ask them what other things can they inherit? Tell the students that their traits will also be passed down to their children, and the cycle will continue.	out the details of how these features are passed from generation to generation. A trait is a characteristic or property of an organism that may be inherited, environmentally determined, or somewhere in between. Some traits are features of an organism's physical appearance, such as eye color, height, or weight. There are other types of traits that range from aspects of behavior to resistance to disease. Traits are often inherited; for example, tall and thin people tend to have tall and thin children. Other traits come from the interaction between inherited features and the environment. For example, a child might inherit the tendency to be tall, but if there is very little food where he lives and he is poorly nourished, he will still be short. The way genetics and environment interact to produce traits can be complicated: for example, the chances of somebody dying of cancer or heart disease seem to depend on both family history and lifestyle.
Closure	
Conclude the lesson by projecting a family picture of yourself on a screen. Ask students which traits they see that are similar between all the people in the picture and which traits are different. **Homework** Ask students to bring a picture of their family to school tomorrow that can be used for further student exploration in the next lesson. Also ask students to bring information back to class regarding facial features of their parents. The data they will be gathering are the four physical features: earlobe attachment, nose shape, hair type, and the ability to roll one's tongue. In addition, have them gather information on their parents' hair and eye color. To record their data, they can use the worksheets that are provided at the following website: *The Science Behind Family Portraits* and produced by the DNA Diagnostics Center (http://www.dnacenter .com/science-technology/dna-education/ family-portraits.html).	I will show a picture of my family. I have a large family and it is always fun to be able to connect with the students by showing them that their teacher is also a regular person with a family just like themselves. My family is unique because of its large size and because I have triplet sisters. Students can look at the picture and see similarities in the faces of all seven of my brothers and sisters, but also see that each one of us is uniquely different. These concepts of image and expression of traits will continue to be brought up and discussed throughout the unit.

Unit Sequence—Core Curriculum	Teacher Reflections
Close the lesson by discussing the goals of this unit, provide an overview of the types of learning experiences they will encounter in this unit, and the types of questions they will ask and seek to answer. Some questions to pose to students may include the following: • What does genetics have to do with me? • How does genetics affect the world around me? • How do scientists study genetics?	Discussing with students the overview of the unit provides a scaffold for their upcoming work and creates a sense of interest prior to instruction. If they are excited about what they are doing, they will learn more in the process.

Lesson 1.2: Punnett Squares and Predicting Heredity

Time allocation: 2–3 class sessions

Concepts

M1	Form and Function	M4	Chance
M2	Expression	M5	Order
M3	Image	M6	Cycles

Principles

P1   Genetics is the science of genes, heredity, and the variation of organisms.

P2   Heredity involves probability and predicting the likelihood of a certain genotype to occur.

P4   Outward expression of a characteristic or trait depends on the individual's genes and specific genotype.

P5   An individual's genes play a part in an individual's identity but do not control everything about the individual.

Skills

S1   Questions that can be answered through scientific investigations.

S2   Design and conduct a scientific investigation.

S3   Use appropriate tools and techniques to gather, analyze, and interpret data.

S4   Develop descriptions, explanations, predictions, and models using evidence.

S5   Think critically and logically to make the relationships between evidence and explanations.

(Continued)

(Continued)

Standards

SD1 Every organism requires a set of instructions for specifying its traits. Heredity is the passage of these instructions from one generation to another.

SD2 Hereditary information is contained in genes, located in the chromosomes of each cell. Each gene carries a single unit of information. An inherited trait of an individual can be determined by one or by many genes, and a single gene can influence more than one trait. A human cell contains many thousands of different genes.

SD3 The characteristics of an organism can be described in terms of a combination of traits. Some traits are inherited, and others result from interactions with the environment.

Guiding Questions

Students will learn the basics of predicting heredity and how traits are passed on to offspring. They learn how to use and implement the key terms genotype, phenotype, heterozygous, homozygous, parent generation, F1 generation, allele, and Punnett squares to predict probabilities of the F1 generation having a certain trait. They will create and use Punnett squares to predict the traits of offspring. They will realize that a large amount of heredity is left up to chance.

1. What does genetics have to do with me?
2. Why are some traits expressed and others not?
3. How can we predict heredity and why is it important?

Unit Sequence—Curriculum of Connections	Teacher Reflections
Preparation	
In advance, prepare a student worksheet with information about gene expression and include key terms and important information involved in predicting inheritance. Use the **Talking Points and Examples** (Appendix 1B) to guide your discussion with your students. **Key Terms** • Punnett square • Genotype • Phenotype • Heterozygous • Homozygous • Parent generation • F1 generation • Allele	Introducing the vocabulary in genetics is necessary so that students can discuss the relationship between these various words, their functions, and purposes. The vocabulary can be introduced prior to this lesson or within the context of the lesson. The **Visual Organizer for Key Terms** (Appendix 1C) that I use is called the Frayer model, which is a type of graphic organizer that helps students develop relationships and categories associated with vocabulary. Students use the graphic to explain and elaborate their understandings of a concept, work, or issue. I vary the version of the chart based on the headings that are best suited for the concept or word. Students use the Internet or other

Unit Sequence—Curriculum of Connections	Teacher Reflections
	sources of text to help define the words as they work in small groups or as we discuss these concepts or vocabulary in class. This format can also be recorded on chart paper and then posted on a word wall in your classroom for future use.

Teaching Strategies and Learning Experiences

Introduction for Predicting Pose the following question to students: How can we predict what traits we will pass on to our offspring? Using their ideas, students examine the picture they brought from home. On a sheet of paper, have them list traits that they have that are similar to and traits that are different from their parents. Ask them why they look different and why they look similar to their parents and siblings. To enhance this discussion, use the noninteractive activity called The Science Behind Family Portraits produced by the DNA Diagnostics Center and located at this website: (http://www .dnacenter.com/science-technology/ dna-education/family-portraits.html). Hand out the worksheets that are available at this site while you project the interactive on a whiteboard for students to engage with as they create their individual portraits. Students will then create their portraits using the information that they gathered and how their facial features compare with their biological parents'. Provide students will large portraiture paper to enlarge their images.	By having students look at their own family, it brings a personal touch to the topic and gives them something they can relate to while teaching them about inheritance.
The Role of Chance Lead the students in a discussion about heredity and the role of chance and its function in the process of heredity. Start off by having students, in pairs, flip a coin 10 times. Ask them to record their results and report them back to the class. The result should be about equal numbers of heads and tails. Tell the students that you could then make a prediction about how often you would toss a coin and get heads and how often you would get tails. This is the probability of that event happening. There is a 50% chance of the coin landing on heads and a 50% chance that the	Probabilities are powerful tools for making predictions over a large number of events. The more events you observe, the closer to predicted results the actual results will be. For example, if you flip a coin 10 times, probability predicts that the coin will land heads-up five times and tails-up five times. However, when you actually do this experiment, your results could be quite different. If you tossed the coin 100 times, you are more likely to obtain results closer to the predicted 50% of each, and tossing the coin 1,000 times will probably give you results even closer to those predicted by probability.

(Continued)

(Continued)

Unit Sequence—Curriculum of Connections	Teacher Reflections
coin would land on tails. Heredity is similar to flipping a coin in that chance plays a role. Explain to the students, *"As scientists, we can predict the probability of an individual of having a certain trait based on the traits of its parents. We make Punnett squares to show us all the possible outcomes an F1 generation (first filial generation, the parents' offspring) can have based on the traits of the parent generation."*	
Introduction to Punnett Squares Use the **Talking Points and Examples** (Appendix 1B) to guide your discussion with your students about the use of Punnett squares to determine the likelihood that some event will occur. This information can be presented by placing the document on a whiteboard, or you can group students based on their readiness levels to work more independently on their own or with your guidance as they read the information and work through the examples of Punnett squares.	Punnett squares are named for geneticist Reginald Punnett, who developed the square as a tool to help scientists predict the genotypes of offspring. The square is based on probabilities; that is, the likelihood that some event will occur. Punnett squares show all the possible outcomes that the parent generation can produce.
Reinforcing Punnett Squares **Web Lab Activity** Students will further their understanding and skills by engaging in the virtual Web Lab that introduces the concept of Punnett squares. At the Genetics Web Lab Directory there is a web lab called Punnett squares (http://www2.edc .org/weblabs/WebLabDirectory1.html). These web labs are published by Education Development Center and can be used to develop an understanding of Punnett squares as well as other topics. Ask students to work in groups of four based on similar readiness levels and have them complete the activities together. For some groups, you may need to provide more structured support to guide their continued understanding of Punnett squares. Throughout the web lab, students are asked to read and answer questions so they will not record anything during the web lab activity to turn in to the teacher, but some students may require the type of cognitive coaching to support their learning of Punnett squares. This web lab provides the students with good	This web activity helps students to understand that . . . • Heredity is the passing of traits to offspring through genes. • Genes can be dominant or recessive. • If a dominant gene is present, that trait will be expressed. **Ascending Intellectual Demand (AID)** This activity can be adjusted for advanced learners by asking students to locate additional resources or advanced reading on the web to deepen their understanding on genetics. Within this lab, students have several options to consider as they advance their level of understanding of genetics and the use of Punnett squares. Another alternative is to have students explore and then explain situations where Punnett squares do not apply.

Unit Sequence—Curriculum of Connections	Teacher Reflections
foundational information about predicting heredity and the process of setting up and completing Punnett squares. Follow up the experience by asking students the following questions: • What did you come to understand about the use of Punnett squares that you did not understand before? • What considerations did you make when trying to create offspring that had long tails and who were albino? • How do recessive and dominant traits influence the chances of predicting the traits of offspring? **Creating a Species** Students are now asked to create a new species and to identify dominant and recessive traits that the species will have. Have each student create her own creature using the traits she came up with. Pair up the students and have them first create a Punnett square for each trait that will be passed down to the next generation. Then have the students flip a coin (heads is dominant and tails is recessive) to determine which traits their "offspring" will inherit. After they have determined which traits their offspring will inherit, have them make the new creature together. Before they create this new creature, check to make sure that their Punnett square charts are completed correctly. Depending on the amount of time permitted, have students produce several children, or generations. They can name each new offspring and create a family. Possibly have them produce the number of children they have in their family. **Assessment** The Punnett squares students create for their creatures and offspring should be evaluated to check student skill level and understanding of how squares assist in determining the likelihood of the possible outcomes.	Students can take this activity in many directions. Their new species can be made of food and snack items or of different shapes of paper and other craft related items. It is up to them which direction they go to making the species. It is often fun to use different snack and candy items to make creatures because the students get to eat their creatures when they have finished. Paper and other craft items are also good because they do not attract bugs and the teacher would not have to worry about students being allergic to different foods. By allowing students to create the list of traits and the dominant and recessive traits for the "creature," they become excited because they have a personal interest in their creation. Making the new creature makes the abstract ideas more concrete and reinforces the ideas of inheritance and heredity. Pairing up the students for the F1 generation, the first generation after the parent generation, helps to ensure all students understand heredity. If a student doesn't understand, he or she now has a built-in support system to help determine the next generation. By using a coin, students can see the role of chance in heredity. They have a visual example with the flipping of the coin to see that not all the alleles or form of genes present are transferred to their offspring and therefore their "children" were not the same even though they came from the same parents. Each parent contributed one allele for each trait.

(Continued)

Unit Sequence—Curriculum of Connections	Teacher Reflections
	Each time the dice are rolled to choose an allele for the new creature, a separate cross is performed. The students will be able to see how some traits are passed to several of the offspring but others aren't. They should begin to realize why they express some features that look like their biological father and some that look like their biological mother. What also needs to be mentioned to students is that while there were only two choices for their "creature," traits often are carried on many different genes and are not controlled by just one gene.
Closure	
How is your "creature" family similar in form to your actual family in the picture? How is it different? Lead a discussion about the similarities and differences between the creature and actual people. To close the lesson, students will be asked to complete an exit card before they leave the class to check for understanding: • *What is the chance that two parents with homozygous recessive traits will pass on a dominant trait to their offspring? Answer: 0%* • *Explain why your creature did not look just like its parents.* • *Do you have any questions about genetics that you would like discussed or clarified? What questions do you have?*	

Lesson 1.3: DNA

Time allocation: 1–2 class sessions

Concepts

This lesson will introduce students to the power of DNA and its role in our lives and in our cells.

M1	Form and Function	M4	Chance
M2	Expression	M5	Order
M3	Image	M6	Cycles

Principles

P1   Genetics is the science of genes, heredity, and the variation of organisms.

P4   Outward expression of a characteristic or trait depends on the individual's genes and specific genotype.

P5   An individual's genes play a part in an individual's identity but do not control everything.

Skills

S1   Questions that can be answered through scientific investigations.

S2   Design and conduct a scientific investigation.

S3   Use appropriate tools and techniques to gather, analyze, and interpret data.

S4   Develop descriptions, explanations, predictions, and models using evidence.

S5   Think critically and logically to make the relationships between evidence and explanations.

Standards

SD2   Hereditary information is contained in genes, located in the chromosomes of each cell. Each gene carries a single unit of information. An inherited trait of an individual can be determined by one or by many genes, and a single gene can influence more than one trait. A human cell contains many thousands of different genes.

SD5   In all organisms, the instructions for specifying the characteristics of the organism are carried in DNA, a large polymer formed from subunits of four kinds (A, G, C, and T). The chemical and structural properties of DNA explain how the genetic information that underlies heredity is both encoded in genes (as a string of molecular "letters") and replicated (by a templating mechanism). Each DNA molecule in a cell forms a single chromosome.

Guiding Questions

1. What is the structure and function of DNA?
2. How does DNA code the information needed to create life?

Unit Sequence—Core Curriculum	Teacher Reflections
Preparation	
Prepare several "Secret Messages" that the students will have to code for using the four nitrogen pairs. Also, make sure to copy the "code" for each student so that they can code and decode their secret messages. See Appendix 1D for the **DNA Alphabet.**	

(Continued)

Unit Sequence—Core Curriculum	Teacher Reflections
Teaching Strategies and Learning Experiences	

Unit Sequence—Core Curriculum	Teacher Reflections
Key Terms • DNA • Nucleotide • Amino acids • Proteins • Nitrogen bases • Adenine • Thymine • Cytosine • Guanine • Double Helix As a class, define the key terms and introduce students to the structure of DNA. Show the class the structure of DNA (the double helix) and begin by having the students draw a spiral staircase in their journal. (You can get several different pictures of DNA and its structure from www.genome.gov.) After they have drawn the staircase, ask them what advantages there are to using a visual representation of a spiral staircase. Explain to the students that a spiral staircase can contain the same amount of stairs in a smaller space. Continue adding details of the structure of DNA, including the nitrogen bases, adenine, thymine, cytosine, and guanine. Have students draw these illustrations in journals and label the parts. **Creating a DNA Molecule** Have students create a model of the DNA molecule and to code for an "amino acid" that will perform a certain task. Students will use the **DNA Alphabet** (Appendix 1D) to send a secret message to a friend. Each student will select a task to code and give it to another student in the class to decode. They will code it using the DNA nitrogen bases and send it to their fellow students in the room. The other students will have to decode the message and then do what the message told them to do. An alternative to this activity would be to have the students code their name and then use their DNA names as a way to pair up students for future activities. Other students could also create the other side of their partners DNA name to make it a double helix.	You can use this link to take you to the glossary of genetics terms provided by National Human Genome Research institute: (http://www.genome.gov/glossary.cfm). This site has all the genetic terms you will need defined as well as more detailed explanations for a deeper understanding of the topic. Students will need an understanding of DNA and how it uses those nitrogen bases to code for amino acids and protein production. Students will use this information to make sense of the activities in this lesson. For more information about DNA basics, go to either of the following links. *DNA Basics* http://ghr.nlm.nih.gov/handbook/basics/dna *National Human Genome Research Institute* http://www.genome.gov/25520880#1 To further explain how DNA coils around itself to make chromosomes, have two students take a rope and wind it in opposite directions. Soon, the rope will begin to coil in on itself and shrink in length, much like the DNA molecule does. This activity can be completed in several different ways. I use die-cut DNA fragments from http://www.accucut.com ; Item #: D1018. I use a different color of paper for each of the nitrogen base pairs, sugar, and phosphate groups and then place them in envelopes and label each. When the students go to make their name or message in DNA, they use the appropriate nitrogen base and sugar and phosphate group. Students start by making only one side of the double helix. Some of my student's DNA names were several feet long! You can also use multicolored paper clips for the nitrogen base pairs. Students can make these chains of DNA using the multicolored paper clips and attaching

Unit Sequence—Core Curriculum	Teacher Reflections
	them together. This is faster, but doesn't necessarily give the students as good of a picture of what a real DNA molecule looks like.
	This activity helps students understand the complexity of the DNA molecule as well as the basics of how DNA codes for the many different traits living things have.
	Secret messages can be simple things like "Hello" or "Smile;" longer messages such as "put your finger on your nose" or "blink your eyes" would also work but would be more time consuming for students to decipher. All messages need to be rather short because coding these messages using the DNA code is a very long process.
Closure	

Ask the students why they think that a double helix is a good structure for the DNA molecule.
 	
Exit Card
 	
Have students complete an exit card prior to the end of class using the 3:2:1 assessment format.
 	
   3. Name three things you learned today about DNA.
 	
   2. Name two things you found interesting about DNA.
 	
   1. List one thing you would like to learn more about DNA.
	After completing the activity, students should realize that it takes a lot of DNA to code for small amounts of information. The double helix allows all the information coded in DNA to be stored in a small space in the nucleus of the cell.
	
	The exit card will help you assess the level of understanding your students have acquired in this lesson. Use this information to clear up any misconceptions.

Lesson 1.4: DNA Extraction Lab

Time allocation: 2–3 class sessions

Concepts

Students may have the misconception that DNA is only something that is found in humans. By doing this lab, students will discover that all living things contain DNA.

M1   Form and Function
M2   Expression
M3   Image

(Continued)

(Continued)

Principles

P1   Genetics is the science of genes, heredity, and the variation of organisms.

P3   Science as a discipline crosses over, affects, and is affected by other disciplinary fields of study, including history, literature, and mathematics.

P5   An individual's genes play a part in an individual's identity but do not control everything.

Skills

S1   Questions that can be answered through scientific investigations.

S2   Design and conduct a scientific investigation.

S3   Use appropriate tools and techniques to gather, analyze, and interpret data.

S4   Develop descriptions, explanations, predictions, and models using evidence.

S5   Think critically and logically to make the relationships between evidence and explanations.

Standards

SD2   Hereditary information is contained in genes, located in the chromosomes of each cell. Each gene carries a single unit of information. An inherited trait of an individual can be determined by one or by many genes, and a single gene can influence more than one trait. A human cell contains many thousands of different genes.

SD3   The characteristics of an organism can be described in terms of a combination of traits. Some traits are inherited, and others result from interactions with the environment.

SD5   In all organisms, the instructions for specifying the characteristics of the organism are carried in DNA, a large polymer formed from subunits of four kinds (A, G, C, and T). The chemical and structural properties of DNA explain how the genetic information that underlies heredity is both encoded in genes (as a string of molecular "letters") and replicated (by a templating mechanism). Each DNA molecule in a cell forms a single chromosome.

Guiding Questions

1. Where is DNA found?
2. How do we extract DNA?

Unit Sequence—Core Curriculum	Teacher Reflections
Teaching Strategies and Learning Experiences	

Introductory Activity

Have students write in their lab journal where they think they could find DNA. Have them list as many things as they can think of. After they share their lists, prepare students for the lab by explaining to them that today they will be extracting DNA from split peas.

DNA Lab Extraction

The lab that will be used to guide student experimentation comes from http://learn .genetics.utah.edu and is called *How to Extract DNA from Anything Living*. This online resource is produced by the Genetic Science Learning Center, University of Utah.

In pairs have students read through the directions together to understand the procedures to follow to complete this lab. Students are also asked to use the **DNA Extraction Lab** worksheet (Appendix 1E) to record their observations as they work through the steps to the lab.

To prepare students for preparation of the lab, have students look at the ingredients that they find at their lab station. Ask the following questions to begin the process of thinking about the experiment they will be conducting.

One way to purify a molecule is to eliminate everything but that molecule. If we want to isolate DNA from peas, what parts of the cell would we need to get rid of? Some responses might include (*All parts of the cell besides the DNA, i.e., cell wall, cell membrane, mitochondria, Golgi apparatus, endoplasmic reticulum, vacuoles, lysosomes, and nuclear membrane*).

Looking at the materials in your lab toolkit, what would you use to isolate DNA from peas? Some responses might include: *Something to mush the cells (blender or your hands), something to destroy membranes (soap dissolves them), something to get rid of proteins and carbohydrates (salt causes them to precipitate), something to separate insoluble cell material from soluble DNA, and something to help get the DNA (alcohol precipitates it).*

There are many labs that can be conducted by students to extract DNA. Fruits and vegetables can be used to conduct the experiment. Students should be encouraged to try different detergents to see how these change the experimentation.

Background Information: All living things store their DNA inside their cells. Cells also contain other chemicals, such as proteins, carbohydrates, and lipids, surrounded by a cell membrane. In this lab students first break the cells open. The blender breaks the peas into single cells. The detergent helps dissolve some of the chemicals in the cell membranes, letting the DNA and other chemicals out. Once the DNA is removed from the cells, students separate the DNA from the other chemicals by placing it in alcohol.

It is important to prepare students prior to the lab experiment to ensure that as they work through the steps they are observant and record even the slightest of actions. This brainstorming prepares students for the inquiry that will take place during the experimentation.

(Continued)

(Continued)

Unit Sequence—Core Curriculum	Teacher Reflections
What can we do with the DNA once purified? Some responses might include: *Use it in DNA fingerprinting (solve a crime, see a genetic defect), put it into another organism to give it specific traits (this is called transformation or genetic engineering), other?*. After students complete the lab, have them return to these questions and write responses based on their findings to clarify their thinking.	
DNA Virtual Lab Extraction Students should now be prepared to complete this virtual lab to perform a cheek swab and extract DNA from human cells. This lab is located at http://learn.genetics.utah.edu/content/labs/extraction/ and produced by Learn.Genetics, Genetic Science Learning Center at The University of Utah. Ask students how this lab was similar to and different from the lab where they extracted DNA from peas.	**AID** Students who are ready for more advanced work can select through the other virtual labs at this site to understand how advanced technologies are being used to investigate diseases and healthy cells versus unhealthy cells. Students will be asked to describe how these technologies work.
Closure	
Close these lab activities by asking students the following questions: • What did the DNA look like? (Pea Experiment) • What did you think of the DNA that you saw? (Pea Experiment) • Did you see what you expected? Why or why not? (Pea Experiment) • How was the DNA similar to and different from the way you thought it would be? (Pea Experiment) • Why might it be useful to extract DNA from cells? (Virtual Lab) • What social and ethical issues might scientists confront as they begin to work with DNA testing? (Virtual Lab)	

Lesson 1.5: DNA Fingerprinting and Crime Lab Investigations

Time allocation: 2–3 class sessions

Concepts

M1	Form and Function	M4	Chance
M2	Expression	M5	Order
M3	Image	M6	Cycles

During this lesson, students will get to meet and hear from a police officer or crime lab worker as they discuss how what they do is related to genetics. Students seeing and hearing from people in the community is important so that they know that science is used in the real world, not just in school. If it is possible to have them come in and speak to your classes that would be best. If this is not possible, there are several popular television shows and movies that show DNA being used to help solve crimes. This would also allow students to see how science is used in the real world.

Principles

P1 Genetics is the science of genes, heredity, and the variation of organisms.

P3 Science as a discipline crosses over, affects, and is affected by other disciplinary fields of study including history, literature, and mathematics.

P4 Outward expression of a characteristic or trait depends on the individual's genes and specific genotype.

P5 An individual's genes play a part in an individual's identity but do not control everything.

Skills

S1 Questions that can be answered through scientific investigations.

S2 Design and conduct a scientific investigation.

S3 Use appropriate tools and techniques to gather, analyze, and interpret data.

S4 Develop descriptions, explanations, predictions, and models using evidence.

S5 Think critically and logically to make the relationships between evidence and explanations.

Standards

SD2 Hereditary information is contained in genes, located in the chromosomes of each cell. Each gene carries a single unit of information. An inherited trait of an individual can be determined by one or by many genes, and a single gene can influence more than one trait. A human cell contains many thousands of different genes.

SD3 The characteristics of an organism can be described in terms of a combination of traits. Some traits are inherited, and others result from interactions with the environment.

SD5 In all organisms, the instructions for specifying the characteristics of the organism are carried in DNA, a large polymer formed from subunits of four kinds (A, G, C, and T). The chemical and structural properties of DNA explain how the genetic information that underlies heredity is both encoded in genes (as a string of molecular "letters") and replicated (by a templating mechanism). Each DNA molecule in a cell forms a single chromosome.

Guiding Questions

1. What is DNA fingerprinting?
2. How does our DNA help police officers solve crimes?

Unit Sequence—Curriculum of Practice	Teacher Reflections
Teaching Strategies and Learning Experiences	
Introductory Activity Introduce the class to the guest speaker. He or she will introduce the topic of crime scene investigations and the role of DNA in solving crimes. Prior to this presentation, have students generate a series of questions that they wish to ask the speaker. After the speaker has finished presenting, have students recall key facts about DNA they have learned. Place the students in cooperative learning groups (based on readiness levels) and then take them to the computer lab where they will solve crimes and extract DNA from a virtual crime scene using the virtual lab, *DNA Fingerprinting*, found at the following website created by the Education Development Center. This virtual lab is for students who have an understanding of DNA extraction and need a challenge (http://www2.edc.org/weblabs/WebLabDirectory1.html) For students who require more guided support and virtual prompting, have these students use the web lab, *CSI: The Experience-Web Adventures* produced at Rice University (http://forensics.rice.edu/). After students complete the web labs, have them respond in groups to the following questions and then debrief their responses. • How is DNA used to fight crime? • What techniques and tools are used to process DNA? What reasoning skills do forensic scientists, detectives, or anyone involved in this type of work have to be able to use to conduct this work well?	During this lesson, students will get to meet and hear from a police officer or crime lab worker and they will discuss how what they do is related to genetics. Students seeing and hearing from people in the community is important so that they know that science is used in the real world, not just in school. If it is possible to have them come in and speak to your classes, that would be best. If that is not possible, there are several different television shows and movies that show DNA being used to help solve crimes. Detectives also have good information about crime scenes and genetics. These web labs are interesting for students to complete and provide them with the know-how and skill of extracting DNA and learning about the tools and techniques used to solve crimes. The first web lab uses advanced vocabulary words and introduces students to the technology involved in DNA extraction and fingerprinting at a more complex and abstract level. The second web lab is more user-friendly for students who may struggle with the vocabulary of genetics.
Closure	
Pass out individual index cards to the groups that worked together on the lab activity to respond to the following questions as homework. Summarize how DNA fingerprinting is used to help solve crimes. • How have DNA extraction, technology, and coding helped to assist society in the area of crime investigation? Think of positive and negative examples. • Challenge: Explain the process of DNA fingerprinting.	Use these two questions to check for student understanding. The first question should be less complex to answer, and the third question will be a challenge for most of the students. Students may need to return to the web lab to answer the question.

Lesson 1.6: Genetics and European History

Time allocation: 2–3 class sessions

Concepts

M1	Form and Function	M3	Image
M2	Expression	M4	Chance

This lesson looks at the concepts of form and function, image, chance, and expression through the scope of the royal family. Instead of focusing on the form and function of DNA, they examine how form and function can be destroyed due to image, chance, and expression.

Students will examine the pedigree and make predictions about how hemophilia affected the royal families of Europe. The presence of hemophilia in the royal family of England spread throughout Europe as royals intermarried. This caused problems for the royal families in Europe and eventually lead to the Russian Revolution and Rasputin's rise in power.

Principles

P1   Genetics is the science of genes, heredity, and the variation of organisms.

P4   Outward expression of a characteristic or trait depends on the individual's genes and specific genotype.

P5   An individual's genes play a part in an individual's identity but do not control everything.

Skills

S1   Questions that can be answered through scientific investigations.

S2   Design and conduct a scientific investigation.

S3   Use appropriate tools and techniques to gather, analyze, and interpret data.

S4   Develop descriptions, explanations, predictions, and models using evidence.

S5   Think critically and logically to make the relationships between evidence and explanations.

Standards

SD1   Every organism requires a set of instructions for specifying its traits. Heredity is the passage of these instructions from one generation to another.

SD2   Hereditary information is contained in genes, located in the chromosomes of each cell. Each gene carries a single unit of information. An inherited trait of an individual can be determined by one or by many genes, and a single gene can influence more than one trait. A human cell contains many thousands of different genes.

(Continued)

(Continued)

SD3 The characteristics of an organism can be described in terms of a combination of traits. Some traits are inherited, and others result from interactions with the environment.

SD4 Disease is a breakdown in structures or functions of an organism. Some diseases are the result of intrinsic failures of the system. Others are the result of damage by infection by other organisms.

Guiding Questions

1. What are some genetic diseases?
2. How are genetic diseases passed on to offspring?
3. How can the study of genetic diseases help scientists find cures for genetic diseases?
4. What do genetic diseases and royal families have in common?
5. How have genetic diseases impacted societies today?

Key Terms

- Hemophilia
- Genetic diseases
- Pedigrees
- Sex-linked traits

Unit Sequence—Curriculum of Practice	Teacher Reflections
Teaching Strategies and Learning Experiences	
Introduction to Pedigree Charts A pedigree chart is a way to record all the known phenotypes for an organism and its ancestors. There are also used to track disease transmission. Pedigrees are also family trees that explain genetic history and can be used to find out the probability of a child having a disorder in a particular family. To provide an overview of the symbols that are used to read these charts, a PowerPoint presentation is recommended to guide students through how to read and interpret these charts. **Pedigree Chart Reading Lab Experience** Using the **Pedigree Studies Lab Experience** (Appendix 1F) set up file folders that contain the two lab experiences for students to complete. Students will randomly be placed in pairs based on your arrangements (readiness for the experience, style, or interest).	I simply went to the Internet and typed in the phrase "Pedigree Chart PowerPoints" or "how to read a Pedigree Chart" and many sources were available for me to use.

Unit Sequence—Curriculum of Practice	Teacher Reflections
Students will be asked to read through the background information on these two labs prior to start of these activities. As students work on these activities, rotate around the room, providing assistance and support. Ask questions that support your assurance that students understand how to read the chart, how to create a pedigree chart, and how to read and determine the genotypes of the families.	
Royal Families Activity Begin the lesson by reviewing what they know about pedigree charts showing the students a pedigree of the royal families of Europe. Teach them how to read the pedigree chart and discuss how sex-linked traits such as hemophilia are passed on to offspring. Use the information in Appendix 1G to discuss these traits. Introduce students to the case study from the National Center for Case Study Teaching. The case study is called *Hemophilia: "The Royal Disease"* written by Yelena Aronova-Tiuntseva and Clyde Freeman Herreid, from the University at Buffalo, State University of New York (http://www.sciencecases.org/hemo/hemo.asp). This case study uses the spread of hemophilia through successive generations of Europe's royal families through Queen Victoria's descendants to illustrate classical principles of genetics. Within this case study there are questions that guide student learning. Arrange students in groups of three so that each group has someone who can read the site, someone who can write down the responses to the questions that are posed, and someone who has the type of leadership skills to keep students managed during this process. Have the students read the case study about hemophilia (see Appendix 1G) and its impact on the royal families of Europe. After they complete the questions, work as a whole class to discuss the findings. The answers are available online, and a teacher can request access to the answers.	Students will need to understand what a pedigree is as well as understand basic information about sex-linked traits. The sex-link trait we will focus on is hemophilia, but make sure the students realize that there are several sex-linked traits. The case study that I recommend comes from National Center for Case Study Teaching in Science, whose purpose is to promote the development and dissemination of innovative materials and sound educational practices for case teaching in the sciences. The Center's website provides access to an award-winning library of case materials. Its work has been supported over the years by the National Science Foundation, The Pew Charitable Trusts, and the U.S. Department of Education (see Appendix 1G for hemophilia readings and the case study outline). **Guidelines for Using the Case Study Method** 1. Before you have students read through the case, prompt students to consider the impacts of genetic diseases on a society. Do they ever help to shape the way a society views people? Does the disease ever help to shape historical events? 2. Open the case by posing an interesting question to consider. Why would royal family be concerned about genetic diseases? Have students establish group rules to ensure cohesion in the group. Each group can come up with a list of rules and agree to sign it like a contract.

(Continued)

(Continued)

Unit Sequence—Curriculum of Practice	Teacher Reflections
Closure	
Provide students with these two journal prompts based on their work on this case study. 1. Why would hemophilia be such a devastating disease to the royal families of Europe? Think about form, function, image, chance, and expression as you form your response. 2. How did genetics (in particular hemophilia) affect history, politics, and geography? Provide evidence to support your response to this question.	

Lesson 1.7: Genetics in Practice

Time allocation: 1 class session for the introduction; 2–5 class sessions for research, evidence gathering, constructing an argument, and presentations

Concepts

M7   Controversy
M8   Change

Principles

P1   Genetics is the science of genes, heredity, and the variation of organisms.

P3   Science as a discipline crosses over, affects, and is affected by other disciplinary fields of study, including history, literature, and mathematics.

P5   An individual's genes play a part in an individual's identity but do not control everything about who they are.

Skills

S1   Questions that can be answered through scientific investigations.

S3   Use appropriate tools and techniques to gather, analyze, and interpret data.

S4   Develop descriptions, explanations, predictions, and models using evidence.

S5   Think critically and logically to make the relationships between evidence and explanations.

Standards

SD1 Every organism requires a set of instructions for specifying its traits. Heredity is the passage of these instructions from one generation to another.

SD2 Hereditary information is contained in genes, located in the chromosomes of each cell. Each gene carries a single unit of information. An inherited trait of an individual can be determined by one or by many genes, and a single gene can influence more than one trait. A human cell contains many thousands of different genes.

SD3 The characteristics of an organism can be described in terms of a combination of traits. Some traits are inherited, and others result from interactions with the environment.

SD4 Disease is a breakdown in structures or functions of an organism. Some diseases are the result of intrinsic failures of the system. Others are the result of damage by infection by other organisms.

Guiding Questions

1. How does the process of inquiry lead to discovery and change?
2. Does discovery and exploration always lead to positive outcomes?
3. What role does the government play in protecting society against the negative outcomes of exploration, experimentation, and discovery?

Unit Sequence Curriculum of Practice	Teacher Reflections
Teaching Strategies and Learning Experiences	
Warm-Up Activity Use the guiding questions to begin to ask students to reflect on how scientific inquiry relates to the words discovery, exploration, and change. Ask students what they think drives the work of practitioners in the field of genetics? Have them write down their responses into their journals. The teacher should use these responses to guide a group discussion about the process of scientific inquiry—its pros and cons. **Calling All Researchers Scenario Task** Give students a short list of some of the areas of research that genetic practitioners investigate. The field of genetics is broad in its approach to discover the secrets of life, so	Science is the process of inquiry into the unknown. Genetic practitioners and scholars work in a large field of study performing a wide variety of tasks. Some research focuses on curing diseases, others on ending world hunger, and others on discovering our history. The process begins with observation, which is followed by experimentation until findings help them to draw conclusions. Out of this inquiry approach comes controversy and change. It is not uncommon for scientists to run into ethical, social, and legal conflicts that result from their work. Some of these conflicts will include: How will they use the information they obtain? Will the research lead to new materials, inventions, or new products that will affect society? Will those products be harmful or helpful?

(Continued)

(Continued)

Unit Sequence—Curriculum of Practice	Teacher Reflections
this list could include others. Briefly explain each area of research and have students choose one area in which they express an interest in investigating. Some areas of research may include the following: • Stem Cell Research • Genetically Enhanced Foods • In-vitro Fertilization • Forensics and Paternal Testing • Uncovering the Past with DNA Research • Preimplantation Genetic Diagnosis • Genetic Diseases • Intelligence • Athletics Have students write down their first and second choice for research on an exit card at the close of this introductory discussion and then match these cards so there are four students assigned to a research team. Each team needs to have someone who considers the perspective of the scientist, general public (including a parent or farmer, or child of diabetes, ethicist), political leader, and governmental official. Introduce the scenario by distributing the handout from Appendix 1H. After students select an area of genetics to investigate, generate a list of questions to guide their research. Ask them to add to this list other questions of interest. 1. Why/ How does your field of genetic research enhance or help society today? 2. Why would anyone want to research in this particular field? 3. What specifically do researchers in your particular field of genetics look at and work with? (What specific genes or chromosomes do they deal with? What do they do with them?) 4. Are there any ethical, moral, or legal concerns that practitioners in your field of genetic research have to deal with? How have these concerns been handled? 5. Who would directly and indirectly benefit from the research these practitioners are doing in your particular field?	Will there be a need to control the use of these products? In this lesson students will look more closely at one area of research in which practitioners in genetic research may focus. They will find how interest in this research contributes to the betterment of society as well as any ethical issues that the practitioners in the field may encounter. After they have completed their research, each group will prepare a 30-minute presentation that shares their perspective on the future funding of the research agenda they have chosen to explore. **AID** Have students work on problems currently posing difficulties for experts in the discipline. These roles include individuals who have vested interests in the research that is conducted by scientists. The scientist plays one role, while the general public typically is interested in how the research helps them medically and socially. Ethicists have a perspective of what they believe is ethically, morally, and socially right and wrong with this type of research or what concerns a special interest group may hold. Political leaders try to understand how to address the social, moral, and ethical issues of the research, and governmental officials may be concerned with laws that would govern the regulation of certain research recommendations. These questions are designed to get the students to consider the ethical or moral and political concerns that face researchers as they conduct their research.

Unit Sequence—Curriculum of Practice	Teacher Reflections
Allow students time to investigate and research their individual topics. Encourage students to contact medical personnel in your community that might provide them with information on the disease or issue they are investigating, stem-cell researchers who would provide them with information on the current research in the field, and so on. The research should include accessing the National Institute of Health and other major medical databases of information that will provide students with the most current research. The **Calling All Researchers Scenario** (Appendix 1H) lists a series of steps that can guide the research process for the students.	Since this scenario contains multiple steps to the research process, it will be important for the groups to establish group rules, determine how they will gather the data to address their questions, and a procedure for reaching consensus. Students will also need support in addressing the perspectives that each major stakeholder holds. It is best to support some groups (those who may need this type of structure and scaffolding) by directing them to have each member of the group select a certain role, generate the questions that will be of concern to this stakeholder group, and then conduct the research to construct an argument or provide evidence to address the potential concerns that may arise from these special interest groups. For those groups who are able to manage this process, the teacher should remain the "guide on the side" to assist them in the process when necessary.
Construction of the Scientific Argument and PowerPoint Presentation When students have completed the work, ask them to gather in their research group to construct a scientific argument that they can use for their presentation. Students can use the **Construction of the Scientific Argument Worksheet** to guide their group thinking (Appendix 1I). **Presentation of Response to Scenario** After students have completed their research and constructed their argument, they will present their information to a community of people who will judge their presentations and scientific arguments. Select individuals from your community that will encourage, applaud, and celebrate your students' thinking, yet provide feedback to their presentations. Community participants can use the **Calling All Researchers Rubric** (Appendix 1J) to judge the quality of the presentation and argument.	Argumentation is what scientists do and is essential to performing science and communicating scientific claims. It is important to share with students that in conducting scientific investigations, scientific argumentation assists the scientist in constructing scientific knowledge claims, to evaluate claims constructed by other researchers, and to establish objectivity. Argumentation is also used when scientists communicate about their findings and when they justify a collection of evidence with supporting or contradictory evidence. To facilitate good scientific argumentation, the teacher should provide resources (links, books, or research articles) that take into account a wide variety of contradictory evidence instead of individual pieces of evidence. Encourage your students to evaluate claims against empirical evidence or data from other sources rather than solely on intuitive and surface ideas.
Closure	
After providing a review of key concepts, principles, and skills used within this unit of study, provide students with a copy of the **Final Assessment** found in Appendix 1K. This final assessment will require several days for students to complete and should serve as a performance task that can be evaluated and combined with other students learning experiences.	

Unit 1 Appendixes

APPENDIX 1A

Figure 1.1

DOMINANT AND RECESSIVE CHARACTERISTICS

	Dominant Traits	Recessive Traits
Eye coloring	brown eyes	grey, green, hazel, blue eyes
Vision	farsightedness	normal vision
	normal vision	nearsightedness
	normal vision	night blindness
	normal vision	color blindness*
Hair	dark hair	blonde, light, red hair
	nonred hair	red hair
	curly hair	straight hair
	full head of hair	baldness*
	widow's peak	normal hairline
Facial Features	dimples	no dimples
	unattached earlobes	attached earlobes
	freckles	no freckles
	broad lips	thin lips
Appendages	extra digits	normal number
	fused digits	normal digits
	short digits	normal digits
	fingers lack 1 joint	normal joints
	limb dwarfing	normal proportion
	clubbed thumb	normal thumb
	double-jointedness	normal joints
Other	immunity to poison ivy	susceptibility to poison ivy
	normal pigmented skin	albinism
	normal blood clotting	hemophilia*
	normal hearing	congenital deafness
	normal hearing and speaking	deaf mutism
	normal—no PKU	phenylketonuria (PKU)

Source: http://www.blinn.edu/socialscience/LDThomas/Feldman/Handouts/0203hand.htm

*Sex-linked characteristic.

Figure 1.2

GENETIC TRAITS AND ME

Name:_____ Hour:_____ Date:_____

Use the chart, your partner, and a mirror to determine what genetic traits you have. After you make your observations, determine which of your traits are dominant and which are recessive. Record your answers below.

Trait	Observation	Dominant or Recessive?
Eye color		
Hair color		
Facial feature: dimples (yes or no)		
Facial feature: earlobes (attached or free)		
Facial feature: Freckles (yes or no)		
Facial feature: lips (broad or thin)		
Facial feature: tongue rolling		
Appendages: double jointed (yes or no)		
Vision: farsightedness or normal		
Vision: normal or colorblind		

Thinking Critically

1. Did you have more dominant or recessive traits? _____

2. Which do you think occurs more often, dominant traits or recessive traits? _____

3. Blonde hair and blue eyes are recessive traits. In Scandinavian countries a majority of people you see have blonde hair and blue eyes. If you answered in question 3 that dominant traits occur more often, how can you account for this? If you answered anything else in question 3, cite an additional example of a recessive trait being more common than a dominant one or explain why you answered the way you did in question 3.

_____

_____

_____

APPENDIX 1B: TALKING POINTS AND EXAMPLES

Genetics is the study of heredity or the passing on of genetic material from one generation to another. The passing on of genetic material takes place in genes, which contain the actual information that gets passed on to you from birth. Only one gene from each parent is passed to each offspring for a particular trait.

There are different forms of a gene that are referred to as alleles, which are traits for which two or more possibilities exist, only one of which may be expressed in a single individual. In humans, one allele is inherited from one's biologic father and one allele from one's biologic mother for each genetic trait. Alleles are forms of the same gene with small differences in their DNA sequence. This pair of alleles can be dominant (BB), recessive (bb), or hybrid (Bb). The dominant and recessive conditions are called pure or homozygous since both genes present are identical. The hybrid condition possesses one of each gene type and is called heterozygous. The genetic structure is called the genotype.

Dominant alleles overpower recessive alleles and are always expressed in offspring. Recessive alleles are only expressed in offspring if both parents contribute a recessive allele. For example, in human eye color, the allele for brown eyes is dominant, and the allele for blue eyes is recessive. Therefore, if the offspring receives a brown eye allele from either parent, the offspring will have brown eyes. The offspring would have to receive a blue eye allele from each parent to have blue eyes.

Although the genotype of an individual may differ from another's, their outward appearance for a particular trait may be identical. The outward appearance is called the phenotype.

The laws of inheritance are based on the laws of chance. In a hybrid cross (the case where the mother and father are both heterozygous for a given trait) every offspring has a 50:50 chance of inheriting the dominant or recessive gene. A common way of illustrating this is with a Punnett square, which is one tool that scientists use to predict the outcome of potential crossings of two parents. By using the Punnett square, you can figure out the likelihood that living organisms whose parents have particular gene patterns (genotypes) will develop particular characteristics (phenotypes).

Use this demonstration on the board to investigate and understand that organisms change over time. The key concept included in this lesson is that genetic variation can lead to diversity of organisms. Let's look at how this works:

Mother's Phenotype

		B	b
Father's Phenotype	B	BB	bB
	b	Bb	bb

1. Ask students to describe how a dominant gene is written and how a recessive gene is written (i.e., B and b). They will describe this through a prompt of brown eyes being dominant over blue eyes.

2. In the example above, ask students to consider a gene with dominant B and recessive b flavors (alleles). What happens if two parents each carrying one of each allele (Bb) (heterozygous) mate? Put the possible eggs for the mother along the top of the square, and the possible sperm for the father along the side. Ask students to fill each box with the allele above it from the mother and the allele beside it from the father. This is a possible combination of alleles of that gene in a child. The four boxes in the Punnett square represent the four possible combinations of the alleles.

3. Discuss with students how this cross yields three possible genotypes in the offspring (BB, Bb, and bb). In addition to showing the possible genotypes of offspring, the Punnett square also indicates how likely a particular child of this mating is to have a given genotype. In this case, there is a one in four (25%) chance that the child would be BB, two in four (50%) that it would be Bb, and one in four (25%) that it would be bb. This outcome is similar to tossing a four-sided die, with BB written on one side, Bb written on two sides, and bb written on the other side. This die gets tossed once for each child. If the cross produces several children, each gets one toss of the die, with the exception of identical twins. On the average, about 25% of the children of this cross should have a genotype

of bb. However, remember that this is a separate combination of egg and sperm, and a separate toss of the dice for each individual. It is possible to throw the dice four times and get bb each time; likewise, it is possible to get four out of four bb children from this cross. It is simply less probable than one out of four having a genotype of bb.

4. Now let's look at this example. We have one gene with two alleles: B-dominant, b-recessive. Since an individual has a pair of each chromosome, they have two copies of the gene. An individual can have a genotype of BB (homozygous dominant), Bb (heterozygous), or bb (homozygous recessive). Any of these individuals could mate with any other; thus, several possible crosses are available as shown in the Punnett squares below:

Mother's Phenotype

		B	B
Father's Phenotype	B	BB	BB
	B	BB	BB

Mother's Phenotype

		B	B
Father's Phenotype	B	BB	BB
	b	Bb	Bb

Mother's Phenotype

		B	b
Father's Phenotype	B	BB	bB
	b	Bb	bb

Mother's Phenotype

		B	b
Father's Phenotype	b	Bb	bb
	b	Bb	bb

Mother's Phenotype

		b	b
Father's Phenotype	b	bb	bb
	b	bb	bb

5. Students will then be prompted as to which eye color will be seen with each combination.

6. Using the Punnett squares above, ask students to determine the number of different offspring genotype combinations. Have them calculate the percent of the genotype offspring combinations. Assist students by helping them to fill in the Punnett squares and instructing them as to how to calculate the percents for each cross. Ask the following questions each time.

(Continued)

(Continued)

How many BB are there? _____

How many Bb are there? _____

How many bb are there? _____

What percent of BB are there? _____

What percent of Bb are there? _____

What percent of bb are there? _____

Genotypes of Parents _____

Genotypes of Offspring _____

Phenotypes of Parents _____

Phenotypes of Offspring _____

The cases listed above are called monohybrid (one trait) crosses, which means that there is one gene and two possible alleles for that gene. To provide Ascending Intellectual Demand, have students examine what happens when a dihybrid cross occurs. This cross occurs when two genes are independent, such as crossing attached earlobes and curly hair with unattached earlobes and straight hair.

APPENDIX 1C: VISUAL ORGANIZER FOR KEY TERMS

Figure 1.3

VISUAL ORGANIZER FOR KEY TERMS

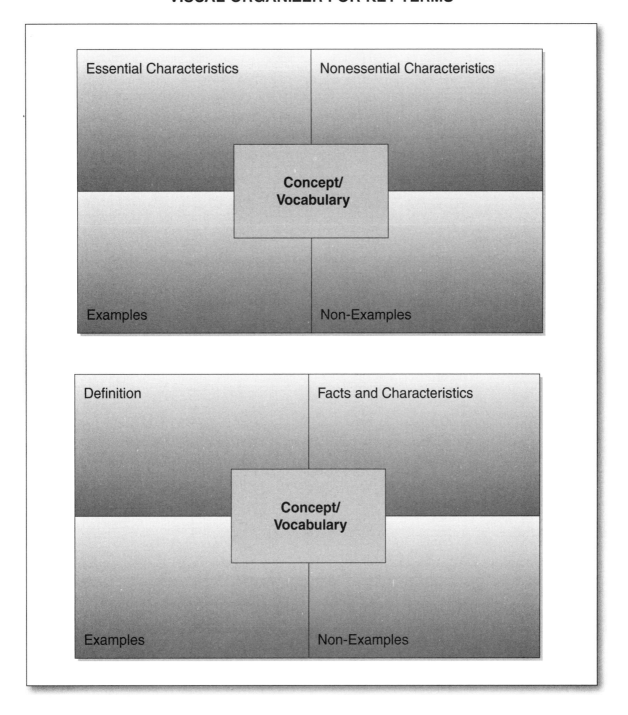

APPENDIX 1D: DNA ALPHABET

Use the following sites to obtain information about the DNA alphabet.

Step 1:   First click onto the following site to read about the DNA alphabet. This site is produced by the Wellcome Trust Sanger Institute. Link to the DNA Code Activity: http://www.yourgenome.org/dgg/gen

Step 2:   Then go to this site to conduct the activity called "DNA Detectives: What is your DNA Alias?" This site is produced by the Canadian Museum of Nature (http://nature.ca/genome/05/051/0511/0511_m205_e.cfm).

Step 3:   You can also use the decoder found at the Name in DNA website: http://www.ebi.ac.uk/training/schools/decode/, which is produced by the European Bioinformatics Institute.

APPENDIX 1E: DNA EXTRACTION LAB

For this experiment, your group will be extracting DNA from green split peas. As you conduct each step, please record your observations and findings.

Step 1: When you separated pea cells from each other, what did you observe?
Observations:

Step 2: When you added the liquid detergent what did you observe?
Observations:

Step 3: When you added the meat tenderizer for enzymes, what observations did you make?
Observations:

Step 4: As you added the rubbing alcohol into the tube, what did you observe?
Observations:

This recording sheet is to accompany the *How to Extract DNA from Anything Living*, which can be downloaded from http://learn.genetics.utah.edu.

APPENDIX 1F: PEDIGREE STUDIES LAB EXPERIENCE

Introduction

This should help you to understand how to read a pedigree chart. Pedigree charts show the phenotype of genetic traits and how they are expressed in a family from one generation to the next. The pedigree can help predict the genotype of each person for a certain trait.

Background Information

- In a pedigree chart, generations are represented by Roman numerals. Each person in each generation is numbered.
- Males are represented by a square and females by a circle.
- A horizontal line connecting a male and a female is called a marriage line.
- Vertical lines represent children.
- Children on the vertical line are always placed from left to right, with the child on the left being the oldest.

Let's Get Started

Examine Figures A and B found below. Answer the questions that follow concerning each figure.

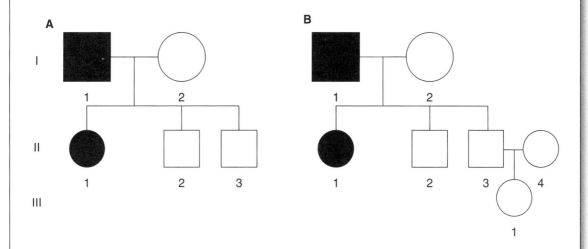

1. What is the sex of the oldest child in Figure A? _____

2. What is the sex of the youngest child in Figure A? _____

3. Which person in Figure B is the daughter-in-law? _____

4. To whom is she married? _____

5. What is the sex of their child? _____

Determining Genotypes

If we look at a specific trait (earlobe shape), two general shapes of earlobes exist: the dominant, *free ear lobes* (E) and the recessive, *attached ear lobes* (e). Individuals on a pedigree chart who have unshaded symbols have at least one dominant gene and show the dominant trait.

(Continued)

(Continued)

Background Information

- Any person on a pedigree chart who has a shaded symbol must be assigned two (2) recessive genes.
- Place lowercase letters under the person's symbol.
- Any person on a pedigree chart who has an unshaded symbol must be assigned a dominant gene.
- Place a capital letter under the person's symbol.
- To determine the second gene for persons who show a dominant trait, a Punnett square must be used.

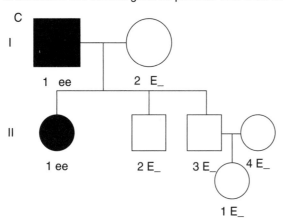

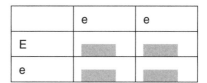

By examining Figure C, you can determine that the grandfather (I-1) is ee. The grandmother, we know, has one dominant allele. By looking at her three children, can we determine whether her second gene is dominant or recessive? If the grandmother were to be dominant (EE), would she be able to have a child with the genotype ee? By using the Punnett square, you will be able to see that this would be impossible. Thus, the grandmother must be heterozygous (Ee).

Answer the following questions using Figure C.

1. Can an Ee parent and an ee parent have the results shown in generation II? _____

2. Predict the second gene for person II-2. _____

3. Predict the second gene for person II-3. _____

4. Could child II-2 or II-3 be EE? Explain. _____

To predict the second allele for person II-4, a different method must be used, since she could be either EE or Ee.

5. Can an EE person married to an Ee person II-3 have children with free earlobes? _____

6. Can an Ee person married to an Ee person II-3 have children with free earlobes? _____

In this case, the second gene from person II-4 cannot be predicted using the Punnett square. Either genotype EE or Ee may be correct. When this occurs, both genotypes are placed under the person's symbol. Predicting the second gene for III-1 results in her not being able to be predicted because if you look at your Punnett square, she could be either EE or Ee, since her father is heterozygous. At some time in the future, if II-3 and II-4 have many more children, one might be able to predict II-4. When both parents show a dominant trait and their children all show a dominant trait, one cannot predict the second gene for anyone if only a small family is available.

Summary

Draw a complete pedigree.

1. Label each of the main parts for a family showing two parents and four children.

2. Make the oldest two children boys and the youngest girls.

3. Indicate, on the pedigree, that child II-2 has attached earlobes.

Using pedigrees 13, 14, and 15 below, predict the genotype of these families.

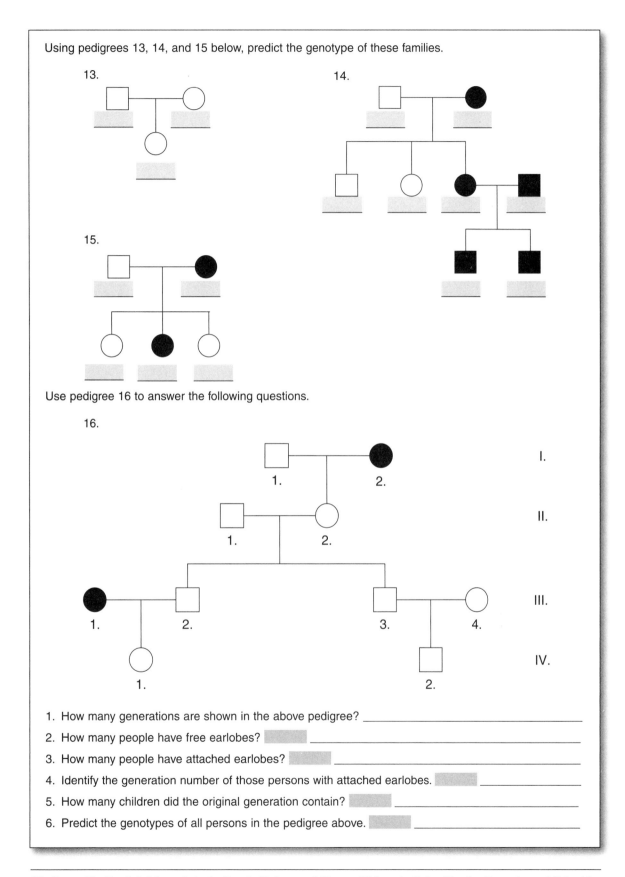

Use pedigree 16 to answer the following questions.

16.

1. How many generations are shown in the above pedigree? _____

2. How many people have free earlobes? _____

3. How many people have attached earlobes? _____

4. Identify the generation number of those persons with attached earlobes. _____

5. How many children did the original generation contain? _____

6. Predict the genotypes of all persons in the pedigree above. _____

"Pedigree Studies Lab" from *Introduction to Biology* and *Honors Biology,* both by Charles Zaremba published by Teaching Point (see www.teaching-point.net).

APPENDIX 1G: INFORMATION TO USE WITH THE CASE STUDY

1. Use the following Internet site to access information about hemophilia to explain the visual aspect of the disease: (http://www.emc.maricopa.edu/faculty/farabee/biobk/BioBookhumgen.html). Work through the visual to assist students in understanding how the allele was passed through the family. Start the discussion where you see "Sex-Linked Traits" discussed.

APPENDIX 1H: CALLING ALL RESEARCHERS SCENARIO

Directions: You will work with a team of three other students to research your area of interest to form a consensus on why this type of research should be funded by the federal government. Each member of your team will choose one of the given aspects of your topic to research. You will discuss your findings and decide the team's stance on funding allocation. Together you will determine the type of persuasive argument to construct and the type of persuasive presentation to create in order to convince a group of concerned citizens to support your topic for further research.

Calling All Researchers

The President has announced plans to fund a new program for scientific research. He wants to spend the money in the most efficient way possible that would be of benefit to society. In his proposal to the scientific community of scholars, he has asked that they prepare a presentation that would address the following issues. These issues and others the researchers wish to include must be addressed in the presentation. Priority will be given to those who address these questions:

- Why should the federal government fund research in this area?
- How does this research benefit society?
- How does this research improve the human condition?
- How can the research that you are advocating for connect to other teams of researchers from other fields of science (e.g., biology, geology, chemistry, and physics) to open new lines of communication among researchers?
- What ethical, moral, or political issues may surface as a result of this funding? How would you recommend that these issues be addressed?

Your presentation will be given to a representative group of scientists, community members, political leaders, and governmental officials who will serve as an advisory committee. The President has called these special interest groups together to make recommendations to his federal policy committee to determine which research to sponsor.

Starting the Research Process

Step 1: Everyone must understand the background information on the type of research you have collected, so make sure that the team understands the information.

Step 2: It's always best that you know what the concerns will be of each member of the review panel so you can consider this when preparing your argument. It is helpful to assign team members to investigate how you would address their concerns. Start this process by brainstorming a list of questions that may surface from these members. Remember your audience will include scientists, community members (ethicists, families, or careers that are affected by the area of research you conduct), political leaders, and governmental officials.

Step 3: Decide as a team which questions should guide your research. Divide the roles and questions among your group. Conduct your research so you can respond to the types of questions these stakeholders may ask.

Step 4: Construct your persuasive argument that uses the format listed below.

Step 5: Create a PowerPoint presentation to present this argument. You have a 30-minute time frame to deliver your presentation.

- **Introduction.** In this section, you need to inform your audience about the issue that you have researched. You will want to state your facts and statistics that address your topic.
- **State Your Case.** You must convince your audience why funding this type of research is the most important to consider. You can share expert opinions that you have found by conducting interviews and any other evidence to support the position you are presenting.

(Continued)

(Continued)

- **Examine and Refute the Opposition.** Knowing your opposition is important, so consider how you will address the concerns that each member of your audience may have. Their concerns can be used to support your position, and their opposing viewpoints will help you to consider how to address their concerns.
- **Reconfirm Your Position.** At the end of your presentation, you will want to review and summarize the main points of your argument and then conclude that your position is the most effective option to consider based on the information you provided.

APPENDIX 1I

Figure 1.4

CONSTRUCTION OF THE SCIENTIFIC ARGUMENT WORKSHEET

Directions: Use the graphic organizer below to organize your scientific argument, support or evidence, and conclusion for each argument. You must remember that in constructing an argument, it must be stated fairly, that your evidence must support the argument, and that your conclusions follow your reasoning. To make your case to the major stakeholders, you will need to include several arguments to prove your case.

The Argument/Claims	The Support or Evidence	The Conclusion
Present your argument supported by data. Consider the following: 1. Does anything seem wrong with this logic? Is this argument fair? Reasonable? Balanced? Informed? 2. What assumptions, perspectives, viewpoints, and biases may be present? 3. Do these influence the validity or strength of the argument?	Gather evidence from investigations, reading information, archived data, or other sources of information. You could also conduct some interviews or gather quotes from experts. Consider the following: 1. What data (facts, statistics, examples, comparisons, or expert viewpoints) support my argument? 2. Are my statistics presenting an honest view of what is really happening? 3. When quoting an expert, is this expert qualified to address this research topic? Are there controversial viewpoints or research that needs to be presented?	In the conclusion, review the evidence that you have provided to support your claims. Make connections between the evidence your group gathered and the claims that you are making. Consider the following: 1. Are the uses of the statements, arguments, and evidence valid? 2. Is this argument effective? 3. Is this argument persuasive?

Figure 1.5

CONSTRUCTING AN ARGUMENT WORKSHEET

The Argument: What argument do you want to prove?
The Support/Evidence:
What facts, statistics, examples, or expert viewpoints support your argument?
What facts, statistics, examples, or expert viewpoints do not support your argument?
The Conclusion: What is the conclusion of your argument? What do you want the stakeholders to think, believe, or know about the research?

APPENDIX 1J: CALLING ALL RESEARCHERS RUBRIC

Scoring Level	Science and Society	Basic Concepts and Fundamental Principles	Scientific Approach	Nature of Science
4-Accomplished	Developed and defended an informed position, and discussed how science and its applications interact with three or more of the following factors (social, economic, political, environmental, cultural, and ethical).	Integrated and applied basic scientific concepts and principles. Explained all scientific ideas and concepts thoroughly.	Demonstrated comprehension of the scientific approach; illustrated with examples. Major points were supported with relevant facts, statistics, and/or examples.	Demonstrated scientific reasoning across multiple disciplines.
3-Competent	Correctly described the position taken, and how science and its applications interact with two or more of the following factors (social, economic, political, environmental, cultural, and ethical).	Showed clear comprehension of basic scientific concepts and principles. Explained some of the scientific ideas and concepts.	Accurately expressed concepts related to the scientific approach. Major points were supported with facts, statistics, and/or examples, but the relevance of some of this information was questionable.	Interpreted related scientific results in a way that showed a clear recognition of the nature of science.
2-Developing	Recognized the place of science in human affairs, but was unable to communicate its roles and its interactions with at least one of the following factors (social, economic, political, environmental, cultural, and ethical).	Able to state basic scientific concepts and principles in simple recall fashion only.	Uses vocabulary related to scientific methods in a rote manner or showing simple conceptualization. Some major points were supported well while others were not.	Provided simplistic or incomplete explanations of the nature of science.
1-Beginning	Did not visualize a role or need for science in human affairs, could not address how science and its applications interact with any of the following factors (social, economic, political, environmental, cultural, and ethical).	Lacked an understanding of basic scientific concepts and principles. Does not recall or has faulty understanding of the scientific ideas and concepts.	Showed minimal understanding of scientific methods. Major points were not supported with evidence.	Did not distinguish between scientific, political, religious, or ethical statements.

APPENDIX 1K: FINAL ASSESSMENT

1. Select two of the following problems to solve by constructing a Punnett square to respond to the questions posed.

2. In rabbits the allele for black coat color (B) is dominant over the allele for brown coat color (b). What is the genotypic ratio and phenotypic ratio for a cross between an animal homozygous for black coat color and one homozygous for brown coat color?

3. Albinism is recessive in humans. An albino man marries a woman who is not albino but had an albino father. What is the probability of this couple having a child that is not an albino? What are the genotypic and phenotypic ratios?

4. In "Teenage Mutant Ninja Turtles," green shells are dominant over brown shells. Leonardo, who is heterozygous for a green shell, marries the lovely Mona Lisa, who has a brown shell. What are the genotypic and phenotypic ratios?

5. In humans, polydactyly (an extra finger on each hand or toe on each foot) is due to a dominant gene. When one parent is polydactylous, but heterozygous, and the other parent is normal, what are the genotypic and phenotypic ratios of their children?

Dihybrid Problems for Advanced Level Students

1. In humans, aniridia (a type of blindness resulting from absence of an iris) is due to a dominant gene. Migraine (a sickening headache) is due to a different dominant gene. A man with aniridia, whose mother was not blind, marries a woman who suffers from migraine. The woman's father did not suffer from migraine. In what proportion of their children would both aniridia and migraine be expected to occur?

2. Using the DNA Coding Chart that was used in class, create the DNA code for the following words:

Science

Genetics

3. Using the *Cartoon Guide to Genetics* written by Larry Gonick and Mark Wheelis, select one of the cartoons that you think you can interpret using the principles, concepts, and skills from this lesson. You should select the cartoon from the folder that contains photocopies of each of them. Take this copy and then select from the following ideas that you wish to explain in your own words. Remember you are providing additional information so someone can get the real insider joke of the cartoon and yet a thorough scientific explanation of the ideas behind its meaning. Try to use some of the genetics vocabulary words that you learned in this unit and that are posted on wall charts throughout our classroom.

4. Choose two from the following questions to respond to and provide examples.

- What concerns do you have about the practices of genetic research?
- What do practitioners in this field think about?
- To what degree is this intriguing, familiar, and/or surprising to me?
- What difficulties do/would practitioners in this field encounter? How do they cope with them? How would I cope with them?
- What have I learn about myself by studying the practitioners in the field of genetics?
- What is the wisdom that this discipline has contributed to the world? How could I see myself contributing to this wisdom?

APPENDIX 1L: REFERENCE SHEET FOR ADVANCED OR INTERESTED STUDENTS AND TEACHERS IN THE FIELD OF GENETICS

Biology is defined as the branch of science dealing with the study of living organisms while genetics is the science of genes, heredity, and the variation of organisms.

1. What kinds of questions are asked in the subdivision? Students can select from these questions as more challenging questions to pursue in this unit.

   - What factors contribute to genetic disorders and diseases? How can studying genes help eliminate painful genetic disorders?
   - Where are certain genes located within the human genome?
   - What are the chances of a person having children with a certain genetic disease?
   - What are the moral implications of stem-cell research?
   - How can genetic engineering help the human race?
   - What can and should be done with unused embryos left over after *in vitro* fertilization?
   - How can and will genetic engineering impact the daily lives of ordinary citizens? Professional athletes?
   - How is DNA fingerprinting performed and how reliable is it?
   - Is there a possibility of recreating extinct animals using their DNA?
   - What type of testing should be done to an infant during pregnancy? Should babies with genetic disorders be aborted before birth?
   - How does genetic engineering and human equality fit together?
   - What happens to DNA during replication?
   - What is the structure and function of DNA and how does that create genetic material that makes organisms function?
   - How can DNA fingerprinting help to solve present-day crimes and historical mysteries such as "Did Thomas Jefferson father a child with his slave Sally Hemings?"
   - How do paternity tests determine a baby's father?
   - Should genetic engineering be regulated by the government or other authority?
   - When and where does life begin?
   - What things have been cloned and what are the benefits and drawbacks involved with cloning?
   - What were Mendel's discoveries about the patterns of inheritance?
   - What is DNA and why is the human genome project studying it?

2. What are key basic reference books in the discipline or subdivision?

Brooks, M. (1998). *Get a grip on genetics.* New York: NY. Ivy Press and Time Life Books.

This is an excellent small reference to help anyone get acquainted with the field of genetics. It is written in an easy to read language and contains information about the beginnings of the field of genetics, DNA, mapping genes, and the uses of genetic knowledge.

Burian, R. (2005). *The epistemology of development, evolution, and genetics.* Cambridge: United Kingdom. Cambridge University Press.

This collection of essays examines the developments in three fundamental biological disciplines: embryology, evolutionary biology, and genetics.

Endelson, E. (1990). *Genetics and heredity.* New York, NY: Chelsea House Publishers.

The history of genetics and application of genetics up until 1990 are discussed in this book. Although dated, the book does contain reader-friendly applications about beginnings and applications of genetics and heredity as well as confer a basic understanding about genetic diseases and how they are passed on to offspring.

(Continued)

(Continued)

Keller, E. F., (1995). *Refiguring life: Metaphors of twentieth-century biology.* New York: NY. Columbia University Press.

This book discusses how genes are the primary agents of life and describes how they function.

Kristol, W., & Cohen, E. (2002). *The future is now: America confronts the new genetics.* Oxford, England: Rowman and Littlefield Publishers.

Excerpts from Huxley's *Brave New World* begin this book, which asks essential questions about genetic engineering and where it is taking the human race.

Noble, D. (2006). *The music of life.* New York, NY: Oxford University Press.

The subjects of genetics and music combine for an alternative perspective; specifically, the book delves into the similarities between genetics and the structure and function of music.

Reilly, P. (2006). *The strongest boy in the world: How genetic information is reshaping our lives.* Cold Springs Harbor, NY: Cold Springs Harbor Laboratory Press.

Genetic engineering is approached from many different angles in this book. *The Strongest Boy* examines genetic engineering's potential impact on professional sports and humanity, diseases, animals and plants, and society. It discusses ethical and moral debates associated with stem-cell research and talks about futuristic impacts of genetics on the whole of society.

Shannon, T. (2005). *Genetics: Science, ethics, and public policy.* Lanham, MD: Rowman and Littlefield Publishers.

Bioethics in four areas—reproductive technologies, genetic technologies, death and dying, and health care policy—are the focus of this book.

Starr, C., & Taggart, R. (2004). *Biology: The unity and diversity of life.* Belmont, CA: Brooks/Cole.

This is a college text on cell biology and genetics. It provides essential information about basic concepts in the field of genetics, including: Mendel's experiments, DNA structure and function, and genetic engineering.

3. What are some selected examples of insiders' knowledge, such as discipline-specific humor, trivia, abbreviations and acronyms, "meccas," scandals, hidden realities, or unspoken beliefs?

- Re-creation of the dodo bird? Possibility of using DNA of extinct animals to recreate them.
- DNA fingerprinting—your DNA fingerprint is as unique as your real fingerprint. This can be used to solve crimes and trace your relatives. It has been used to identify remains of soldiers from the Korean War by matching DNA and the soldiers' old shaving kits. It can also be used to identify paternity mysteries. Not only ones from today but also mysteries of the past.
- Early genetic misconceptions—pregnant women used to be discouraged from eating strawberries because they were believed to cause birthmarks in babies.
- During World War II, the birth of mentally retarded children was thought to be caused by trauma suffered by expectant mothers during bombings.

2

The Exxon Valdez Oil Spill: What's at Stake?

The Convergence of Science and Society, Grade 6

Julie Martinek

INTRODUCTION TO THE UNIT

When disaster occurs, society and science often find themselves in conflict with one another based on the various perspectives each possesses. An important goal in science education should be to assist students in understanding the relationship between how scientific knowledge is constructed and how it is used by society when a problem needs to be solved. This problem-based unit is structured to provide students an opportunity to make this connection by studying a real-world event shaped by conflicting perspectives. As these connections are made, students will understand how science and society shape decisions made when disaster occurs.

Students will be investigating the events of the March 1989 Exxon Valdez oil spill in Prince William Sound. They will be introduced to the actual event as if it were happening in real time. This allows students to generate their own questions (which reflect their own personal lens) about this event and then to compare these questions with those posed through a scientific lens. At this point in the unit, students realize that the real challenge in solving problems can occur when personal perspectives shape and drive the decision-making process. They also come to appreciate the role of science in helping to shape an argument or position.

After they have discussed how personal perspectives differ from scientific perspectives, students are introduced to a more complicated and more authentic situation when they are asked to assume the role of multiple and competing stakeholders whose job it is to prioritize and recommend cleanup efforts in seven sites located in Prince William Sound. In teams they will be assigned roles based on various stakeholders who have perspectives regarding this decision. As they try to prioritize the sites, they will gather, analyze, interpret, and draw conclusions about the vulnerability of animals, shorelines, and the livelihood of the people in each site by using scientific information, data, and computer modeling maps. After they make their decision, each team will construct a persuasive essay to convince their classmates that the site they have chosen should receive priority.

Toward the end of this unit, students present their decisions and participate in a scientific colloquium activity where they consider how mixed stakeholder groups can renegotiate the priority assigned to those sites that brought about the most disagreement. These activities help students to realize that science does not operate in a vacuum but rather is an integral part of a social system. As a result of these activities, they are able to reflect on the final question: What is the role of science in our society?

The ultimate goal of this unit is for the students to *feel* the scientist perspective, contrast it with the other stakeholder perspectives, and ultimately come to appreciate and understand the conflicts that can arise when trying to solve problems that are faced by a society.

BACKGROUND TO THE UNIT

It is important to stress with students that as humans we all have a natural desire to explain why something happens. Human societies have always been curious about why and how things happen and have asked questions, made observations, collected data, and created explanations for natural phenomena. In science, there is a similar purpose, which is to explain and predict events. Although many scientific theories have withstood the test of time, other knowledge claims are altered by new scientific evidence. Scientific evidence and knowledge are distinguished from other ways of knowing in terms of the criteria that must be met. These criteria include the use of empirical standards and rules of evidence, a logical structure, rational thought, questioning, and openness to criticism.

In this unit, students vicariously experience how scientific explanations and evidence also interact with human social systems and cause great challenges, as varying perspectives can alter how data are interpreted. They will come to understand the difference between objective and subjective data. Data are objective, but the meaning-making of the data can become subjective. Students arrive at a situation in their learning where their classmates are using the same data but the interpretation being assigned to these data are shaped by varying personal or stakeholder perspectives. What they come to understand is that in the grand scheme of things, although we all look at the same data, the use and interpretation of these data will be shaped by perspective. Through this experience, students begin to realize that there are many voices (personal, stakeholder, and scientific) that can arise when problems occur within a society. Students will ponder questions that ask: What is the role of science in a society? Is it possible to have a personal perspective while possessing a scientific perspective? What role do activists play when solving problems? Which role(s) match my personal identity?

CONTENT FRAMEWORK

Organizing Concepts

Macroconcepts

M1   Systems

M2   Perspectives

M3   Cause and Effect

M4   Change and Patterns

M5   Properties and Measurement

M6   Models and Evidence

Discipline-Specific Concepts

Personal

Scientific

Social

Interactions

Ecosystem

Vulnerability Scales

Environmental Sensitivity Index Maps

Scientific Inquiry

Reliability

Principles and Generalizations

P1   External factors can influence a system.

P2   Personal, social, and scientific perspectives interact to shape decisions.

P3   A cause can have multiple effects.

P4   An effect can have multiple causes.

P5   By examining cause and effect relationships, predictions and hypotheses can be formulated.

P6   Natural processes and human activity cause change.

P7   Changes may result in patterns to allow for predictions of future events.

P8   Symbolic representations show how the quantity of something changes over time or in response to other changes.

P9   Data can be used to describe or predict an event.

P10   Collection and analysis of measurements can solve a problem and determine a new problem.

P11   The process of scientific inquiry and technological design enhances a scientist's ability to investigate questions and solve problems.

Skills

S1   Identify the cause-effect relationships within systems.

S2   Refine and refocus broad and ill-defined questions.

S3   Access, gather, store, retrieve, and organize data using hardware and software.

S4   Use appropriate tools, technologies, and metric measurements to gather and organize data and report results.

S5   Describe how interactions within a system can be described, measured, and calculated.

S6   Construct explanations on what is observed and differentiate explanation from description—providing causes for effects and establishing relationships based on evidence and logical argument.

S7   Interpret and evaluate data in order to formulate logical conclusions.

S8   Demonstrate that scientific ideas are used to explain previous observations and to predict future events.

S9   Review and summarize data to form a logical argument about the cause-and-effect relationships.

S10   Listen to and respect the explanations proposed by other students, remain open to and acknowledge different ideas and explanations, accept the skepticism of others, and consider alternative explanations.

S11   Identify how personal and social perspectives shape decisions.

S12   Identify and evaluate alternative explanations and procedures.

S13   Identify the changes in environmental conditions that affect the survival of individual organisms, populations, and entire species.

S14   Identify and describe forces that destroy landforms.

S15   Construct arguments to write a persuasive essay.

National Science Standards

NSD1 Science as Inquiry—Use appropriate tools and techniques to gather, analyze, and interpret data.

    a. Identify questions that can be answered through scientific investigations.
    b. Develop descriptions, explanations, predictions, and models using evidence.
    c. Think critically and logically to make the relationships between evidence and explanations.
    d. Recognize and analyze alternative explanations and predictions.

NSD2 Science in Personal and Social Perspectives—Natural hazards can present personal and societal challenges because misidentifying the change or incorrectly estimating the rate and scale of change may result in either too little attention or not enough significance.

NSD3 Science as a Human Endeavor—The work of science relies on basic human qualities, such as reasoning, insight, energy, skill, and creativity—as well as on scientific habits of mind, such as intellectual honesty, tolerance of ambiguity, skepticism, and openness to new ideas.

NSD4 Life Science—Living things interact with each other and their environment.

NSD5 Physical Science—Land forms are the result of a combination of constructive and destructive forces. Constructive forces include crustal deformation, volcanic eruption, and deposition of sediment, while destructive forces include weathering and erosion.

Table 2.1 Making Sure the Parallels of Connections, Practice, and Identity Remain Central in Teaching and Learning

Curriculum Component	To Ensure Focus on Key Concepts for Each Parallel
Content	Students will use general scientific methodologies, such as gathering, analyzing, and interpreting data, as they examine the effects of the Exxon Valdez oil spill in Prince William Sound to explore how the causes and effects or interactions affect an ecosystem.
	Curriculum of Connections: Students compare and contrast the differences between how personal, scientific, and stakeholder perspectives shape the interpretation of data and impact the decisions that are made when disaster occurs.
	Curriculum of Practice: Students develop skills to analyze and interpret situations in the role of multiple stakeholders in order to understand methods of gathering relevant information and analyzing its implications. They will apply the advanced-level thinking skills mentioned above as they conduct research using information and data to construct and defend positions.
	Curriculum of Identity: Students understand the role of science in society as well as how multiple perspectives can influence the outcome of decisions. They will question their own behavior and that of society at large while considering the wider implications of choices made by individuals and groups that hold varying perspectives.
Assessments	A variety of assessments are embedded throughout the unit to allow the teacher to assess students' development of thinking skills needed to eventually conduct their own research, make decisions, and construct effective arguments. Journal prompts are used as students explore essential questions posed throughout the unit; teacher observations are made to know when to scaffold student learning; and rubrics are used to guide the writing of persuasive arguments.
	Conversations between the teacher and students about the various tasks within the unit and the teacher's evaluation of their performances provide students with necessary information to assess their own work. These conversations are encouraged throughout the unit as a means for encouraging students to take responsibility for their own learning.
	Types of performances include making class or public presentations, discussing scientific matters with peers or teachers, and conducting research. Products of student work include journal notes and data gathering information, diagrams, and persuasive essays.

(Continued)

Table 2.1 (Continued)

Curriculum Component	*To Ensure Focus on Key Concepts for Each Parallel*
Introductory Activities	Introductory activities focus on a series of question prompts that build an understanding of the principles and key concepts. Curriculum of Connections: The introductory activities require students to look at how systems can change and are affected by causes and effects; and how perspective shapes question generation and data interpretation. Curriculum of Practice: The introductory activities invite students to consider how environmental disasters can affect living organisms, how data can be used to determine environmental impacts, and how to view these impacts through varied perspectives. Curriculum of Identity: The introduction asks students to recognize their own place in society, and their ability to perform the type of science that relies on basic human qualities, such as reasoning, insight, energy, skill, and creativity—as well as on scientific habits of mind, such as intellectual honesty, tolerance of ambiguity, skepticism, and openness to new ideas.
Teaching Strategies	Problem-based teaching strategies are used in this unit to engage students in a task that requires complex thinking. It is assumed that a teacher who uses this unit is skilled in scaffolding thinking and feels comfortable teaching skills within the context of a problem or as students demonstrate refinement or advancement in its use.
Learning Activities	Students are assigned to stakeholder teams as they conduct research in order to prioritize for cleanup efforts the seven sites in the Prince William Sound. The learning activities mirror the type of work that is carried out by groups who share a certain perspective as they try to form a convincing argument for public presentation.
Grouping Strategies	Various grouping strategies ensure that all students have access to the concepts and principles of the unit. During the earliest stages of the unit, students work in small groups to allow them to share a variety of personal perspectives. When students are assigned roles, they can be assigned based on interest or readiness levels.
Products	Ongoing products and planned student reflections are organized around students demonstrating and providing evidence of understanding the key principles and concepts.
Resources	Online resources include scientific information and data related to the Exxon Valdez, Environmental Sensitivity Index Maps, Shoreline Vulnerability readings, and Internet sites have been written into the unit to ensure that students and teachers have the resources available to complete the unit. Resources that are included in the Science Data and Information Learning Stations have been created so teachers can simply reproduce them for their students. Stakeholder Folders include the task cards, role descriptions, graphic organizers, and site information that can be reproduced for student use. PowerPoint slides are included within the unit to guide a teacher's instruction.
Modifications for Learner Need (Including Ascending Intellectual Demand)	Materials, tasks, and criteria for success are modified in response to learner readiness and interest. All students are asked to engage in research, and Ascending Intellectual Demand activities are created for advanced students to explore more complex perspectives, use advanced resources like the Environmental Sensitivity Index Maps, and to approach expert-like thinking.

UNIT ASSESSMENTS

The preassessment asks students to explore the cause-and-effect relationship within a system. Questions about this relationship are linked to the key principles of the unit to determine the level at which students are currently thinking about this topic. The information gathered may help the teacher make instructional decisions about the pacing, resources, and scaffolding students may require.

Periodic assignments and research tasks are given to students throughout the unit to provide structure to prioritizing which site will be selected for cleanup efforts. Conceptual understanding is assessed through the use of rubrics, conferencing, and discussion. Proficiency of skills and evidence of personal growth are demonstrated as students are asked to work as researchers in gathering, analyzing, and interpreting data to make a decision, constructing arguments, and creating persuasive essays as a way to explain their decision.

UNIT SEQUENCE, DESCRIPTION, AND TEACHER REFLECTION

Lesson 2.1: Pretest: The Cause-and-Effect Relationship Within a System

Time allocation: 2 class periods

Concepts

M1	Systems
M2	Perspectives
M3	Cause and Effect

Principles

P1	External factors can influence a system.
P2	Personal, social, and scientific perspectives interact to shape decisions.
P3	A cause can have multiple effects.
P4	An effect can have multiple causes.
P5	By examining cause-and-effect relationships, predictions and hypotheses can be formulated.

Skills

S1	Identify the cause-effect relationships within systems.
S2	Refine and refocus broad and ill-defined questions.

(Continued)

(Continued)

Standards

NSD1   Science as Inquiry—Use appropriate tools and techniques to gather, analyze, and interpret data.

       a. Identify questions that can be answered through scientific investigations.
       b. Develop descriptions, explanations, predictions, and models using evidence.
       c. Think critically and logically to make the relationships between evidence and explanations.
       d. Recognize and analyze alternative explanations and predictions.

Guiding Questions

The objective of this pretest is to see how students have processed previous discussions about the following concepts: system, cause and effect, and perspectives. Since one purpose of science is to understand how things change, this unit requires students to identify and describe how a system has changed as a result of the ecologic disaster, the Exxon Valdez. The unit learning experiences require students to identify and analyze the primary forces acting on the system from both natural and human activities; to acquire knowledge of how the Earth system responds to change; and to consider the consequences of these changes for human civilization from a scientific perspective and from other major stakeholders' perspectives invested in the Prince William Sound.

1. How do we define systems in science?

2. What is an example of a system in science that we have studied?

3. How does cause-and-effect thinking play a role in looking at a system?

4. What role does science play in studying man-made disasters?

5. How does perspective shape the outcomes or decisions of an action?

Unit Sequence—Core Curriculum	Teacher Reflections
Teaching Strategies and Learning Experiences	
Brainstorming and Synthesizing Conceptual Ideas (System and Cause and Effect) Prior to Instruction Begin this unit by grouping students in small, heterogeneous groups of three or four and asking them to brainstorm a list of topics in science and in any other field of study that can be viewed as a system. Students should also be encouraged to list events in their daily lives that can be viewed as a system.	This brainstorming activity is used to set the stage for the type of thinking that will be necessary as students begin the problem-based unit. Students have had lots of experience discussing and defining what is meant by the concept of system, and how this idea is viewed in science as in other disciplinary fields of study. This activity helps them to first generate and warm up to thinking together as a group and then to individual selection of an idea to illustrate their personal understanding.

Unit Sequence—Core Curriculum	Teacher Reflections
After 5 minutes of brainstorming, tell the groups that each individual within the group must select one idea from the list or generate any other idea they can think of that can be illustrated showing all the parts within the system they have chosen. Have students create a three-part illustration using chart paper. In the first column, ask students to create their system. When this illustration is complete, ask students to consider some act or event that might cause harm or disruption to this system and illustrate it in the second column of the chart paper, and in the third column illustrate the possible effects on the system.	
When students have completed their illustrations, they should present their ideas to the rest of the class. Discussion should be held to ask students to characterize the relationship between the terms cause and effect as viewed from a personal lens and a scientific lens. The following questions can be used to guide the discussion. • How would you define a system? • How does your example fit the definition of a system? • How does cause-and-effect thinking play a role in looking at a system? • What role does science play in studying phenomena? Disasters? Cause-and-effect relationships? • How does perspective shape the outcomes or decisions of an action? • If a scientist were to look at your cause-and-effect relationship, what actions would he or she take? How does this compare to a personal action that we would take? Are they different? Why or why not? • Is there a difference between scientific perspectives and personal perspectives?	The discussion is necessary to link the unit concepts together: system to cause-and-effect relationships and personal and scientific perspectives. It is important for students to make the connection that the role of science is to bring an objective, data-driven perspective to these situations rather than a personal perspective that individual stakeholders may hold that are less objective and more subjective.
Homework The students' assignment is to tell about a time in their own lives when they experienced or witnessed a cause-and-effect relationship. They are to choose one of the following formats to explain this relationship: Short story, poem, song or rap, cartoon, collage, detailed drawing, or drama.	This preassessment homework assignment will be used to check students' individual ability to identify a cause-and-effect relationship and to discuss it in class the next day.

(Continued)

(Continued)

Unit Sequence—Core Curriculum	Teacher Reflections
Sharing of Homework and Large-Group Discussion of Cause and Effect Encourage students to share their homework products with the class. On the overhead use the **Cause-and-Effect T-Chart** (Appendix 2A) graphic organizer to record student examples from their homework assignment. Pose the following questions and then record student examples: • What is another effect of this cause? • What could be another cause of this example? • Could you see this effect coming? Why or why not? • Does the effect always follow this cause? • What type of questions would a scientist ask about the cause or effects? • What would a person who is experiencing the effects question? • Is there a difference between these two types of questions? • How might a scientific perspective vary from a personal perspective?	
Debriefing and Closure	
When the class has generated a variety of examples, discuss the relationship between the two sides of the organizer. Guide students toward forming generalizations about cause and effect. List these statements or chart paper and display them in the classroom. This chart can be added to throughout the unit of instruction.	Possible generalizations that students will generate about cause-and-effect relationships might include: • A cause can have multiple effects. • An effect can have multiple causes. • By examining cause-and-effect relationships, predictions and hypotheses can be formulated.

Lesson 2.2: Introduction to the Exxon Valdez Problem

Time allocation: 2 class periods

Concept

M6   Models and Evidence

Principle

P11   The process of scientific inquiry and technological design enhances a scientist's ability to investigate questions and solve problems.

Skills

S2　Refine and refocus broad and ill-defined questions.

S3　Access, gather, store, retrieve, and organize data using hardware and software.

S4　Use appropriate tools, technologies, and metric measurements to gather and organize data and report results.

S11　Identify how personal and social perspectives shape decisions.

Standards

NSD1　Science as Inquiry—Use appropriate tools and techniques to gather, analyze, and interpret data.

　　a. Identify questions that can be answered through scientific investigations.
　　b. Develop descriptions, explanations, predictions, and models using evidence.
　　c. Think critically and logically to make the relationships between evidence and explanations.
　　d. Recognize and analyze alternative explanations and predictions.

NSD2　Science in Personal and Social Perspectives—Natural hazards can present personal and societal challenges because misidentifying the change or incorrectly estimating the rate and scale of change may result in either too little attention or not enough significance.

Guiding Question

1. How does your personal lens or perspective shape an understanding of data that you might collect and analyze to answer your questions?

Unit Sequence—Core Curriculum	Teacher Reflections
Introduction	
Say to the students, *"Today we are going to examine a disaster that is similar to the cause-and-effect relationships that we have discussed in our previous lessons. As we explore this disaster, I want you to be thinking about the event and the potential causes and effects that could arise from such a disaster."*	In preparation for this lesson, make sure that students have access to computers.
Teaching Strategies and Learning Experiences	
Activity 1: The Day of the Disaster Open today's session by creating a problem-based scenario using the disaster of the	This problem-based scenario was intentionally started by letting students listen to the recording of the first call that was made by

(Continued)

Unit Sequence—Core Curriculum	Teacher Reflections
Exxon Valdez by saying, "*Today we are going to listen to an event that took place in March of 1989. You are going to listen to an audio recording and read the transcript of the reported event to try to piece together what actually occurred on this day. Using your computers, you are going to work with a partner to play this recording and then read the transcript to gather some information about this event. You will have to determine who is involved in this recording to gather information to explain the event using the graphic organizer* **Who, What, When, Where, and Why** *(Appendix 2B), I have provided to your team.*" At this point, students will play the audio recording and read the transcript from Captain Hazelwood called *The First Call: Hazelwood Radios in to Inform the Valdez Traffic Center He Has Hit Bligh Reef with the Exxon Valdez Oil Tanker,* found at the website The Whole Truth: History of the Exxon Valdez Oil Spill (http://www.wholetruth.net/history.htm) and record the information that they hear.	Captain Hazelwood. This helps to establish a feeling of "fuzziness" about the event and in turn prompts student inquiry. When pairing students at the computer make sure that you have made provisions to match students together based on their readiness levels. For example it would be helpful to have teams where one member of the team has reasonable and efficient use of the computer while the other member of the team has writing skills to help record the data.
Activity 2: Furthering Student Understanding of the Exxon Valdez Oil Spill After students have recorded the preliminary information about this event, have them share their findings and discuss what other information is necessary to put together a more complete understanding of this event. At this point, share the slides that are provided in the **Exxon Valdez PowerPoint** to further explain the event to the students. Say to the students, "*I would like to provide you with other information that might help you understand the event much better. As I show you these slides, I want you to take notes using the* **Note-Taking Graphic Organizer Example** *and* **Note-Taking Graphic Organizer** *(Appendix 2C and Appendix 2D) to record information about this historic event.*"	As students viewed the transcript and listened to the audio, they were motivated to learn more of the story and asked questions that lead up to the PowerPoint presentation that was prepared by the teacher. The information gathered for the PowerPoint provides students with the following information about how the event started and the problems that resulted from this disaster. 1. What the area looked like prior to the oil spill. 2. Where the oil spill occurred. 3. An enlarged picture of Prince William Sound. 4. The number of gallons of oil that was spilled. *Note:* The PowerPoint presentation is available on the book's companion website at (www.corwin.com/sciencecurriculum).
Activity 3: Generating Questions Based on Personal Lens/Scientific Lens Say to students, "*When we learn about an event and we understand its importance, this often generates more questions that we want answered.*"	**AID** For some students, you can encourage them to generate more scientific and less personal questions. During the academic year, students in this science class have learned that scientists

Unit Sequence—Core Curriculum	Teacher Reflections
What questions would you like to have answered about this disaster? Using the **Questions Graphic Organizer** *(Appendix 2E), I want you to individually brainstorm questions that you would like answered about this event in the first column. For example, you might ask, What happened to the animals?"* After students brainstorm these questions, have them categorize these questions by the topics they address, such as animals, economy, people, tourists, and so on, and then categorize each of these questions by those that are generated from a personal or scientific perspective. Ask students to then complete an analysis of their own form of questioning to consider the consequences on their own thinking as they view or analyze data about an event in which they hold personal interest. Ask students: *"Why are there more personal concern-type questions than scientific inquiry-posed questions?"* and *"How do those personal questions help reveal to us what you care about? Would these varying perspectives ever cause conflict when individuals are asked to solve a problem?"*	use techniques for investigating phenomena that they are puzzled by, acquiring new knowledge to understand phenomena, or correcting and integrating previous knowledge. The method of inquiry that they use is based on observable, empirical, and measurable evidence. Learning to think like a scientist allows them to see things (or perceive problems) in a different way than we normally would. For example, if you were a scientist, you would think about the weather one way. If you were a student getting dressed for school in the morning, you might think of weather differently. What other ways might a scientist think about things differently than you might? How might their scientific perspective differ from your personal perspective? For students who are ready to ask these types of questions, encourage them to generate their questions from a scientific lens; for other students, let their personal interest guide their questions.

Debriefing and Closure

A Personal Lens Provide closure to these activities by saying to students, *"The activities that you have experienced today have helped you to create an understanding of the Exxon Valdez Oil Spill. In most cases, you have also generated questions that come from your 'personal lens' or questions that you care about answering, while some of you have created more scientific questions that intrigue you about this event. So I want you to consider the following questions before you leave class today:* • *Based on the questions you have asked, how will this shape your understanding of the disaster?* • *What if you were actually assigned to figure out for the Alaskan government which area to clean up first? Would your personal lens pose a problem for you as you try to investigate the disaster? Why or why not?"* Let students share their comments with each other before they leave class. Then say, *"Tomorrow, I will be asking you to assume the role of another perspective or lens as we study this event— one that might be quite different than your personal lens. Come prepared to do some real thinking!"*	It is important to close this section by focusing on the fact that most of us first consider finding information that matters to us most or ideas that bother us. The questions that the students have generated are more than likely structured around a personal perspective of what they are worried about as it related to the Exxon Valdez Oil Spill. This is an important perspective to consider, but it is also one of many perspectives that may influence someone's decision-making ability. Close this session by asking the questions posed in the left-hand column. It is important to discuss with the students that even as scientists, it is a real challenge to remain objective and not biased. The field itself has a set of criteria that provides peer-reviewed criteria to judge the merit of the research that a scientist conducts as a method to prevent bias from occurring in experimental research.

Lesson 2.3: Setting Up the Stakeholders' Research Activities

Time allocation: 3–5 class periods

Concepts

M2	Perspectives	M5	Properties and Measurement
M3	Cause and Effect	M6	Models and Evidence
M4	Change and Patterns		

Principles

P2   Personal, social, and scientific perspectives interact to shape decisions.

P5   By examining cause and effect relationships, predictions and hypotheses can be formulated.

P6   Natural processes and human activity cause change.

P7   Changes may result in patterns to allow for predictions of future events.

P8   Symbolic representations show how the quantity of something changes over time or in response to other changes.

P9   Data can be used to describe or predict an event.

P11   The process of scientific inquiry and technologic design enhances a scientist's ability to investigate questions and solve problems.

Skills

S2   Refine and refocus broad and ill-defined questions.

S3   Access, gather, store, retrieve, and organize data using hardware and software.

S4   Use appropriate tools, technologies, and metric measurements to gather and organize data and report results.

S5   Describe how interactions within a system can be described, measured, and calculated.

S7   Interpret and evaluate data in order to formulate logical conclusions.

S13   Identify the changes in environmental conditions that affect the survival of individual organisms, populations, and entire species.

S14   Identify and describe forces that destroy landforms.

Standards

NSD1 Science as Inquiry—Use appropriate tools and techniques to gather, analyze, and interpret data.

   a. Identify questions that can be answered through scientific investigations.
   b. Develop descriptions, explanations, predictions, and models using evidence.
   c. Think critically and logically to make the relationships between evidence and explanations.
   d. Recognize and analyze alternative explanations and predictions.

NSD3   Science as a Human Endeavor—The work of science relies on basic human qualities, such as reasoning, insight, energy, skill, and creativity—as well as on scientific habits of mind, such as intellectual honesty, tolerance of ambiguity, skepticism, and openness to new ideas.

NSD4   Life Science—Living things interact with each other and their environment.

NSD5   Physical Science—Land forms are the result of a combination of constructive and destructive forces. Constructive forces include crustal deformation, volcanic eruption, and deposition of sediment, while destructive forces include weathering and erosion.

Guiding Questions

1. How does your personal lens shape your interpretation of the data?
2. How does your stakeholder lens affect how you interact with data to help you make a decision?
3. What is the role of science in this whole decision-making process? How does it vary from the stakeholder's perspective?
4. How do environmental changes influence an ecosystem?
5. How can data be used to predict something?
6. Why is it important for data to be reliable and repeatable?

Unit Sequence—Curriculum of Connections	Teacher Reflections
Introduction	
Begin this activity by reviewing the following information that the students have come to understand about this event. *"Yesterday we started out with a problem involving the Exxon Valdez, and we found out that it was filled with 53 million gallons of oil. It has now lost 11 million gallons in the Prince William Sound area. We identified that Prince William Sound is a huge area, with 5,000 miles of shoreline, which is an incredibly large area to clean up and protect at the same time. On the day of the accident, no one was present to assist in efforts to immediately respond to this disaster. Additionally, you generated lots of questions about this event that pertained to how the people who lived there would be affected, what happened to the animals, and how the oil moved through the area. When you generated these questions, you realized that if a team of people had to decide a site in which to begin the cleanup efforts, that this site would more than likely be chosen based on their personal lens or what they personally cared about most.*	Provide this review of information from previous lessons to remind students of what they know about the Exxon Valdez disaster. These points can be summarized on an overhead projector or included in a PowerPoint presentation. During this presentation, students should be asked to consider how taking on another role would widen the understanding of the problem for them rather than to pursue this investigation through their own personal lenses.

(Continued)

(Continued)

Unit Sequence—Curriculum of Connections	Teacher Reflections
"As a group, you also identified that you believed the following people would be invested in the oil spill including: the governor, tourists, environmentalists, people who care about certain plants and animals, people who work there, and people who live in Prince William Sound, particularly those who are the Alaska Natives and have villages there. *"Today, I am now giving you a new task to perform. This task will require you to consider seven areas or sites within the Prince William Sound that could be affected by the oil spill. Your job will be to analyze data to determine which site is most vulnerable and should receive top priority in the cleanup efforts."*	

Teaching Strategies and Learning Experiences

Providing an Overview of the Learning Tasks

Activity 1: Perspective Shift

"Today you are going to make an identity or perspective shift. You are no longer going to be yourself. You are going to assume the role of certain stakeholders. You will be divided into research teams that require you to take on their perspective as you make a decision as to which site should be selected for the cleanup efforts. Your team will be asked to analyze the maps and other data that are available to you at the Science Data and Information Stations located around the room in folders, using the lens or stakeholder perspective you are assigned to as you try to ultimately make recommendations for which of the seven sites you believe should be prioritized to begin the cleanup efforts."

Now ask students these questions: *"Why wouldn't I assign you your personal lens? What research techniques will yield us the more objective or complete picture of the problem? What is the value of having to assume a perspective or lens that wasn't your own personal lens?"*

Continue by saying, *"So the task today is to assume a stakeholder perspective and make a recommendation as to which site should be cleaned up first."* Ask students to think aloud about these questions: How will you do this? How will you decide which site to prioritize? What do you need to consider? How are you going to learn about these seven sites so you can make a decision? (Let students share their responses with the whole class.)

In the **Science Data and Information Learning Stations** scattered throughout the classroom, there are folders that contain pictures and information, websites, and graphs and charts that will assist students in their investigations. There are eight folders that include the specific information to help students make their decisions. The information and photos used in these stations are included on the **online Resources for Exxon Valdez Oil Spill Disaster** that can be found at (www.corwin.com/sciencecurriculum). See Appendix 2M for resources.

Station 1: Computer Modeling (Environmental Sensitivity Index [ESI] Maps); a computer station that has sites bookmarked to explain ESI Mapping; and Oil Spill Trajectories

Station 2: Overview of Prince William Sound (Articles and Photos)

Station 3: Shorelines and Shore Responses to Oil

Station 4: Native Alaskan Villages/Tourism in Prince William Sound

Station 5: Open Water Animals (Orca Whales)

Station 6: Birds and Inter-Tidal Zone Animals (Mussels and Clams)

Station 7: Fish and Fish Hatcheries (Salmon and Herring)

Station 8: Shoreline Animals (Otters, Seals, Sea Lions, and Harbor Seals)

Unit Sequence—Curriculum of Connections	Teacher Reflections
"To assist you in your research, I have prepared some information for your team that is included in the **Stakeholder Folder** *that I created for you to help you organize your research. This folder contains:* 1. *An Outline of the Task* 2. *A Description of your Stakeholder Role* 3. *Map of Prince William Sound* 4. *Site Maps* 5. *Pictures of Each Site* 6. *A Data Collection Graphic Organizer to record your observations, questions, data, and conclusions* 7. *A Summary Data Matrix* *"After you read through the description of your stakeholder role, you should read the site information provided to you in your folder and decide how to understand if the sites are vulnerable in the first place. The site information will provide you with some facts, and you will have to consider how these facts may affect your stakeholder's position. By also using the information at the* **Science Data and Information Stations**, *you will find resources to assist you in gathering more facts to help you draw some conclusions about which sites are most vulnerable based on your stakeholder's perspective. At the end of this research process, all this information will help you to develop an argument for how you will prioritize the sites.*	You will have to create 5 **Stakeholder Folders** containing the information listed in the left-hand column. The outline of the task is a description of the work that the students will perform. Each of the 5 stakeholder teams has a description of its role. There are maps of Prince William Sound, a map of Prince William Sound with the 7 sites listed on the map, and pictures of each of the 7 sites. There are also two graphic organizers to assist students in recording data about the sites. The **Data Collection Graphic Organizer** (Appendix 2F) is used to gather data about the questions students ask about each site. The **Summary Data Matrix to Compile Your Findings** (Appendix 2G) should be used by students to construct an overview of what they found out about each site prior to a final decision being made about which site to prioritize. All the information at these stations was provided to the students because I wanted them to focus more on the analysis of data and how to use these data to shape their argument.
"Before I model how this research process works. I want to hand out to your teams their **Stakeholder Role Cards**. *In your prior thinking about who might be affected by this disaster, you identified a list of potential people and animals. I have turned this list into potential stakeholders and create your roles from your advice. The stakeholders include:* • *State Tourism Board Member* • *Native Alaskan Tribe Member Living in Chenega Village* • *Fisherman* • *Manager of a Pacific Herring Hatchery* • *Manager of Salmon Hatchery"* Distribute these **Stakeholder Role Cards** to the teams and let them read through their description. After they read through their roles,	Have a discussion with students about how scientific perspectives differ from social perspectives in a society. Ask students to consider what types of questions the stakeholders would generate or be interested in knowing vs. scientists. Which perspective(s) would be more objective? Which perspectives would be more subjective? Why do different stakeholders ask different questions?

(Continued)

(Continued)

Unit Sequence—Curriculum of Connections	Teacher Reflections
have them discuss with each other why this particular role or perspective would be interested in the Exxon Valdez oil spill. At this point it is important to try to keep these ideas isolated from the other teams. *Activity 2: Modeling the Research Process* Begin by saying, *"Before you begin your investigation, I would like to model for you how to think through the research process you are being asked to conduct."* (On a large classroom screen, project the map that shows the seven sites in Prince William Sound.) *"Each number on the map represents one of the seven sites that I want you to consider in your decision-making process. Each site in Prince William Sound has a story. Your job is to the find the story of each site and then use this information to help you frame the story of each site based on your team's stakeholder perspective as you work toward constructing an argument to help persuade the class which site should be prioritized for the cleanup efforts. Your team is going to put together the research you need to make the most persuasive argument to the class. Do you think that each stakeholder will tell the same story?* *"Let's take site 6 and try to model the kind of thinking that your team is required to perform."* (Show information from The **Site 6 PowerPoint** by projecting the slides on the screen for the students to view and handout the **Data Collection Graphic Organizer** [Appendix 2F].) *"Using the graphic organizer I just handed out to you, I want you to make some observations of the Site 6 pictures that are projected on the screen. What do you see?"* (Students responses might include: trees, look like islands, lots of rocks on the shoreline.) *"Do all the shorelines look the same? Might one shoreline be more vulnerable to damage from the oil spill than others? This is what you will need to find out by using the resources located in the shoreline information at the **Science Data and Information Stations**. So using your graphic organizer, in the first column where it says Observation, you can record Rocky Shores since you can make this observation from the pictures. In the second column, you can create a question like, Does this shoreline have a problem with oil? At this point you will want to go to a station that can provide you with data and information so you can answer your questions. When you find information that helps to answer your questions, record it in the Data column*	Use the **Site Six PowerPoint** presentation to introduce students to Site 6. This site has been chosen for this modeling exercise because Site 6 is typically ruled out when students conduct their research because the wind trajectory research demonstrates that over time the oil moves away from Site 6. Support student thinking by asking them to consider the types of questions that should be asked about the shoreline of this site and the surrounding area. Then work toward an explanation of how these data would have to be viewed in two ways. First the recording of data must be factual in order to understand how the area is being affected by the oil spill. Secondly, these data will have to be viewed through the lens of their stakeholder's perspective in order to shape an argument that will support their decision. During this modeling it may be important to have a discussion about the objective and subjective nature of interpreting data. I found that when students began their team research they became so invested in the role they played that if they found data that did not support their perspective they discarded it rather consider using it when they constructed their arguments. This also led to a class discussion about the ethical challenges placed on individuals when deciding to ignore data to justify a particular perspective or cause which required them to wonder if they should be concerned about this and who takes the responsibility to look at the whole picture rather than individual perspectives. **Ascending Intellectual Demand** Advanced level students can be asked to become experts in using the resources located in the Computing Modeling Station since the maps are difficult to interpret. In this center there are Environmental Sensitivity Index Maps that are designed to provide the necessary environmental information to the user from which a decision can be made

Unit Sequence—Curriculum of Connections	Teacher Reflections

of your graphic organizer. Finally, you will use the last column to derive a conclusion of these facts."
 	
    Ask students to consider other questions that they might ask about the shorelines? (Student responses vary but some possible questions include: How long has the shoreline been there? What life is there? What plants and animals might be living here? Continue the discussion by saying, *"To answer these questions, you may need to visit other stations to conduct your research. For example, one station includes Environmental Sensitivity Maps."* (Project the Spring Environmental Sensitivity Map that illustrates what types of birds and animals live in the area.) *"You will have to read the map's key legend in order to interpret the data so that you can draw a conclusion. Since the oil spill occurred close to Site 7, you have to ask yourself, How likely will it be that Site 6 will be affected? What station do you think would provide you with this information? (Right, the station that discusses the wind currents is called the Computer Model and Oil Spill Trajectories.)*
 	
    *"After you record your information on the **Data Collection Graphic Organizer** (Appendix 2F) for each site, you will begin to use this information to draw some conclusions between these sites prior to making your final decision. **The Summary Data Matrix to Compile Your Findings** (Appendix 2G) can help you to organize your overall findings. This graphic organizer will help you to record information about each site's shoreline and its vulnerability, animals and plants that may be affected, human resources (what do the people in this area depend on), and historical and cultural sites in the immediate area that may be affected. This summary of information might be used as you begin to decide which of the 7 sites should receive top priority for cleanup efforts.*
 	
    "Now you are ready to begin. Today we will complete the research for one site only, and then we will spend two to three days gathering this information for the other sites." (At this point, distribute the folders for the students to begin their research.)
	regarding spill response priorities and appropriate clean-up methods. Students can be asked to find out how these sensitivity maps are displayed, read, and interpreted as well as what information they do or do not provide. At the end of this unit there is an **Online Resource List** that includes the references that I used to create the data stations. Under the ESI Maps category a teacher can locate resources that students can use to become experts in using these maps. Their expert-like skill can be used to assist other students in the class as they gather data that will assist them in their research and decision-making activities.
	
	    *The **Summary Data Matrix** was created to help students organize their thinking prior to the decision making process which follows in another lesson.* A teacher may find that this form is not necessary if teams can organize and keep track of their findings.
	
	    Throughout the investigation, the teacher should rotate around the room to address the questions, skills, and standards listed for this lesson. Help students refine their data recording experiences, how to read and interpret the computer modeling maps found in the **Science Data and Information Learning Stations**, and to inquire how students are analyzing data to construct an argument based on their stakeholders' perspectives.

Debriefing and Closure	
While students are working on their research, rotate around the room to visit with the teams and to check the graphic organizers for the quality of the information that students are recording. Ask each group these essential questions:	To vary this approach, you can ask students to respond to these questions in their science journals or on an exit card, which is an index card where students record their responses to these questions and turn it in to the teacher prior to the end of class.

(Continued)

Unit Sequence—Curriculum of Connections	Teacher Reflections
• How does your personal lens shape your interpretation of the data? • How does your stakeholder lens affect how you interact with the data to help you make a decision? • What is the role of science in this whole decision-making process? How does it vary from the stakeholder's perspective?	After students complete their research have them use the **Evaluate the Quality of Your Thinking Chart** (Appendix 2H) to document evidence to support their assessment of how they performed these skills and carried out these dispositions during their site investigations.

Lesson 2.4: Prioritizing the Sites and Constructing a Persuasive Argument/Essay

Time allocation: 2–3 class periods

Concepts

M2	Perspectives	M4	Change and Patterns
M3	Cause and Effect	M6	Models and Evidence

Principles

P2   Personal, social, and scientific perspectives interact to shape decisions.

P5   By examining cause-and-effect relationships, predictions and hypotheses can be formulated.

P6   Natural processes and human activity cause change.

P11   The process of scientific inquiry and technologic design enhances a scientist's ability to investigate questions and solve problems.

Skills

S6   Construct explanations on what is observed and differentiate explanation from description, providing causes for effects and establishing relationships based on evidence and logical argument.

S7   Interpret and evaluate data in order to formulate logical conclusions.

S8   Demonstrate that scientific ideas are used to explain previous observations and to predict future events.

S9   Review and summarize data to form a logical argument about the cause-and-effect relationships.

S10   Listen to and respect the explanations proposed by other students, remain open to and acknowledge different ideas and explanations, accept the skepticism of others, and consider alternative explanations.

S11   Identify how personal and social perspectives shape decisions.

S12   Identify and evaluate alternative explanations and procedures.

S15   Construct arguments to write a persuasive essay.

Standards

NSD1   Science as Inquiry—Use appropriate tools and techniques to gather, analyze, and interpret data.

    a. Develop descriptions, explanations, predictions, and models using evidence.
    b. Think critically and logically to make the relationships between evidence and explanations.
    c. Recognize and analyze alternative explanations and predictions.

NSD2   Science in Personal and Social Perspectives—Natural hazards can present personal and societal challenges because misidentifying the change or incorrectly estimating the rate and scale of change may result in either too little attention or not enough significance.

NSD3   Science as a Human Endeavor—The work of science relies on basic human qualities, such as reasoning, insight, energy, skill, and creativity as well as on scientific habits of mind, such as intellectual honesty, tolerance of ambiguity, skepticism, and openness to new ideas.

Guiding Questions

1. How are arguments supported?
2. How does one's perspective shape an argument?
3. What was the role of science data in constructing arguments?
4. What does it take to reach consensus regarding controversial issues?

Unit Sequence—Curriculum of Practice and Identity	Teacher Reflections
Introduction	
Prioritizing Your Site and Constructing an Argument Say to the students, *"Now that you have completed your investigation, it is time to begin your work with your stakeholder team to construct an argument and develop a persuasive essay to explain the prioritizing of the seven sites within the Prince William Sound. Today your task will be to decide in your team what priority you will assign to the seven sites, use the evidence you collected to construct an argument, and then to create a persuasive essay to persuade your classmates why you have chosen a particular site and why you think this is the best site in which to begin the cleanup efforts. Let's begin with the first task of making a decision."*	During the decision-making process, students should develop the ability to listen to and respect the explanations proposed by other students. They should remain open to and acknowledge different ideas and explanations, be able to accept the skepticism of others, and consider alternative explanations. This is part of the dispositions of being a scientist. In this decision-making activity, there will be much argumentation even among team members who share the same perspective. This should be respected and even celebrated.

(Continued)

(Continued)

Unit Sequence—Curriculum of Practice and Identity	Teacher Reflections
Teaching Strategies and Learning Experiences	

Activity 1: Learning How to Make a Decision

By this time students have collected data and must now make a decision of which site will receive the topic priority based on the role that they played. Distribute the **Decision-Making Matrix** (Appendix 2I) to guide student thinking.

Say to students, *"I want you now to work in your teams to finalize your priority list. You need to make a decision on a site that will receive your top priority recommendation. In order to make this decision, I am handing out a matrix to help you organize this process. In the first box you list the* **Alternatives** *or options from which you must choose. Notice that I have written this in the box for you. In the second box, you have to list* **Selection Criteria** *you can use for judging these options. What kinds of questions or criteria would help your team make a selection of one site."* (At this point have students generate five criteria or questions that address the concerns of their stakeholders and would help them choose a site.)

"Now in the next box, **Decision Matrix**, *you get to take the first step in converting your decision into numbers. The rows and columns of the table correspond to your judgment criteria and options/ alternatives, respectively. The columns going across the table list all selection criteria you are considering when making this decision. The boxes going down list your alternatives.*

"Since you have seven alternative sites to consider, you will use a 1 (not a very good alternative) to 7 (best alternative) scale as you weigh the importance of each criterion against the seven sites. You can only use the number once as you evaluate each criterion to the sites. The more important a given criterion feels to you when you think about each site, the higher number you give it, within your chosen range.

"Next, based on all those numbers you can calculate the **Total Score** *(overall desirability) of each alternative in the weighted decision-making matrix. The alternative that has the highest total score is your decision matrix's conclusion on what is your best choice.*

It is important to let middle school students know that the advancement of science occurs through legitimate skepticism. Asking questions and querying each other's explanations is part of scientific inquiry. To evaluate the explanations proposed by their teammates, students should be asked to examine evidence, compare evidence, identify faulty reasoning, point out statements that go beyond the evidence, and suggest alternative explanations for the same observations.

Students should base their explanation on what they observed, and as they develop cognitive skills, they should be able to differentiate explanation from description— providing causes for effects and establishing relationships based on evidence and logical argument. What you want students to realize is that by developing explanations, they can make connections between the content of science and the contexts within which students develop new knowledge.

An important purpose of these activities is to give students a means to understand and act on personal and social issues. These activities help students develop decision-making skills and to establish a foundation on which to base decisions they will face as citizens.

As students generate criteria to guide the selection process, teachers may find it useful to help them to establish some ideas to consider such as the size of impact that the alternative will have on people in the area, the food chain, and so on. If students are in charge of generating their own criteria, often their stakeholder bias will show up; if they pick the criteria that benefit their lens, can they really claim objective decision making was done? It might be a good idea to post criteria ideas as a class and discuss how different criteria can lead to different conclusions. It's a great opportunity to discuss how the seemingly objective can still be subjective. Alternatively, this discussion could be an AID piece.

It may be helpful to distribute the **Decision-Making Rubric** (Appendix 2J) to students as they

Unit Sequence—Curriculum of Practice and Identity	Teacher Reflections
"Finally, I want you to tell me your decision and then provide reasons for this site selection in the box called **Decision and Reasons.** *You can begin the process now."* After students complete this process use these questions to guide the class discussion. • In what way did this process assist you in making a decision? • What role does collaboration play in the decision-making process? Was this difficult? • How did your perspective shape your decision? Did you ever feel drawn to shaping your decision on your personal perspective rather than your stakeholder's perspective? • What was the role of science data in constructing your argument? • What else did you experience during this decision-making activity? **Activity 2: Constructing a Persuasive/ Argument Essay** Say to the students, *"Now it is time for your team to construct an argument and to write your persuasive essay to defend, to convince, and to inform your classmates of your decision. Persuasive writing, also known as argument essay, utilizes logic and reason to show that one idea is more legitimate than another idea. It attempts to persuade a reader to adopt a certain point of view or to take a particular action. The argument must always use sound reasoning and solid evidence by stating facts, giving logical reasons, using examples, and quoting experts.* *"An argument has several purposes: to communicate, to motivate, and in this case to persuade an audience. First you must make a claim and then you must support this claim with evidence. The facts and statistics that you have gathered will make a difference in constructing this argument. By using these facts, you can turn your claim into a*	complete the decision-making activity. This rubric should help to guide their performance. During this process, students experienced the difficulty of making a group decision. They found out first-hand that individual team members vary in their willingness to make a decision that is based on data and/or return to personal belief systems to guide their decision-making. A teacher may find it helpful to discuss the type of strategies members within the same team employed to reach consensus during the decision-making activity. My students reported that when conflict emerged within their team, they found it helpful to return to the data to analyze them more carefully, which is exactly what scientists do. Through this experience, they learned that the objective is the foundation for justifying a more subjective perspective. This also brought up questions about the role science plays in constructing arguments. Does and should it serve as a lens for making decisions based on varying perspectives? Should this be the general rule applied to all decisions that individuals make when they take on a personal or stakeholder's lens to support a cause? As students were constructing their arguments, we discussed how to "play fair" or objectively with the facts and data while still using a voice that is more subjective or related to stakeholder roles. Students discussed that they have seen times when people construct arguments based more on the subjective interpretation of data and how these individuals make themselves vulnerable to having their arguments dismissed by an audience as they are questioned as to their credibility. My students found this ironic when they realized that the voice of the stakeholder could be more effectively considered when it is shaped and moderated by the voice of the scientist. Of course this discussion brought up all sorts of issues concerning biases that can exist within any reporting made in journals and newspapers, on TV, and on the Internet. **AID** Students who really understand this decision-making dilemma can be challenged by asking

(Continued)

(Continued)

Unit Sequence—Curriculum of Practice and Identity	Teacher Reflections
message that has solid support. To assist you in planning this essay, I have provided you with a ***Persuasive Essay Graphic Organizer*** *(Appendix 2K). So use these steps to guide your thinking:* 1. *Choose your position. Which site have you decided to prioritize? This becomes your claim.* 2. *Structure your essay using the graphic organizer. Figure out what evidence you will include and in what order you will present the evidence. Remember to consider your purpose, your audience, and your stakeholder role.* 3. *Use what you have brainstormed to write the essay into paragraph form. Members of your team can be assigned to different sections of the essay."* **Activity 3: Presenting Stakeholder Priorities and Hosting a Scholarly Colloquium** After students complete their persuasive essays have each team present their findings to the class. Discuss with the students how their argument was shaped by data and by their stakeholder's perspective at the same time. Ask teams to respond to the following questions: • Why didn't we all reach consensus on a particular site to clean up? • Is it ever possible to reach consensus when you have multiple perspectives? • How can our differences actually be constructive when trying to reach consensus? • What is the role of science in making decisions that are filtered through varying perspectives? • Which presentation seemed more credible and why? • What do these presentations have in common and is there a way to consider all these perspectives in order to shape a decision?	them to construction their persuasive essays using third-person passive voice. As a teacher you will also experience varying developmental and readiness levels emerge as some advanced-level students become more concerned with how to construct an essay using more objective data to support their arguments, while others are clearly more focused on winning or losing the argument and not paying enough attention to constructing an argument using reliable and credible evidence. By asking advanced-level students to construct an essay using third-person passive voice, the objective voice can be heard. This assignment modification may better match the readiness level of advanced students. As students construct their essays, distribute the **Persuasive Essay Rubric** (Appendix 2L) to guide their performance. This rubric can be used to guide teacher-student conversations about the quality of their arguments within the essay. During this activity, the teacher should purposely rotate to the teams to elicit and analyze the explanations that students are constructing as well as the evidence they are documenting in order to effectively construct their arguments. They should be encouraged to consider how to use alternative or counter positions to support their arguments as well. This assessment technique is useful in assessing the reasoning students are using as they construct an argument and prepare for their final presentations. A teacher may find it necessary to work with students in small groups to refine student reasoning during these assignments. By providing skills training while students are working on the learning tasks helps to refine student thinking and promote skill transfer. **Other Discussions That Emerged During Student Presentations:** Many discussions and questions emerged during the presentations made by the various stakeholder teams that I chose to follow-up on with the students. I found that during the presentations, students came to question the relationship between society and science. They began to wonder how this relationship could coexist while still being true to individual or group perspectives that

Unit Sequence—Curriculum of Practice and Identity	Teacher Reflections
• How could we analyze all of these decisions in order to see a pattern of concern that would help us select one or more of these sites that would be best for beginning our cleanup efforts? (Some students suggested the use of a Venn diagram to analyze an overlap of these decisions and to identify where all or at least most of the stakeholders' choices were in agreement. This helped them to see the complexity of making a decision that is in the best interest of all groups.)	will exist in a society. They also wondered under what conditions do we typically see this relationship coexist and began to question whether this should occur or does it benefit scientific research when these varying perspectives reveal themselves. They asked should science operate in partnership with varying stakeholders? What are the merits and challenges this relationship would pose? All of these student questions help me to realize the importance of helping students understand that science can't tell us what is right or wrong, good or bad, but it can provide objective data that are often filtered through many lenses (ethical, socially driven group perspectives, individually held personal decisions) to generate decisions. The challenging question for all humans is to consider is how these varying perspectives ever reach consensus . . . can they, do they, under what conditions should they? **AID** Ask students to consider to what degree their personal lens shaped their scientific perspective or vice versa. Is it possible to still be a scientist and possess a personal perspective about an issue or idea? Do you have to give up your personal perspective to become a scientist or is this tension the angst that helps to create a scientist's research agenda? Ask them to research these questions to find out how scholars resolve this paradoxical situation.
Debriefing and Closure	
Ask students to select from the various journal prompts and to respond to these statements or questions in their science journals. These prompts vary in complexity, so you may need to assist students in making the appropriate selection based on their readiness and interest. **Prompt 1** What have you learned about yourself in this unit? Consider this as you read the statement below. Do you agree or disagree with this statement? Provide support for your position based on your learning experiences in this unit.	I chose to create several prompts from which students could select to reflect on how their identity was influenced or changed by the learning in which they were engaged. The first two choices ask students to reveal how their personal identity has been changed as a result of their learning experiences in this unit, while the third prompt requires them to consider how varying voices are necessary to solve complex problems. The first prompt requires students to analyze how their skills have changed as a science student when they reflect on a statement that is often quoted about the type

(Continued)

(Continued)

Unit Sequence—Curriculum of Practice and Identity	Teacher Reflections
The work of science relies on basic human qualities, such as reasoning, insight, energy, skill, and creativity—as well as on scientific habits of mind, such as intellectual honesty, tolerance of ambiguity, skepticism, and openness to new ideas. **Prompt 2** Think about your own personal identity and voice as you respond to the following questions: • How do I keep my own voice in a group while other voices vary in their perspectives? • Why is it important for me to recognize my personal voice and perspective while simultaneously exploring the possibilities that may occur when I consider other perspectives? • Is it possible to have both an objective and subjective voice? • Can I be a scientist and still hold a personal perspective? **Prompt 3** What is the role of science in our society? To explore this question conduct the following performance tasks: 1. Compare and contrast the voices of two people involved with global climate change by reading the interview of Susan Solomon, who is an atmospheric chemist involved in global climate change research, and viewing excerpts of Al Gore, who is a former politician and currently an environmental advocate on global climate change and featured in the movie An Inconvenient Truth (see Online Resources to find these references). 2. As you read the interview and view excerpts from the film, discuss the importance of hearing both voices; one whose role it is to represent the scientific community (Solomon) and the other voice that represents the climate policy advocate (Gore). Identify the relationship that exists between these two voices. Ask yourself: Do they need each other? Does science need a storyteller? Why? Can science operate without advocates/policymakers?	of skills and dispositions required in the scientific world. The second prompt asks students to reflect on the struggle to maintain a perspective or voice in the midst of professional standards and/or when considering other perspectives. In the third prompt, students are asked to consider the role that varying voices can have in the shaping of major scientific decisions. I want them to consider the possibilities that exist between and among these voices and in particular to question the possibility of being able to maintain an objective perspective while simultaneously being personally vested in an issue. This prompt should lead students to explore the notion that credible stakeholders don't have much of a voice or argument without considering objective data gathered from scientists, and the reverse to this argument is that the objective voice often is not heard until it is revealed through a voice that does hold a more subjective perspective.

Unit 2 Appendixes

APPENDIX 2A: CAUSE-AND-EFFECT T-CHART

Figure 2.1

GRAPHIC ORGANIZER: CAUSE-AND-EFFECT T-CHART

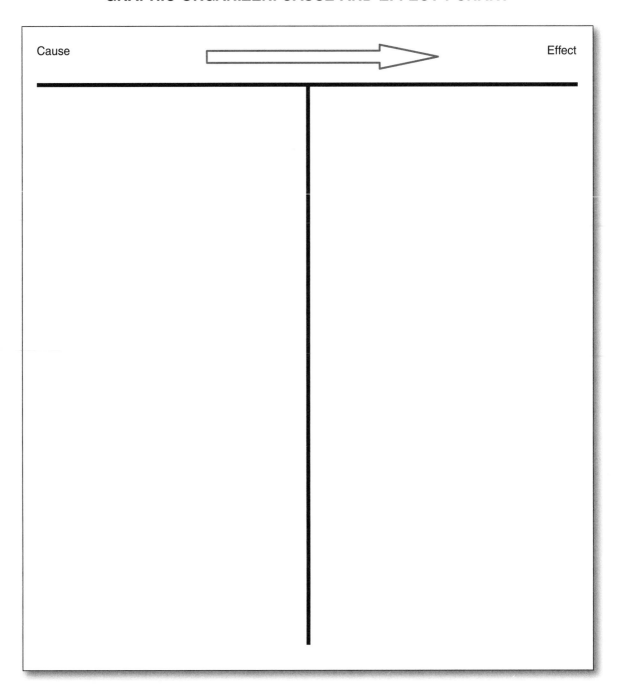

APPENDIX 2B: WHO, WHAT, WHEN, WHERE, AND WHY

Figure 2.2

GRAPHIC ORGANIZER: WHO, WHAT, WHEN, WHERE, AND WHY

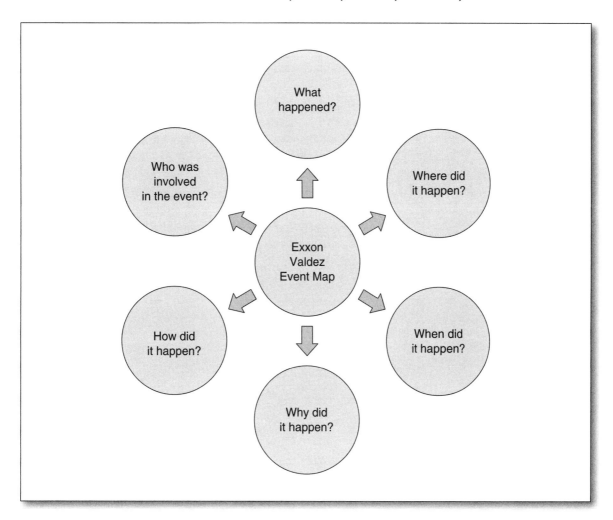

APPENDIX 2C: NOTE-TAKING GRAPHIC ORGANIZER EXAMPLE: CORNELL NOTE-TAKING FORMAT

Figure 2.3

NOTE-TAKING GRAPHIC ORGANIZER EXAMPLE: CORNELL NOTE-TAKING FORMAT

Subject: **Note-taking**   Date: _____

Main Ideas	*Details*
• Cornell notes Semantic map or web 	• There are a couple of ways you can take notes. The Cornell method is best when the information is given in a sequential, orderly fashion and allows for more detail. The semantic web/map method works best for information that provides a "big picture" when you're previewing materials or getting ready to study for a test. • Students have learned that they can use this side of the graphic organizer to capture the main idea of the information being read or from information presented in lecture format. • Students also have been taught to use this column to define terms or explain concepts listed on the left side.

Summary:

• After class, write a summary of what you learned to clarify and reinforce learning and to assist retention.

APPENDIX 2D: NOTE-TAKING GRAPHIC ORGANIZER

Subject: _____   Date: _____

Main Ideas	Details

Summary:

APPENDIX 2E: QUESTIONS GRAPHIC ORGANIZER

Directions: Use this graphic organizer to create questions about the Exxon Valdez Oil Spill that are of interest to you. For example, you may have a question like, "What happened to the animals?" As you learn more about this event, these questions may change.

Questions that I have about this disaster.	Categories that these questions address.	Are these questions based on personal or scientific perspectives?	What could be the consequences of my thinking in this manner?	What group of people or scientists would be interested in this question?

APPENDIX 2F: DATA COLLECTION GRAPHIC ORGANIZER

(Use one form for each site.)

Site: _____

Observation	Question(s)	Data	Possible Conclusions

APPENDIX 2G: SUMMARY DATA MATRIX TO COMPILE YOUR FINDINGS

Use this matrix to compile your findings for each site. This summary should give you an overview of the categories that are affected most at each site and whether this site should be considered in your final analysis. You can simply record a check mark in the boxes to indicate if each category is vulnerable or record brief notes about what you found out in your research.

Site	Shores	Animals	Human Resources	Historical/Cultural Resources	Other?

APPENDIX 2H: EVALUATE THE QUALITY OF YOUR THINKING CHART

Assessment of Skills and Dispositions	Teacher Comments/Student Comments
I use a variety of sources during my research.	
I asked questions to clarify meaning or confirm my understanding.	
I assess problems or situations by careful analysis of the evidence gathered.	
I critically evaluate the inferences and conclusions I make by basing arguments on facts rather than opinion.	
I honestly report and record observations.	
I choose to consider situations from multiple perspectives.	
I usually remain skeptical of a proposal or argument until evidence is offered to support it.	
I can pick out biased and inaccurate interpretations.	
I willingly repeat measurements or observations to increase the precision of evidence.	

APPENDIX 2I: DECISION-MAKING MATRIX

Directions: Use this decision-making matrix to select your site priority.

Alternatives: Site 1, Site 2, Site 3, Site 4, Site 5, Site 6, Site 7

Selection Criteria

1. _____
2. _____
3. _____
4. _____
5. _____

Decision Matrix

Alternatives	Criterion 1	Criterion 2	Criterion 3	Criterion 4	Criterion 5	Total Score (Add across)
Site 1						
Site 2						
Site 3						
Site 4						
Site 5						
Site 6						
Site 7						

Selection Criteria

Scoring

1–7=low score; 7=high score

Decision and Reasons

Researchers' Names: _____   Site Number Priority: _____

Stakeholder Lens: _____

Priority for Clean Up: _____   Because _____

_____

_____

_____

_____

APPENDIX 2J: DECISION-MAKING RUBRIC

Stakeholder Group Members: _____

Stakeholder Role: _____

Trait	3	2	1
Identifies Alternatives	Identifies alternatives that include the 7 sites.	Identifies only a portion of the alternatives.	Identifies alternatives that are not related to the decision.
Identifies Selective Criteria for Assessing Alternatives	Identifies important and less obvious criteria reflecting a thorough understanding of the situation.	Identifies the important criteria that should be considered.	Identifies only some important criteria.
Applies Criteria to Alternatives on the Decision-Making Grid	Determines the extent to which each alternative possesses each criterion and justifies this with appropriate information or knowledge at an unusual level of depth.	Determines the extent to which each alternative possesses each criterion and justifies this with appropriate information or knowledge.	Can't determine the extent to which some of the alternatives possess some of the criteria.
Evaluates Results, States the Decision, and Provides Reasons	Evaluates whether important scores or criteria should be changed or dropped in a way that reflects an in-depth understanding of the subject. Supports decision with reasons.	Evaluates whether important scores or criteria should be changed or dropped in a way that reflects understanding of the subject. Supports the decision with few reasons.	Has difficulty evaluating whether important scores or criteria should be changed or dropped. Can't support their decision with reasons.

APPENDIX 2K: PERSUASIVE ESSAY ORGANIZER

Researchers' Names: _____

Date: _____

Introduction

Main Idea/Topic Sentence: _____

_____

Supporting Reasons

Body 1 _____

_____

Body 2 _____

_____

Body 3 _____

Conclusion sentence: _____

_____

Body 1

Reason 1 _____

_____

Detail/Example 1 _____

_____

Detail/Example 2 _____

_____

Detail/Example 3 _____

_____

Conclusion sentence: _____

_____

Body 2

Reason 2 _____

_____

Detail/Example 1 _____

_____

Detail/Example 2 _____

_____

(Continued)

(Continued)

Detail/Example 3 _____

_____

Conclusion sentence: _____

_____

Body 3

Reason 3 _____

_____

Detail/Example 1 _____

_____

Detail/Example 2 _____

_____

Detail/Example 3 _____

_____

Conclusion sentence: _____

_____

Conclusion

Restate Main Idea: _____

_____

Restate Supporting Reasons

1. _____

_____

2. _____

_____

3. _____

_____

Recommendations and/or Predictions: _____

_____

APPENDIX 2L: PERSUASIVE ESSAY RUBRIC

Criterion	3	2	1
The claim	We make a claim and explain why it is controversial.	We make a claim but don't explain why it is controversial.	Our claim is buried, confused, and/or unclear.
Reasons in support of the claim	We give clear and accurate reasons in support of our claim.	We give reasons in support of our claim, but we may overlook important reasons.	We give 1 or 2 weak reasons that don't support our claim and/or irrelevant or confusing reasons.
Reasons against the claim	We discuss the reasons against our claim and explain why it is valid anyway.	We discuss the reasons against our claim but leave some reasons out and/or don't explain why the claim still stands.	We say that there are reasons against the claim but don't discuss them.
Organization	Our writing has a compelling opening, an informative middle, and a powerful conclusion.	Our writing has a beginning, middle, and end. It is persuasive but not compelling.	Our writing is organized but sometimes gets off topic.
Voice and tone	It sounds like we care about our argument. We show how we think and feel about it.	Our tone is OK but we need to tell more about how we think and feel.	Our writing doesn't show how we think and feel about the argument.
Conventions	We use correct grammar, spelling, and punctuation.	We generally use correct conventions.	There are too many errors in our essay that will distract a reader.

APPENDIX 2M: ONLINE RESOURCES FOR EXXON VALDEZ OIL SPILL STATIONS

These resources were used to create the PowerPoint presentation, create the learning stations, and to gather photographs, articles, and information to share with the students.

General Background on the Exxon Valdez Oil Spill

Exxon Valdez Oil Spill Trustee Council: http://www.evostc.state.ak.us/facts/index.cfm

The U.S. Department of Commerce: http://oceanservice.noaa.gov/education/stories/oilymess/oily01_infamous.html

Teachers' Domain: http://www.teachersdomain.org/resource/ess05.sci.ess.watcyc.exxon/

NOAA Fisheries: http://www.fakr.noaa.gov/oil/default.htm

National Oceanic and Atmospheric Administration (NOAA) 200th Year Celebration: http://celebrating200years.noaa.gov/events/exxonvaldez/welcome.html

Survivors of the Exxon Valdez: http://www.jomiller.com/exxonvaldez/manipulation.html

Newspaper Articles

Anchorage Daily News: http://www.adn.com/evos/pgs/sp2.html

Online Articles

E-TECH INTERNATIONAL, INC.: ESI PUBLICATIONS

http://www.oil-spill-info.com/index.htm

SCIENCE/AMERICAN ASSOCIATION FOR THE ADVANCEMENT OF SCIENCE

http://www.sciencemag.org/cgi/content/abstract/302/5653/2082

NOAA

http://response.restoration.noaa.gov/book_shelf/967_TM125.pdf

UNIVERSITY OF ALASKA: MARINE ADVISORY PROGRAM

http://seagrant.uaf.edu/bookstore/pubs/QTR-VII-3.html

Photographs

E-TECH INTERNATIONAL, INC. EXXON VALDEZ OIL SPILL PHOTOGRAPHS

http://www.oil-spill-info.com/

Audio/Visual Resources

THE WHOLE TRUTH: EXCERPTS OF AUDIO TRANSMISSION OF GROUNDING; MOVIE OF EXXON REPRESENTATIVE SPEAKING TO TOWN HALL MEETING

http://www.wholetruth.net/history.htm

NOAA: Oil Spill Trajectory Model (Specific to Prince William Sound)

http://oceanservice.noaa.gov/education/stories/oilymess/supp_trajmodel.html

Exploring Earth: What Happens When an Oil Spill Occurs?

http://www.classzone.com/books/earth_science/terc/content/investigations/es0703/es0703page01.cfm?chapter_no=investigation

Maps

Bearfoot Guides: (Download General Map of Prince William Sound)

http://www.alaska101.com/exploreAlaska/maps/

NOAA: Prince William Sound Environmental Sensitivity Index Atlas (Download the Spring Summary Map; pictures and data for stations)

http://www.asgdc.state.ak.us/maps/cplans/pws/esi/esi.html

NOAA: Site Pictures and Ecosystem Data (simplified graphic information software (GIS)-type software environment—ArcGIS not needed)

http://mapping.fakr.noaa.gov/Website/ShoreZone/viewer.htm

This is where I created the site maps for students to view. There are not specific names for each site, but if you take a look at the website's interactive map, you will see lots of red dots (each is a separate picture!). All I did was go to areas of Prince William Sound that seemed to match the sites I had chosen and selected pictures to represent these sites. I also specifically chose pictures with varying shorelines.

National Biological Information Infrastructure

Type in "ESI Maps" into the Search Box to retrieve resources for a more advanced exploration of ESI maps using GIS software (http://metadata.nbii.gov/clearinghouse/)

NOAA: Background on ESI Maps (how to use and how to download more detailed maps—PDF or ArcView GIS)

http://response.restoration.noaa.gov/type_subtopic_entry.php?RECORD_KEY%28entry_subtopic_type%29=entry_id,subtopic_id,type_id&entry_id(entry_subtopic_type)=74&subtopic_id(entry_subtopic_type)=8&type_id(entry_subtopic_type)=3

Additional Resources

Susan Solomon Interview on NPR

http://www.npr.org/templates/story/story.php?storyId=7126121

An Inconvenient Truth (Amazon.com)

http://www.amazon.com/Inconvenient-Truth-Al-Gore/dp/B000ICL3KG/ref=sr_1_1?ie=UTF8&s=dvd&qid=1237225625&sr=1–1

3

Systems

An Integrated Approach to Science and English Instruction, Grades 9–10

Kristina J. Doubet, PhD

INTRODUCTION TO THE UNIT

This group of lessons represents a snapshot of how ninth-grade English and biology curricula can be united in a meaningful, mutually beneficial manner. By exploring the interdependent nature and function of *systems*, students can delve deeply into virtually every major topic in ninth-grade biology: cell biology; genetics; evolution; ecology; plant and animal structure, growth, and reproduction; and human biology. Likewise, the study of English revolves around the study of systems; every story is itself a system with interdependent elements. Each of those elements comprises its own complex system: setting, plot structure, character development, the cyclical nature of conflict, and the interworking of the former elements to produce theme. By examining the systemic nature of both *life* (biology) and the attempt to capture the *human experience* of life (English literature), students can tunnel deeply into the essence of each discipline and discover its purpose and organization (The Core Curriculum). At the same time, students can use what they discover about each discipline to deepen their understanding of the other (The Curriculum of Connections). In other words, students should be able to apply their grasp of the complex nature of systems in science to better understand systems in English, and vice versa.

The portion of the unit included here is designed to serve as a course opener; thus, it begins with an interdisciplinary investigation of the concept of *systems*. The exploration asks students to connect the concept with areas of their interest/choice, including politics, music, sports, and astronomy. Next, students use their newfound understanding of systems to review and solidify prior subject-specific learning (biology—cell building blocks; English—story elements).

From there, the unit diverges into separate lessons for English and biology. The two English lessons explore the systems that lie at the heart of John Steinbeck's *The Pearl* (1945)—a novella typically featured in ninth-grade English curricula. These systems include the self (psyche), the family (nuclear and extended), and the larger community. The two science lessons, designed to be implemented at about the same time as are the English lessons, focus on cell structure as well as cell transport. A final integrated performance task allows students to connect what they've learned in both courses with the goal of demonstrating a sophisticated grasp of how systems operate at the heart of both content areas. At this overview's conclusion, suggestions for future applications outline how the concept of systems and its related principles can be woven into successive topics in both content areas.

This unit was inspired by the successful collaboration of a seventh-grade life science teacher and a seventh-grade language arts teacher working in an interdisciplinary team setting. Lisa Wells (Biology) and I (English) were both certified secondary teachers and true lovers of our content areas. Since we shared the same students and a preparation period, we often planned in the same room; consequently, we—at first serendipitously, later purposefully—discovered many areas of conceptual overlap between our two seemingly unrelated curricula. We decided to take advantage of these opportunities to reinforce one another's instruction. For example, when Lisa taught the scientific method, I taught characterization; our uniting concept was *investigation,* and students found that—as readers—they followed the same steps as a scientist when trying to determine what a character was like. First, they *observed* what the character did, said, thought, and how others responded to him or her. Next, they *drew inferences* from these observations, and then *gathered more data* (more of the character's thoughts, words, actions, and interactions). They used these new data to either *reinforce or revise their hypotheses.* The lightbulbs went off for many more students when we taught this way. Students who typically excelled in science were able to apply the conceptual scaffolding to English, and vice versa. Lisa and I, thrilled with our students' engagement and success, strove to make these connections whenever possible. Examples included ecosystems in science paired with plot structure in language arts (concept—*cause and effect*), and cell structure in science taught in consort with paragraph structure in language arts (concepts—*structure and function*).

Although Lisa and I eventually moved on to different schools and pursuits, we have never forgotten the sweetness of seeing our students catch and hold onto learning in such a powerful way. In fact, we discovered that teaching in a conceptual, connected fashion is actually *more efficient* than the traditional divide and conquer approach to teaching and learning! This ninth-grade unit on systems seeks these same goals of both efficiency and power in student learning. In the process, it explores questions posed by both the Core Parallel and the Parallel of Connections:

- What is the structure of this discipline? (*Core*)
- What are the key concepts and principles in this discipline? (*Core*)
- How are these key concepts and principles related to other topics or disciplines? (*Connections*)
- How are these key concepts and principles in biology/English related to those same concepts and principles in English/biology? (*Connections*)

- How might I use what I already know about these concepts and principles in (biology/English) to acquire a deeper understanding of those same concepts and principles in (English/biology)? (*Connections*)

BACKGROUND TO THE UNIT

Designed to introduce the courses of ninth-grade biology and English, this unit outtake assumes a certain degree of prior subject-specific learning. The biology portion begins with a *review* of the organic compounds, or building blocks of the cell (lipids, proteins); students must have at least a *familiarity* with these topics to be successful in this lesson. The English portion operates under the premise that students possess a relatively *high degree of comfort* with story elements (plot structure, conflict)— enough to be able to manipulate them and examine their interdependence. Although the opening activity is interest based, the unit includes preassessments designed to determine whether or not students possess the prior knowledge (for both content areas) necessary to successfully engage in the opening activity. Each preassessment enables the teacher to gauge the readiness of the entire class (to see if an introductory lesson or two are necessary before launching the opening activity) as well as the readiness of individuals (to determine the need to pull small groups, provide certain students with additional scaffolding, and so on).

AS TEACHERS PREPARE TO TEACH THESE LESSONS, THEY MAY WANT TO GATHER . . .

- Websites for Lesson 3.1's interest-based groups (astronomy, music, sports, government)
- Materials to familiarize one's self with the operation of an offensive line in football team (Biology Lesson 3.2)
- Access to software programs "Sim City" or "The Incredible Machine" (anchor activity for all lessons)
- Information (electronic and print at various levels) about how a pearl is formed (all English lessons)
- Information (electronic and print) on-the-job descriptions, requirements, and responsibilities of a psychologist, a microbiologist, and an anthropologist (throughout the entire unit, students can research these fields as anchor activities or a chance to deepen their understanding of subject matter).
- Videos on diffusion, osmosis, active and passive transport; labs to supplement.

CONTENT FRAMEWORK

Organizing Concepts

Macroconcepts

M1 System

M2 Survival

M3 Balance

Macroprinciples

MP1   The survival of a system depends upon the successful operation of each of its interdependent parts.

MP2   Change to one part of a system results in change to the rest of the system.

MP3   Systems strive to achieve and maintain balance.

Discipline-Specific Concepts

C1   Identity (English)

C2   Environment (biology and English)

C3   Function (biology and English)

C4   Conflict (biology and English)

Discipline-Specific Principles

P1   One's sense of identity is shaped, in part, by one's environment (English).

P2   The function of an organism reflects the environment in which it operates (biology):

   (P1 + P2 = Function/identity reflects the environment in which it operates).

P3   Function dictates structure (English and biology).

P4   Conflict can strengthen or destroy a system (biology and English).

National or State Standards

Virginia Standards of Learning for Secondary Biology

BI0.4   The student will investigate and understand relationships between cell structure and function. Key concepts include the following:

   a. Characteristics of prokaryotic and eukaryotic cells;
   b. Exploring the diversity and variation of eukaryotes;
   c. Similarities between the activities of a single cell and a whole organism; and
   d. The cell membrane model (diffusion, osmosis, and active transport).

(*Note:* This standard applies to the lessons featured herein.)

BI0.5   The student will investigate and understand life functions of plants and animals, including humans. Key concepts include the following:

   a. How their structures and functions vary between and within the kingdoms;
   b. Comparison of their metabolic activities;
   c. Analyses of their responses to the environment;
   d. Maintenance of homeostasis; and
   e. Human health issues, human anatomy, body systems, and life functions.

(*Note:* This standard applies to content to be explored later in the course.)

Virginia Standards of Learning for English, Grade 9

Reading Analysis

9.3 The student will read and analyze a variety of literature.

   a. Identify format, text structure, and main idea.
   b. Identify the characteristics that distinguish literary forms.
   c. Use literary terms in describing and analyzing selections.
   d. Explain the relationships between and among elements of literature: characters, plot, setting, tone, point of view, and theme.
   e. Explain the relationship between the author's style and literary effect.
   f. Describe the use of images and sounds to elicit the reader's emotions.
   g. Explain the influence of historical context on the form, style, and point of view of a written work.

(*Note:* This standard applies to the lessons featured herein as well as to content to be explored later in the course.)

Writing

9.6 The student will develop narrative, expository, and informational writings to inform, explain, analyze, or entertain.

   a. Generate, gather, and organize ideas for writing.
   b. Plan and organize writing to address a specific audience and purpose.
   c. Communicate clearly the purpose of the writing.
   d. Write clear, varied sentences.
   e. Use specific vocabulary and information.
   f. Arrange paragraphs into a logical progression.
   g. Revise writing for clarity.
   h. Proofread and prepare final product for intended audience and purpose.

(*Note:* This standard applies to content to be explored later in the course.)

Skills

S1 (B)   Analyze systems to determine cause–effect relationships within cell makeup, structure, and function.

S2 (B)   Analyze systems to determine cause–effect relationships within and among various biologic systems.

S3 (B)   Evaluate the importance/role of each part of a given biologic system.

S4 (E/B)   Make/demonstrate connections between systems in English and in biology and in the world beyond the classroom.

S5 (E)   Analyze literature to determine cause–effect relationships within story structure and among character relationships.

S7 (E)   Evaluate the effectiveness of authors' portrayals of characters, conflicts, and themes.

LESSON/UNIT ASSESSMENTS

Preassessment

To determine student readiness (included at the end of Lesson 3.1):

- Story Elements Preassessment
- Organic Compounds/Cell Building Block Preassessment
- Cell Structure Preassessment

Formative Assessments

- Literary Elements (English Lesson 3.2)
- Evaluating Kino's Decisions (English Lesson 3.3)
- Cell Structure (eukaryotic) (Science Lesson 3.2)
- Cell Survival Mechanisms Description/Concept Map (Science Lesson 3.3)

It is important to note that two copies of each preassessment are provided for the teacher. The first copy is a blank that is ready for copying and distribution to students. The other copy contains an answer key on which correct responses are shaded.

Postassessment

Assignment description and planning sheet included at the end of Science Lesson 3.3.

Essay: Compare and contrast the cell's operation as a system to the operation of one or more systems from *The Pearl*. You may include diagrams to supplement your written discussion. Make comparisons based on THREE of the unit's six principles:

1. The *survival* of a *system* depends upon the successful operation of each of its interdependent parts.

2. Change to one part of a *system* results in change to the rest of the *system*.

3. *Systems* strive to achieve and maintain *balance*.

4. *Function/identity* reflects the environment in which it operates.

5. *Function* dictates structure.

6. *Conflict* can strengthen or destroy a *system*.

Criteria for Success

Although the primary purpose of the preassessments is to drive instruction, two of the preassessments can also be used to measure growth. The "Story Elements Preassessment" and the "Cell Structure Preassessment" can serve as both pre- and postassessments, giving the teacher a clear picture of how students have progressed in their learning. The "Cell Structure" preassessment can be given as is both at the beginning and the end of the unit as a means of objectively tracking growth. To best utilize the "Story Elements" preassessment as a tool to measure growth, the teacher should select an alternate familiar tale for students to analyze (rather than reusing "The Boy Who Cried Wolf"). If students are able to apply what they've learned to a new yet parallel situation, it will be clear that they have mastered the content.

Mastery of the content in both content areas will be measured via student performance on the essay assessment administered at the close of the unit. Criteria for success on this assessment are outlined in the essay's rubric and include the following:

- Demonstrates a strong grasp of each of the unit's principles through providing appropriate examples of these principles at work in both systems discussed.
- Thoroughly and accurately discusses the cell's (eukaryotic) interdependent structures and operations (cell membrane [marker, receptor, and transport proteins], cytoplasm, cytoskeleton, nucleus, ribosomes, ER, vesicles, lysosomes, Golgi apparatus, mitochondria, DNA, RNA, enzymes, cell wall, chloroplasts, and central vacuole).
- Thoroughly and accurately discuss active and passive transport (osmosis, diffusion, hypotonic, hypertonic, sodium-potassium pump, movement against a concentration gradient, endocytosis, exocytosis, signal molecule, ATP).
- Thoroughly discuss one or more of the following systems from *The Pearl*—the self/psyche; the family (immediate and fishermen's village); the larger community (town)—in terms of its interdependent parts and their relationships.
- Demonstrate a thorough understanding of the characters' identities, conflicts, and perspectives, and discuss how setting impacts them as well as how they work together to shape theme.
- Make genuine connections between the purpose and relationships in literature and cell structure and function.

As with any Curriculum of Connections unit, it is interesting to think of the possibilities a Connection unit opens. To capitalize on the genuine understanding fostered by examining English and science in an interdisciplinary fashion through the uniting concept of *systems,* teachers may want to continue this focus in subsequent units. Several unit suggestions follow, each of which can continue to focus on the macroconcepts and principles outlined at the unit's outset.

Biologic Systems

- Respiratory/circulatory systems
- Digestive/excretory systems
- Endocrine system
- Nervous system
- Immune system

Systems in *Romeo and Juliet*

- Upper levels of hierarchical Verona society in Tudor and Early Stuart societies
- Capulet and Montague feud

- Romeo and Juliet's relationship
- Cycle of misunderstandings

Writing as a System

- Purpose drives form
- Purpose drives organization
- Purpose and audience inform choices about grammar
- Audience determines style
- Audience determines word choice and grammatical conventions
- Organization and expression drive clarity and, subsequently, understanding

LESSON SEQUENCE AND TEACHER REFLECTION

Unit Preparation and Preassessment

Time allocation: 30 minutes for each assessment

Unit Sequence	Reflection
A few days before the unit begins, teachers for both content areas should administer the preassessments designed for their content areas (see the end of Lesson 3.1).	These preassessments are designed to reveal students' grasp of previously studied material (story elements and organic compounds). The results of these assessments should be used to form the readiness groups featured in Steps 7 and 10 (Part 2); however, they may reveal that all students need to review the content. If so, a review should be built in to instruction prior to Lesson 1 or prior to the beginning of Part 2 of Lesson 3.1.

Lesson 3.1: An Introduction to Systems

Time allocation: 90–120 minutes

Concepts

This lesson serves as an introduction to the macroconcepts with which students will be grappling for the entire unit. All aspects of life revolve around these concepts, and this lesson gives students the chance to discover the relevance of these concepts by investigation a system of their choosing—one with which they feel a connection.

M1 System
M2 Survival
M3 Balance

Principles

Students will actually examine and *test* these principles during this lesson in an attempt to establish their truth. If these concepts and principles are going to guide student learning for two entire courses, students must first connect genuinely with them.

MP1 The survival of a system depends upon the successful operation of each of its interdependent parts.

MP2 Change to one part of a system results in change to the rest of the system.

MP3 Systems strive to achieve and maintain balance.

Skills

Although this will be students' first experience exercising these skills, future lessons will call upon students to build upon this skill set with increasing degrees of both complexity and specificity.

Analyze systems to determine cause-and-effect relationships within the parts of a given system.

Evaluate the importance/role of each part of a given system.

Make connections among English, biology, and the world beyond the classroom.

Standards

Although this introductory lesson *sets the stage* for students to master both English and biology standards, it does not call upon students to deal with them directly.

Guiding Questions

These questions should help students unpack the principles. They are the essential questions (Wiggins & McTighe, 2006) with which students will grapple for the remainder of both courses.

1. What is a system?

2. What determines whether or not a system will survive?

3. What happens to a system when we change or take away one of its parts? What happens when we add an additional element?

4. How would you evaluate the role and importance of balance in a system?

Unit Sequence—Core Curriculum	Teacher Reflections
Class Session 1	This interest-based lesson asks students to examine the nature of interdependent systems by investigating a system of their choice. Interest-based groups work together to answer the "guiding questions" about a system in government, music, sports, or astronomy.
<div align="center">**Introduction**</div>	
1. Begin the class by asking students, in think-pair-share format, how they would describe or define a "system." During the share phase, make a web or map of student responses on the board or overhead. Students can work individually or in pairs to generate definitions of "system" that synthesize the information on the board. 2. Pairs "pair up" to form quads; students combine the two definitions into one. 3. Each quad pairs with another quad to recombine once more; these definitions are shared and written on the board. The teacher works with the entire class to fashion one definition that encompasses those contributed by the groups of eight. The class should craft an inclusive yet parsimonious definition. This definition will be posted in the room and referred to throughout both courses.	Asking students to generate a definition rather than simply giving them the definition ensures that they will be more engaged and more likely to remember the definition. They get at it three ways—pulling from their own experience, melding it with others' experiences, and evaluating responses to generate the best definition possible. The teacher can guide students through both of the "share" phases, working to ensure that student definitions approximate the actual definition of a system: <div align="center">*"A set or combination of independent yet inter-related, interdependent parts forming a unified whole working toward a specific purpose"* (paraphrased from The American Heritage Dictionary *and* WordNet)</div>
<div align="center">**Teaching Strategies and Learning Experiences**</div>	
1. Four Corners: Display list of four interest area choices (Music, Politics, Sports, Astronomy). Give students each an index card and ask them to write down the choice that interests them most. Then, assign one corner of the room to each area of interest, and send students to those corners with their index card and a writing utensil. Circulate among the groups to ensure that students have moved to their "corner of choice" rather than to the corner to which their friends have moved. Groups move to an area of the room that is comfortable and provides a workable space for them. They will be responsible for researching and presenting information that answers the following question (on task cards):	The "Four Corners" strategy benefits adolescent learners in three ways: (1) it allows students to enter into learning through an avenue of their choice, thus fostering investment in the task and forging connections with content; (2) it allows students to "join forces" with other students who share similar interests, in the process building connections among peers and fostering community; (3) it gives students a chance to get up and moving, which is no small thing when adolescent development is considered!

Unit Sequence—Core Curriculum	Teacher Reflections

Music
 	
 • Describe the function of each member of a band or vocal group.
 • Explain how the group works as a system.
 • Simulate how they work together to accomplish a purpose (e.g., studio recording, concert, etc.).
 • Demonstrate what would happen if:
 	
  o One part (instrument or vocal part) quit working or began to malfunction.
  o A new part was introduced.
 	
 Government/Politics
 	
 • Describe the function of each part of our three branches of government/system of checks and balances.
 • Explain how they work as a system.
 • Simulate how these parts work together to accomplish a purpose (e.g., make a law; distribute power).
 • Demonstrate what would happen if:
 	
  o One part (branch) quit working or began to malfunction.
  o A new part (branch) was introduced.
 	
 Sports
 	
 • Describe the function of each part (player/position) of a sports team (your choice of sport).
 • Explain how it works as a system.
 • Simulate how these parts work together to accomplish a purpose (e.g., make a play; win a game).
 • Demonstrate what would happen if:
 	
  o One part (player/position) quit working or began to malfunction.
  o A new part (position or player) was introduced.
 	
 Astronomy
 	
 • Describe the function of each part of the Earth's role/place in the solar system (Earth, sun, moon, orbit, gravity).
 • Explain how they work together as a system.
	Music is a powerful source of motivation in the lives of students; thus, this category is likely to have a lot of "takers." It might be helpful to divide students into subgroups based upon more specific interests, such as orchestra, vocal ensemble, and popular music. This subdividing can be done before or after students move to their corner, but in order for this to be efficient, you may want to ask students to write their areas of "special interest" on their index cards.
	
	 Sports, like music, may be a popular topic; therefore, it might also be helpful to divide students into subgroups based upon more specific sports. Again, asking students to write their areas of special interest on their index cards will make the process of subdividing more efficient.
	
	  Every group of students is different, and a few of these suggested areas of interest may not actually interest anyone! A safe substitute category is "school," as all students can relate to it. Students could discuss the school itself as a system, their particular class as a system, or a system within the school system, such as student council. They should still discuss school in the same manner all other topics are discussed (parts, how they work together, and how they do so to attain a purpose, and what would happen if one part quit working and if an additional part was added).

(Continued)

(Continued)

Unit Sequence—Core Curriculum	Teacher Reflections

• Simulate how these parts work together to accomplish a purpose (e.g., sustain life as we know it).
• Demonstrate what would happen if:
 	
  o One part quit working or began to malfunction.
  o A new part was introduced.	

2. After sufficient preparation and rehearsal time (approximately 15 minutes), each group presents its system: (a) at work, (b) with a part removed or malfunctioning, and (c) a new part added. 3. After each group presentation, the teacher records notes (on the board, LCD) about what happened to the system during scenarios b and c. 4. At the conclusion of group presentations, the class should study the list on the board and begin to make connections/groupings to generalize what happens when a system's normal elements and processes are interrupted. Guide student discussions to the following conclusions: When a system's normal parts and processes are disturbed, the system responds by:	To provide students with additional scaffolding, if needed, the teacher might want to be ready with prompting pictures or websites for students to observe to get the initial juices flowing. If students need additional avenues to pursue, check to see if the school has access to the software games "The Incredible Machine" or "Sim City." Students can be encouraged to experiment with either. They provide wonderful examples of interdependent systems.

a. Adjusting or adapting (rebalancing) its processes to incorporate the change; this results in a lasting change to the system itself.
  b. Expelling the addition or change; this results in no lasting change to the system.
  c. Collapsing (destruction of the system).
 	
5. Explain that systems are everywhere. Return to the definition and ask students to give you other examples of systems present in their world. Record these on the board. Instruct students to pick one of these areas to "investigate" for the next class period. They should come to class prepared to share how their chosen system:
 	
  o Adheres to the definition of "system."
  o Deals with changes/additions.
  o Adheres to option a, b, or c (above).
 	
This will serve as closure for this portion of the lesson.
	In essence, the teacher is asking students to examine the ideas probed by the guiding questions:
	
	• What determines whether or not a system will survive?
	• What happens to a system when we change or take away one of its parts? What happens when we add an additional element?
	
	How would you evaluate the role and importance of balance in a system?
	  This at-home activity encourages students to continue making connections on their own. The more students see systems at work in their own lives, the more "glue" they'll have in their brains to which subject-specific information about systems can stick.

Unit Sequence—Core Curriculum	Teacher Reflections
Class Session II 6. Begin with students, in think-pair-share fashion, discussing their findings from their "investigations" (described in Step 5). Use student discussion to transition to the idea that—just as in other areas of life—we can find systems at work in both English and science. 7. Present students with a list of literary terms and definitions (or point them toward the appropriate pages in their literature texts) along with a well-known fable or story (e.g., "The Boy Who Cried Wolf"). Use results of preassessment to divide students into the following groups:	These steps can take place in combined classrooms or within individual subject-area classrooms, depending upon the flexibility of time and space. If implemented in a combined setting, complete Steps 7–12 plus closure together. If implemented in separate classes, complete Steps 7–9, 12, and closure in the English classroom and Steps 7, 10–12, plus closure, in science class.
Setting What would happen to the story's plot, characters, conflicts, and theme if the story were set in modern day New York City (Central Park)? Rewrite or retell the story with this change and explain how the other story elements are affected. Which are affected most by the change in setting? Least?	These group activities require ascending levels of intellectual demand. The "setting" group task calls for students to examine concrete alterations to the story; hence, these students will examine cause-and-effect relationships which yield limited and defined results. This task is well suited for students who need a review of the story elements and/or who require additional scaffolding in examining cause and effect relationships.
Character What would happen to the story's plot, setting, conflicts, and theme if the boy in the story were an old woman…or…if the boy had a "partner in crime?" Rewrite or retell the story with this change and explain how the other story elements are affected. Which are affected most by the character change? Least?	The "character" group's task also requires students to wrestle with concrete alterations to the story, but they will be less restricted in imagining and designing the effects to the other story elements.
Conflict Suppose the boy was acting as a secret government agent responsible for testing the community's emergency response system. Rewrite or retell the story with this change incorporated and explain how the other story elements are affected. Which are affected most by the additional conflict? Least?	The "conflict" group will wrestle with the most abstract changes to the story as well as the most open-ended story alterations. This "twist" can take the story in limitless directions, bringing this group's task closest to an examination of real-world events.
8. Form heterogeneous trios (one each from setting, character, and conflict groups) and ask students to share their rewrites/retellings and findings with each other.	All students will have something unique (and interesting) to bring to the discussion of how this story shifts and changes due to alterations to one or more of its elements.

(Continued)

(Continued)

Unit Sequence—Core Curriculum	Teacher Reflections
After trios have shared, engage in full-group discussion about results: How does a story act as a system? Which elements seemed to "run the show," or have the biggest impact on the other story elements. Which proved immutable? What does that tell us about stories and their dynamics? Which of the following options seemed to fit the story system best?	This "3-dimensional" view of the interdependence of a story system will reveal the interconnected nature of the discipline and prepare students to delve into such cause-and-effect relationships in literature, writing, history, and—of course—science.
a. Adjusting or adapting its processes to incorporate the change; this results in a lasting change to the system itself.	
b. Expelling the addition or change; this results in no lasting change to the system.	
c. Collapsing (destruction of the system).	
9. Use the last question to transition to a discussion of systems in science—more specifically, cell building blocks or molecules. Present students with a list of the definitions and functions of the following terms (or point them to the appropriate pages in their science texts):	These groups will not necessarily be in the same formation as the story elements group, as the two formations are based on different assessments. If these two learning experiences take place in the same classroom, the shifting of students will foster community and an accurate picture of the dynamic nature of human intelligence
• Carbohydrates • Lipids • Proteins (amino acids) • Nucleic acids (DNA/RNA) • ATP	
10. Use results of preassessment to divide students into the following groups:	
Carbohydrates What would happen to a cell's functioning if its carbohydrates disappeared or malfunctioned? How would this affect the functioning and success of the cell itself? The ATP molecules? Write and/or illustrate a description of these changes. You can share them from the point of view of the cell and its parts or from the point of view of a scientist observing this phenomenon.	These activities require ascending levels of intellectual demand. The "carbohydrate" task calls for students to examine a single-faceted change—one that is foundational to the functioning of the system; hence, this task is well suited for students who need a review of the cell building blocks and/or who require additional scaffolding in examining cause and effect relationships.

Unit Sequence—Core Curriculum	Teacher Reflections
Lipids What would happen to a cell's functioning if its lipids disappeared or malfunctioned? How would this affect the functioning and success of the cell itself? The cell membrane? ATP? Write and/or illustrate a description of these changes. You can share them from the point of view of the cell and its parts or from the point of view of a scientist observing this phenomenon.	The "lipids" task requires students to consider a change with a double-pronged "effect" chain. Although there are more facets to consider, they are still relatively well defined.
Nucleic Acids (specifically, RNA) What would happen to a cell's functioning if its ribonucleic acids disappeared or malfunctioned? How would this affect the functioning and success of the cell's proteins/amino acids? The cell itself? The skin and muscles of the organism? Write and/or illustrate a description of these changes. You can share them from the point of view of the cell and its parts or from the point of view of a scientist observing this phenomenon.	The "RNA" group must examine a change with multifaceted results. RNA manufactures proteins, which are the basic building blocks of most tissue. If proteins were disturbed, the effects would be far-reaching. Though the prompt guides students in following the "dominos" involved in this chain of events, students must wrestle with less-defined results, which further approximates real life.
Polarization What would happen to a cell's functioning if a polarizing agent was introduced? This polarizing agent would turn all non-polar molecules to polarized molecules! How would this affect each of the cell's building blocks/organic compounds and the functioning of the cell itself? What would happen to the organism the cells comprise? Write and/or illustrate a description of these changes from the point of view of the cell and its parts or from the point of view of a scientist observing this phenomenon.	The "Polarization" groups must wrestle with the most far-reaching cause-and-effect chain of all the cell groups. This task is well suited for students who may already know the functions of each of the organic compounds, as it asks students to examine them in more depth in order to determine what happens to each building block as well as to the cell as a whole, when an outside force or alteration is applied. This "twist" brings the task closer to what authentic scientists do.
11. Form heterogeneous quads (one each from carbohydrate, lipid, RNA, and polarization groups) and ask students to share their rewrites/retellings and findings with each other. After trios have shared, engage in full-group discussion about results: How do cell building blocks work together as a system? Which elements seemed to be the foundational building blocks, or had the biggest	All students will have something unique (and interesting) to bring to the discussion of how the cell responds to alterations to one or more of its building blocks. This perspective of the interdependence of a cell system will reveal the interconnected nature of the discipline and prepare students to delve into such cause-and-effect relationships in literature, writing, history, and, of course, science.

(Continued)

(Continued)

Unit Sequence—Core Curriculum	Teacher Reflections
impact on the others? The least? What does that tell us about cell functioning? Does the cell respond to change by: a. Adjusting or adapting its processes to incorporate the change resulting in a lasting change to the system itself? b. Expelling the addition or change resulting in no lasting change to the system? c. Collapsing (destruction of the system)? 12. In think-pair-share fashion, ask students to compare and contrast the cell structure response to the story element response (collapsing. expelling, or adjusting). Invite students to form hypotheses to explain why different systems respond to the same disruptions in different fashions? You may want to use the illustration of a schedule change being give to a Type A personality versus a Type B personality to illustrate that the nature and purpose of the system itself can affect how it responds to change.	
Closure	
Ask students to consider both systems studied (story and the cell), and then write a response arguing whether or not they believe the following quote is true of both the story and the cell systems. They may have different opinions for each of the systems, but they must explain why they believe as they do: *It is possible [for a system] to fail in many ways… while to succeed is possible only in one way.— Aristotle*	The teacher may need to prompt students to return to the following: • Does the system adjust or adapt its processes to incorporate the change, resulting in a lasting change (and survival) to the system? • Does the system expel the addition or change, resulting in survival without change? • Does the change result in collapse and destruction of the system?

Lesson 3.2 (English): *The Pearl*, Part 1 (Chapters 1–3)

Time allocation: 90–120 minutes

Concepts

M1	System	C1	Identity
M2	Survival	C4	Conflict

Principles

This lesson snapshot outlines how to discuss the events, characters, conflicts, and themes from a system's perspective—how to study the text via the unit principles. This is not to say that Part 1 of this novella does not warrant further study; depending upon the teachers' goals, she or he may want to spend additional class periods discussing such content as the historical and geographical backdrop for the story, additional vocabulary and character studies, and so on.

MP1   The survival of a system depends upon the successful operation of each of its interdependent parts.

MP2   Change to one part of a system results in change to the rest of the system.

MP3   Systems strive to achieve and maintain balance.

P1   One's sense of identity is shaped, in part, by one's environment.

P4   Conflict can strengthen or destroy a system.

Skills

S5   Analyze literature to determine cause-and-effect relationships within story structure and among character relationships.

S7   Evaluate the effectiveness of authors' portrayals of characters, conflicts, and themes.

S4   Make/demonstrate connections between systems in English, biology, and the world beyond the classroom

Standards

Additional, more subject-specific skills are outlined in the next section (Standards)

Virginia Standards of Learning for English, Grade 9—Reading Analysis

9.3   The student will read and analyze a variety of literature.

a. Identify format, text structure, and main ideas.
b. Identify the characteristics that distinguish literary forms.
c. Use literary terms in describing and analyzing selections.
d. Explain the relationships between and among elements of literature: characters, plot, setting, tone, point of view, and theme.
e. Explain the relationship between the author's style and literary effect.
f. Describe the use of images and sounds to elicit the reader's emotions.

Guiding Questions

These guiding questions are essentially the unit's principles in question form. They refer specifically to the story, making them useful for both the planning and the implementation of this English lesson. Of particular importance, however, is that the guiding questions for this parallel science lesson revolve around the same principles.

(Continued)

The science guiding questions refer specifically to the structure and function of the cell and seek to uncover the same *relationships* as do the English guiding questions—those set forth in the unit's principles.

1. How has Kino's family operated as a successful system thus far? What are the "parts" and their functions? How do we know the system is successful?

2. How has Kino himself strived to maintain "equilibrium" in his own head? How does he know he's achieved this?

3. What happens to change the way Kino's psyche operates? The way the family system operates? Describe the changes that result from the introduction of new "elements" to the systems of psyche and family.

4. What does Kino do to try to maintain balance in the midst of a changing system? How are his reactions similar and different to Juana's? Why?

5. How has Kino's family's environment shaped his identity? Juana's?

6. Do you think the conflict introduced by the scorpion and the Pearl of the World will strengthen or destroy Kino? Juana? Their family's system? Explain.

Unit Sequence—Core Curriculum	Teacher Reflections
This lesson is designed to connect students to the novella's principles, conflicts, and themes by introducing the systems of "the psyche" and "the family." Students will examine these systems, first in terms of their personal lives and then in relationship to the story.	Of special import to this lesson is that the author's use of "song" often parallels this unit's treatment of "system." Highlighting this connection on the front end as students read will help them grapple with the idea of systems.
Introduction	
As the "think" portion of a think-pair-share, ask students to respond to one of the following two writing prompts: 1. What is your "as usual"; in other words, what does a typical day look like for you if it runs according to habit or routine? 2. What is your family's "as usual"; in other words, what roles do your family members typically fulfill if things are running according to habit or routine? After about 10 minutes of free-writing, ask students to share their writing—at least the parts with which they are comfortable—with a partner. Once each partner has shared, ask for volunteers to share examples from each "system." Record representative students' answers on the board.	The introductory activity is designed to (1) flesh out the unit's *principles* by tying them to student's personal lives and (2) foster connection with the *characters* of the novella by establishing "common ground" with them (i.e., we all have a certain sense of how things are "supposed" to run—what's expected or what's typical). With this commonality established, students will be more likely to identify with Kino and Juana, even though they are from a different time and place. Giving students a choice of topics promotes a sense of safety in this portion of the lesson. If family is a particular source of hardship or pain, students can write about their daily "schedule" instead (and vice versa). Allowing students to share only the parts of their free-writes with which they feel comfortable further fosters a sense of safety in the classroom.

Unit Sequence—Core Curriculum	Teacher Reflections
Teaching Strategies and Learning Experiences	

Class Session 1

1. Divide the classroom in two, and ask students to move to the appropriate side of the room (thus dividing into two groups)—one side for those who would like to focus on "the self" and the other side for those who would like to focus on "the family." Students should pick a partner from their group and read the first few pages of chapter one together (aloud in a one-foot voice or silently). They should stop reading after the line, "Kino sighed with satisfaction—and that was conversation."

Again, students have a choice of how they pursue information regarding systems; they will be able to conduct further investigation into the system of their choice as they read this very short 11-paragraph section. This provides focus for students as they read and something concrete for partners to discuss after they read.

2. After partners finish reading the assigned section, they should work together to answer the appropriate prompt for their group:

   • What is Kino's "as usual"; in other words, what does a typical morning look like for him when it runs according to habit or routine? How does he derive his identity from that routine (in other words, how does his "as usual" day make him feel about himself and about life)? Predict how he would react if something happened to interrupt this routine. Would he adjust and adapt? Would he react and continue without change? Would life as he knows it cease? Explain.
   • What is Kino's family's "as usual"; in other words, what roles do Kino, Juana, and Coyotito fulfill in order to make the "Song of the Family" play out as it is supposed to? Predict what would happen to the song if something interrupted it. Would the rhythm of the song adjust and adapt? Would the song ignore the interruption and continue without change? Would the song cease? Explain.

These prompting and predicting questions should be familiar to students:

   • The prompts reflect those used in this lesson's introductory activity.
   • The predicting questions reflect those students discussed in the previous lesson: *What happens to a system when a change is introduced?*

        ○ Does the system adjust or adapt its processes to incorporate the change, resulting in a lasting change (and survival) to the system
        ○ Does the system expel the addition or change, resulting in survival without change?
        ○ Does the change result in collapse and destruction of the system?

3. Students should share their analyses and predictions and explain them. When students defend their predictions, ask them to refer to the previous lesson's systems. The teacher may need to prompt students to remember the definition of a system (*A set or combination of independent yet inter-related,*

The discussion in Step 3 should, in essence, revolve around the following guiding questions:

   • How has Kino's family operated as a successful system thus far? What are the "parts" and their functions? How do we know the system is successful?

(Continued)

(Continued)

Unit Sequence—Core Curriculum	Teacher Reflections
interdependent parts forming a unified whole working toward a specific purpose) as well as the systems illustrated in class (music, sports, government, astronomy, school), and ask them which systems they think the psyche and the family most closely resemble.	• How has Kino himself strived to maintain "equilibrium" in his own head? How does he know he's achieved this?
4. Read aloud the rest of Chapter 1 (from "The sun was warming the brush house…." to "He looked down in wonder at his split knuckles and at the blood that followed down between his fingers."). During and after reading, discuss the following questions: • What was the invading force and what effect did it have on Kino? On "The Song of the Family?" • To what other two systems do we discover that Kino belongs? What is his role in each? How does he handle the disparity in his roles? Compare Kino's roles in these various systems to his role in one of the systems discussed in the previous lesson—an orchestra or band. Compare Kino's role in his immediate family (Juana and Coyotito) to that of his role in the fishing village to that of his role in the larger town. Which instrument would he represent in each? How is he a necessary and vital part of each system? Can you relate to this? How does it make you feel? Predict the role it will have on Kino.	These questions keep students focused on the concepts of systems, survival, identity, and conflict while exploring the interdependence of story elements. Students are, in essence, examining what happens to one's character in the face of conflict, how the time and place in which one lives (setting) influences character and drives conflict, and how one's perspective is shaped by—not only his/her surroundings (setting)—but also by the conflicts they encounter.
5. Exit Reflection (individual responses to be collected after students have time to record their ideas): Do you, like Kino, feel that you hold different roles in the different systems to which you belong? In which system do you have the most power? The least? How do you feel about and this and how does it affect you. If you were Kino, what would you do next?	These principles and literary relationships also hold truth in reality, and so the questions encourage students to compare the character's struggles and decisions to experiences of their own.
6. Assign Chapters 2–3 as at-home reading. As students read, they should attempt to discern whether or not their impressions/predictions about Kino were accurate. In addition, they should record their answers to	Chapters 2 and 3 are short, but are excellent preparation for a **Socratic Seminar**, a strategy that is best used when there are ideas to explore and/or debate because of the potential for multiple interpretations.

Unit Sequence—Core Curriculum	Teacher Reflections
the rest of the lesson's guiding questions. For each question, students should support their assertions with specific textual support: • What happens to change the way Kino's psyche operates? The way the family system operates? Describe the changes that result from the introduction of new "elements" to the systems of psyche and family. • What does Kino do to try to maintain balance in the midst of a changing system? How are his reactions similar and different to Juana's? Why? • How has Kino's family's environment shaped his identity? Juana's? • How does the disruption of the pearl re-shape his identity in each of his "systems"? • Do you think the conflict introduced by the Pearl of the World will ultimately strengthen or destroy Kino? Juana? Their family's system? 7. Students written answers to these questions will serve as their "Participation Ticket" for the following period's "Square-Share" activity. **Class Session 2** 1. Use the previous day's exit reflection to form small processing groups. These groups should consist of students who responded similarly to Kino's predicament and to how they, personally, feel in such power struggles. In these small groups, students should discuss the reading questions from Chapter 2 and be prepared to share their answers in a Socratic Seminar. Students' written answers to these questions with textual support (think) will be their ticket to participate in the small group think tanks (square) and Socratic Discussion (share). 2. **Socratic Seminar** focused on guiding questions from Step 6. Students must cite evidence from the text in their contributions. 3. Distribute literature on how a pearl is formed. Students should compare this explanation with that offered in Chapter 2:	*Socratic Seminar—Teacher's Roles* • Serve as *facilitator*, not director. • Pose well-thought-out, open-ended questions (such as those in Step 6). • Give no response, negative or positive, to the students' discussion. • Pose more questions to "move" discussion from stalemate positions. *Socratic Seminar—Students' Roles* • Be prepared for the seminar • Direct the flow of the discussion within the seminar • Utilize critical thinking, listening, and communicating skills • Pose your own thoughts and respond to classmates' comments • Ask questions of classmates • Respect and honor the opinions and voices of other participants • Support opinions with evidence from the text and cite all sources *Socratic Seminar—Guidelines* • Only students who have prepared for the seminar should participate in the discussion. • The group sits in a circle; all participants to make eye contact. • Silence is not a negative. • Allow discussion to flow. • One student speaks at a time. • Students respond to classmates' comments/questions and pose their own. • Engage in postseminar reflection. *Suggested Rules for Socratic Seminar* • Do not raise your hand. • Use all talking chips (three each). • Do not interrupt another person. • Be respectful of all participants. • Disagree in a respectful manner.

(Continued)

(Continued)

Unit Sequence—Core Curriculum	Teacher Reflections

An accident could happen to these oysters, a grain of sand could lie in the folds of muscle and irritate the flesh until in self-protection the flesh coated the grain with a layer of smooth cement. But once started, the flesh continued to coat the foreign body unit it fell free in some tidal flurry or until the oyster was destroyed (p. 17).
 	
Students should then work in small groups to answer the following:
 	
• How does the formation of a pearl represent the disruption of a system?
• Which of our three options for dealing with change does pearl formation best reflect:
 	
  1. The system adjusts or adapts its processes to incorporate the change.
 	
  2. The system expels the addition or change and remains unchanged.
 	
  3. The change results in collapse and destruction of the system.
	This discussion not only brings students back to the text, but also points them toward the most important symbol in the book—the pearl itself. By investigating this symbol as the result of a scientific system, students will be more prepared to make authentic connections each time Steinbeck returns to this symbol or alludes to it in even the slightest way
	
	Again, the discussion returns "home" to the three options for dealing with system's change (this time, students could debate options A and C). This conceptual focus was introduced in the opening lesson, examined again in Class Session 1 of this lesson, and is used to bring the lesson around "full circle" at the end of Class Session 2.

Closure	
4. In written, visual, or kinesthetic form, answer the following: *How does Kino's response mirror that of the oyster's? In other words, what "grains of sand" get into him and how does he "coat these over?" How does his environment—physical, relational, and emotional—influence this? (HINT: Look for examples from the text referring to "hardening" or muting of one of his many songs.)* Students should work in groups of like-preference and present findings to the class. Teacher can use presentations as a means to formatively assess students' grasp of the plot, characterization, conflict, setting, and themes presented thus far in the novella. Make notes about students' understandings and/or misconceptions. Reteach with small groups if students do not have a firm understanding of the literary elements and how they are used in *The Pearl*. The notes about student strengths will help later on when the teacher will form groups in Lesson Three.	This is the first time students have worked in groups of similar learning profile preferences, and it is an ideal time for them to do so. Students can demonstrate what they've learned via the medium that is most accessible and/or comfortable for them. The products they present will help the teacher see immediately if there are misconceptions or holes in students' understanding about the plot, setting, characters, conflicts, and themes presented thus far in the novel. Each presentation provides the teacher with a chance to provide "on-the-spot" clarification and redirection, if needed. In addition, this activity serves as a formative assessment to let the teacher know if students need re-direction or if the class is ready to move on to the following lesson's activities.

Lesson 3.3 (Science): Introducing Cell Structure

Time allocation: 90–120 minutes

Concepts

M1   System
M2   Survival
C3   Function

Principles

This lesson snapshot outlines how to examine the cell from a system's perspective—how to study content via the unit principles. This is not to say that the cell does not warrant more in-depth study; depending upon the teachers' goals and time allowances, he or she may want to spend additional class periods conducting labs and examining plant (e.g., small leaf from a Elodea sprig) versus animal cells (e.g., epithelial cells).

MP1   The *survival* of a *system* depends upon the successful operation of each of its interdependent parts.

MP2   Change to one part of a *system* results in change to the rest of the system.

P3   *Function* dictates structure (English and biology).

Skills

S1   Analyze systems to determine cause-and-effect relationships within cell structure.

S3   Evaluate the importance/role of each part of a cell.

S4   Make/demonstrate connections between systems in English and biology and in the world beyond the classroom.

Standards

Virginia Standards of Learning for Secondary Biology

Additional, more subject-specific skills are outlined in the next section (Standards).

BI0.4   The student will investigate and understand relationships between cell structure and function. Key concepts include the following:

   a. Characteristics of prokaryotic and eukaryotic cells;
   b. Exploring the diversity and variation of eukaryotes; and
   c. The cell membrane model (diffusion, osmosis, and active transport).

Guiding Questions

These guiding questions are essentially the unit's principles in question form. They refer specifically to the structure and function of the cell, making them useful for both the planning and the implementation of this biology lesson. Of particular importance, however, is that the guiding questions for the parallel English lesson revolve around the same principles. The English-guiding questions refer specifically to the story but

(Continued)

(Continued)

seek to uncover the same *relationships* as do the science guiding questions—those set forth in the unit's principles.

1. How does the *survival* of the cell [*system*] depend on the successful function of each of its interdependent parts (nucleus, mitochondria, Golgi apparatus, ER, ribosomes, lysosomes, cell membrane)?

2. What would happen to the *survival* of the cell if any of its interdependent parts quit working?

3. How does the *structure* of the cell/its organelles reflect the *function* it is to perform?

4. What would happen to the *survival* of the cell if a new element were to be introduced?

Unit Sequence—Core Curriculum	Reflection
This lesson is designed to examine the cell itself as a system and to examine how each of its parts (1) is a system unto itself and (2) a part of the larger system of the complete cell.	Throughout the course of this lesson, students will continually grapple with the guiding questions as they relate to the larger cell system and its constituent parts.
Introduction	
1. Remind students of the definition of "system" they developed in the last class period: *A set or combination of independent yet inter-related, interdependent parts forming a unified whole working toward a specific purpose.* 2. In think-pair-share fashion, ask student to describe their school as system. Prompting questions: • What is the system's (school's) purpose? • What are the interdependent yet interrelated parts that make up the school? These are actually subsystems (systems within a system). • How does each of these subsystems help the school achieve its purpose? • What would happen if any of these systems stopped working?	This introduction serves several purposes: • It activates prior learning (definition and nature of systems). • It connects students to content by asking them to think about systems in terms of the operation of their own school. • It sets the stage for future learning. "School" will serve as the metaphor through which the cell's subsystems (organelles) and their functions will be introduced. Getting students to think about the interdependence of their school's "subsystems" at the beginning of class will make it easier for them to make the metaphorical leap later in small group work.
Teaching Strategies and Learning Experiences	
1. Explain that cells are systems, too, and that some cells (like their school) contain many complex subsystems, making the cell itself complex. These cells are called *eukaryotic* cells. Others cells are more like the one-room schoolhouses of the past, with very few components (students and teacher). These cells are called *prokaryotic* cells.	This rather traditional approach to presenting information is appropriate at this point in the lesson because (a) students have something to which to anchor their new learning (the school/ system metaphor), and (b) the mini lecture will comprise only a small portion of the class period.

Unit Sequence—Core Curriculum	Reflection
2. Use this comparison as a jumping-off place for a mini lecture on the differences between prokaryotic and eukaryotic cells. Major talking points include the following: • Both eukaryotic and prokaryotic cells have a cell membrane, cytoplasm, ribosomes, and DNA. • Prokaryotic cells do not have a nucleus nor do they have organelles; they do, however, have a cell wall and flagella. • Eukaryotic cells have a nucleus, cytoskeleton, organelles, and cilia. Plant cells and animal cells are both eukaryotic, but plant cells also have a cell wall, chloroplasts, and a central vacuole. 3. As an introduction to small group work, explain that students will have a chance to examine some of the eukaryotic cell's subsystems, but that they'll have to choose their subsystem according to the school subsystem to which it is most similar. 4. Four Corners: Display list of four subsystem-function choices (Administration, Teachers, Cafeteria, Offensive Line). Give students each an index card and ask them to write down the choice that interests them most. Then, assign one corner of the room to each area of interest, and send students to those corners with their index card and a writing utensil. Circulate among the groups to ensure that students have moved to their "corner of choice" rather than to the corner to which their friends have moved. 5. Groups move to an area of the room that is comfortable and provides a workable space for them. They will be responsible for researching and presenting information that answers the following question (on task cards): *Administration* The administration of the school organizes the school and ensures there is an appropriate environment for learning. The nucleus performs a similar role in the cell. You are to research and present the structure and function of the following:	Care should be taken to make sure students do not lose interest at this point. Visual examples of each of the cell types, readily available by "googling" (e.g., pictures of magnified prokaryotic cells, diagrams of eukaryotic cells and their organelles), are a must. In addition, the teacher should break up the mini-lecture with think-pair-share questions calling for clarification of material, predictions about functions of cell parts, comparisons to the school or other systems from the previous class period's activity, etc. The "Four Corners" strategy benefits adolescent learners in three ways: (1) it allows students to enter into learning through an avenue of their choice, thus fostering investment in the task and forging connections with content; (2) it allows students to "join forces" with other students who share similar interests, in the process building connections among peers and fostering community; and (3) it gives students a chance to get up and move, which is no small thing when adolescent development is considered! No matter which groups students join, they will wrestle with the following Guiding Questions, although they may be tailored to more specifically address each subsystem's function: • How does the *survival* of the cell [*system*] depend on the successful function of each of its interdependent parts? • What would happen to the *survival* of the cell if any of its interdependent parts quit working?

(Continued)

Unit Sequence—Core Curriculum	Reflection
<ul><li>Nucleus</li><li>Proteins</li><li>ER</li><li>Ribosomes</li><li>Vesicles</li></ul>Be sure to explain how your organelles are like the administration of your school, how they help the cell survive, and what would happen to the cell if your subsystem ceased to work (compare this with the administration, too). *Teachers* Teachers carry out the tasks that help the school meet its goal. Teachers are the disseminators of information. The cell has subsystems that perform similar function. You are to research and present the structure and function of the following:<ul><li>Golgi apparatus</li><li>Proteins</li><li>Vesicles</li><li>Lysosomes</li><li>Cytoplasm</li><li>Cytoskeleton</li></ul>Be sure to explain how your organelles are like the administration of your school, how they help the cell survive, and what would happen to the cell if your subsystem ceased to work (compare this with missing teachers, too). *Cafeteria* We could not function without the cafeteria! Whether or not we like to admit it, the cafeteria is vital to our existence because it provides everyone with food, which in turn gives us energy. The cell has a subsystem that performs a similar function. You are to research and present the structure and function of the following:<ul><li>Mitochondria</li><li>Its inner and outer membranes</li><li>ATP</li></ul>Be sure to explain how your organelle is like the cafeteria in your school, how it help the cell survive, who gets most of the "energy" and why, and what would happen to the cell if your subsystem ceased to work (compare this with a missing cafeteria, too).	<ul><li>How does the *structure* of the cell/its organelles reflect the *function* it is to perform?</li><li>What would happen to the *survival* of the cell if a new element were to be introduced?</li></ul>

Unit Sequence—Core Curriculum	Reflection
Offensive Line on Football Team Your subsystem seems to be a bit off-topic, but you'll see how important it is! In fact, you will close our presentations today and "kick us off" again tomorrow with your presentation because your topic is vital to understanding active and passive transport. Your subsystem is the cell membrane, and its parts include the following: • Lipid bilayer (phospholipids) • Cell-surface marker • Receptor proteins • Transport proteins • Enzymes	
Today I'll want you to present how the cell membrane works as a whole to keep things in/out of the cell (lipid bilayer, phospholipids), but tomorrow I'll ask you to be more specific and explain how each part of the cell membrane operates like a different member of the offensive line (quarterback, center, offensive guards and tackles, running backs and fullbacks). Be prepared to demonstrate your "offensive line/cell membrane" in action, to discuss how it helps the cell survive, and to predict what would happen to the rest of the cell if the cell membrane ceased to work (compare this with a faulty offensive line, too).	Since this particular group must truly understand football in order to make connections, choose its members carefully. Teachers can target students who are knowledgeable about sports, but you can also pull in reticent students and those who learn by doing. Since this activity is so kinesthetic and because it is presented in two parts—one during this lesson and one during the next science lesson—many "outlying" students may be "hooked" to this content through their participation in this small group.
6. Groups present. Teacher prompts students, when necessary, to make sure each group addresses all of the guiding questions. The teacher should also begin to create or reveal a comprehensive illustration/diagram of a eukaryotic cell, and should add to it after each group presents.	
7. After presentations are complete, place students in mixed quads—one from each subsystem group—and ask them to: • Discuss how each subsystem relies on the others for its success. • Discuss what would happen to the other subsystems when each quit working. • Evaluate which subsystem holds the most important role. Defend your position with examples from the other two discussion points.	There is no right or wrong answer to the "evaluate" this discussion; however, there are degrees of expertise when it comes to offering support. As the teacher circulates through the groups, s/he is looking to identify a group that will present to the class. It must be a group that returns to the text and their notes to find specific examples of subsystem's functions and interdependence. A group in which there is some evidence of argument/ disagreement would also be an ideal choice, as they most likely recognize and appreciate the "fuzzy" nature of this question.

(Continued)

(Continued)

Unit Sequence—Core Curriculum	Reflection
Students should take notes on this discussion and be prepared to present their findings. Circulate during presentations and choose one group to present the first point of discussion. All groups should be involved in the discussion of the second point (evaluating).	
Closure	
Ask students, individually, to draw a rough sketch of a eukaryotic cell and to explain—either through writing and/or drawing—the *role*, *importance*, and *interdependence* of the cell's subsystems and their components: • Nucleus • ER • Ribosomes • Proteins • Cytoplasm • Golgi apparatus • Vesicles • Lysosomes • Mitochondria • ATP • Cell membrane	Since so much of this lesson has been completed in small groups, it's important to check for each individual student's understanding of both cell subsystem's structure and function, and how those subsystems work together to form a complete, interdependent system. Teachers may choose to distribute a sketch of the cell without labels and ask students to simply label the parts before discussing the *role*, *importance*, and *interdependence* of cells' subsystems/their components. This option would save class time. Review students' drawings noting students' understandings and misconceptions. If misunderstandings persist, reteach in small groups if necessary.

Lesson 3.4 (English): *The Pearl*, Part 2 (Chapters 4–6)

Time allocation: 90–120 minutes

Concepts

M1	System	M3	Balance
M2	Survival	C4	Conflict

Principles

This lesson snapshot continues to ask students to examine the events, characters, conflicts, and themes from a system's perspective—to study the text via the unit principles. This is not to say that Part 2 of this novella does not warrant further study; depending upon the teacher's goals, he or she may want to spend additional class periods discussing such content as historical backdrop, economic connections, and so on.

MP1   The survival of a system depends upon the successful operation of each of its interdependent parts.

MP2   Change to one part of a system results in change to the rest of the system.

MP3   Systems strive to achieve and maintain balance.

P4   Conflict can strengthen or destroy a system.

Skills

Additional, more subject-specific skills are outlined in the next section (Standards).

S5   Analyze literature to determine cause-and-effect relationships within story structure and among character relationships.

S4   Discover connections among written pieces.

S7   Evaluate the effectiveness of authors' portrayals of characters, conflicts, and themes.

S4   Make/demonstrate connections between systems in English and biology and in the world beyond the classroom.

Standards

Virginia Standards of Learning for English, Grade 9—Reading Analysis

9.3   The student will read and analyze a variety of literature.

   a. Identify format, text structure, and main ideas.
   b. Identify the characteristics that distinguish literary forms.
   c. Use literary terms in describing and analyzing selections.
   d. Explain the relationships between and among elements of literature: characters, plot, setting, tone, point of view, and theme.
   e. Explain the relationship between the author's style and literary effect.
   f. Describe the use of images and sounds to elicit the reader's emotions.
   g. Explain the influence of historical context on the form, style, and point of view of a written work.

Guiding Questions

These guiding questions are essentially the unit's principles in question form. They refer specifically to the story, making them useful for both the planning and the implementation of this English lesson. Of particular importance, however, is that the guiding questions for the parallel science lesson revolve around the same principles. The science guiding questions refer specifically to cell structure and function but seek to uncover the same *relationships* as do the English guiding questions—those set forth in the unit's principles.

   1. How does the *survival* of a *system* (self, family, town) depend on the successful function of each of its interdependent parts?

(Continued)

(Continued)

2. What would happen to the *survival* of the system (self, family, town) if any of its interdependent parts quit working?

3. What would happen to the *survival* of the system if an unwanted element were to be introduced?

4. How does a system strive to achieve and maintain *balance* (self, family, town)?

5. Does *conflict* strengthen or destroy a *system?*

Unit Sequence—Core Curriculum	Teacher Reflections
A unique instructional strategy is used in this lesson to finish discussing *The Pearl* in terms of what outside and inside influences can do to the systems of self, family, and community. It is called Structured Academic Controversy (SAC). Three supporting documents are included at the end of this lesson (Appendixes 3G, 3H, 3I). The first is a two-page synopsis of the strategy that can be used by teachers in preparation for this lesson. The remaining two documents are worksheets for students. A note-taking graphic organizer will help students prepare for their presentation, and a discussion web will help them summarize what they heard during their conversations.	Students will return to the three options for dealing with change (adapt, expel, be destroyed) and discuss the implications for Kino, his family, and his community in the novella's final chapters.
Introduction	
Display or direct students' attention to the following passage from the beginning of *The Pearl*, Chapter 4: *It is wonderful the way a little town keeps track of itself and of all its units. If every single man and woman, child and baby, acts and conducts itself in a known pattern and breaks no walls and differs with no one and experiments in no way and is not sick and does not endanger the ease and peace of mind or steady unbroken flow of the town, then that unit can disappear and never be heard of. But let one man step out of the regular thought or the known and trusted pattern, and the nerves of the townspeople ring with nervousness and communication travels over the nerve lines of the town. Then every unit communicates to the whole. (p. 40)*	This introductory activity serves a multitude of purposes: • It activates prior learning from both English and science class. • It connects them with the material on a personal level (comparing the town to their school). • It asks them to, for the first time, make a direct connection between a system from the novella to the cell system or one of its subsystems. This will become an extremely important reference point when students begin work on the summative assessment (Appendix 3K).

SYSTEMS **137**

Unit Sequence—Core Curriculum	Teacher Reflections
Think-Pair-Square-Share Response • THINK: Individually complete a free write explaining how this passage: (1) describes the town as a system and (2) mirrors their own "school" as a system (discussed in science). • PAIR: In pairs, students discuss the answers to the two questions listed above along with a third question, (3) How is the town like a cell? • SQUARE: Pairs team up to form squares; each square is assigned one question to illustrate and explain. • SHARE: Squares share illustrations and examples.	You can form these squares strategically to get a mix of thinkers; you can also let squares choose the question they want to illustrate, providing all questions are addressed. Presentations need not be long—they need only to demonstrate the three connections outlined in the left-hand column. It might be more efficient to let squares team up with other squares (who illustrated the same connection) for the presentations; that way material is not needlessly repeated.

Teaching Strategies and Learning Experiences

Class Session 1 1. Read aloud the beginning of Chapter 4, pages 40–51 (to "These were proud of Kino"). As you read, ask students to listen for evidence of what is happening to Kino. How has the pearl become a grain of sand in his psyche and in his family life? Is this a good thing or a bad thing? Discuss this question during and after reading. 2. Place students in mixed ability small groups (these groupings can be the same as those from the last lesson's closure activity, or they can be formed using the formative assessment results from the previous lesson's closure activity). 3. Distribute or redirect each group to the last portion that was read aloud from Chapter 4: *Perhaps, some argued, perhaps it would have been better if Kino took the one thousand five hundred pesos. That is a great deal of money, more than he has ever seen. Maybe Kino is being a pigheaded fool. Suppose he should really go to the capital and find no buyer for his pearl. He would never live that down.* *And now, said other fearful ones, now that he had defied them, those buyers will not want to deal with him at all. Maybe Kino has cut off his own head and destroyed himself.*	Reading key portions aloud create a shared experience for the class, allow students to hear the author's rhythm, cadence, and style, and alert students to things they may have missed by reading alone. This particular section sets up the conflict around which the rest of the lesson's teaching strategies and learning experiences revolve, so it is important that students all begin "on the same page." Steps 2–5 require students to return to one of the central questions from the unit: *"What happens to a system when a change is introduced?"* • Does the system adjust or adapt its processes to incorporate the change, resulting in a lasting change (and survival) to the system? • Does the system expel the addition or change, resulting in survival without change? • Does the change result in collapse and destruction of the system? This passage offers a striking portrayal of villagers actually discussing this same question! Interpretations may vary, including: • The first discussion reflects the villagers' opinion that Kino should have *adjusted* to the town's expectations of him and accepted the offer.

(Continued)

(Continued)

Unit Sequence—Core Curriculum	Teacher Reflections
And others said, Kino is a brave man, and a fierce man; he is right. From his courage we may all profit. These were proud of Kino. (p. 51)	• The second explores a combination of B with the outcome of C—he *expelled* the change, which would result in his *demise*.
4. Explain that Kino has introduced a change to the town system when he refused the pearl-sellers' offers. In this passage, the villagers are discussing what will result from this change. Ask students to analyze the options and decide how these three assessments of Kino's reaction to the change mirror the three ways systems handle change: (A) adjust, (B) expel, and (C) collapse.	• The third group seems to believe that Kino's *expulsion* of pearl-sellers' offer would result in his survival (B) and also strengthen the villagers' system by uniting them against those that oppress them (A).
5. Each group should share their classification of villagers' reactions. Spend some time debating classifications, but move students to discussing their own evaluation of which option they believe is the best option for dealing with the pearl-sellers' reaction and the subsequent disruption of Kino's system of self, his family system, and the town system.	
6. As students read the rest of the novella, they are to do so with the following question in mind: *Did Kino make a wise decision when he rejected the pearl-seller's offers and struck out on his own?* Remember, a decision can be wise and still end with bitter consequences. *Be sure to consider the following:* • Kino's psyche (desire to be a man) and dreams for his son • Kino's relationships with his immediate family and extended family (villagers) • Kino's "place" within the town system • Kino's need to survive Students can complete some of Step 6 in class, at home, or in a combination thereof. They should be sure to take notes on the four points above (use the **Note-Taking Graphic Organizer** (Appendix 3H) included at the end of this lesson) to prepare for the academic controversy to occur the following class period.	For the rest of this lesson, students themselves are asked to do what the villagers were doing in the highlighted passage: evaluate Kino's decision making. They will examine his decisions and the effects each had on the three systems of interest in this story—self/psyche, the family, and the town. In addition, students will evaluate Kino's decisions from the perspective of the goal of every system—survival. Did Kino do what he needed to do to survive or did he endanger his survival with his decisions? Although students are asked to find textual support for their views, it is important to stress that students must also rise above the narrative and see the whole picture—the picture that the characters in the story only see parts of. They must use what they have learned *independent of Kino* and synthesize this knowledge with what they have learned *along with Kino* in order to create the most informed opinion possible about the wisdom of Kino's actions.
Class Session 2 1. As students enter the following day, ask them to report to one side of the room or the other:	Now students' individual beliefs and opinions will be challenged and strengthened via discussion and debate with their peers. The Structured Academic Controversy (SAC)

Unit Sequence—Core Curriculum	Teacher Reflections
• Right side: Kino made wise choices, although they turned out badly • Left side: Kino choices were unwise, which is why things turned out badly 2. Ask students to pair up with someone from the opposite side of the room. Depending on numbers, you may have trios or students who are like-minded working together. 3. Students work together to complete the steps of a Structured Academic Controversy (Appendix 3G) in which they argue both for and against the statement: Kino made a wise decision to reject the pearl-seller's offer. 4. Explain that the "gist" of this strategy is that students must take both positions at different points in the proceedings and argue both sides of the issue before arriving at consensus that pulls from each side. 5. A detailed description of this strategy and how it applies to this statement from *The Pearl* is included at the end of this chapter. Basic steps are completed by pairs of students: Step 1: Prepare your position. Step 2: Present and advocate your position. Step 3: Engage in open discussion in which you refute the opposing position and rebut attacks on your own position. Step 4: Reverse positions and repeat steps 1-3. You can use your opponents' arguments against them! Step 5: Synthesize and integrate the best evidence and reasoning into a joint position statement with support. Step 6: Write a joint report that explains the group's synthesis and is based on a group consensus supported by evidence. Step 7: Present an informative and interesting position talking paper to the class. Step 8: Individual response. Give students the Structured Academic Controversy Discussion Web (Appendix 3I) to help them prepare their positions in Steps 1 and 4.	actually provides a prime example of one of the unit's principles: Conflict *can strengthen or destroy a* system. In this instance, the SAC will either strengthen or change students' own belief systems about how conflict affected Kino's personal and family systems! The Structured Academic Controversy Discussion Web (Appendix 3I), included at the end of this lesson, provides further support for students as they begin use of this instructional strategy. The strategy requires students to think in a complex manner about the following unit principles: • The *survival* of a *system* depends upon the successful operation of each of its interdependent parts. • Change to one part of a *system* results in change to the rest of the *system*. • *Systems* strive to achieve and maintain *balance*. • *Conflict* can strengthen or destroy a *system*.

(Continued)

(Continued)

Unit Sequence—Core Curriculum	Teacher Reflections
Closure	
Formative Assessment Students will compose and submit a personal statement on the following topic: *Did your original views about Kino's decision change? If so, how did they change and what particular pieces of information were most influential in swaying your view? If your opinion did not change, what additional information or support did you glean to solidify your original position?* Students should submit this statement along with their original note-taking graphic organizer and their discussion web so that the teacher can see how students' thinking evolved throughout their reading, discussion, and analysis.	This trio of documents (Appendixes 3G, 3H, 3I) will provide the teacher with an evidence trail of how students' thinking progresses throughout their "digestion" of *The Pearl*, Part 2. Each of *the Pearl's* systems is discussed at each point, as is the ultimate goal of every system—survival. This closure activity allows students to synthesize all of this information into an opinion statement that reflects each student's values and beliefs, thus forging deep connection to the concepts, conflicts, and characters that are central to this story.

Note: For more information about this instructional strategy, see the following:

http://www.iasce.net/Conference2004/22June/Edwardnathan/IASCE%20Conference%20Handout%20-%20Edward%20Nathan.doc

http://www.learner.org/workshops/civics/workshop7/readings/controversy.html

Note: For two video clips that showcase SAC in the science classroom, see the following:

http://serc.carleton.edu/NAGTWorkshops/affective/evolution.html

Lesson 3.5 (Science): Movement in Cells

Time allocation: 90–120 minutes

Concepts

M1	System	M3	Balance
M2	Survival	C4	Conflict

Principles

In this lesson, students have a chance to investigate these principles through a variety of modes. Using the first two principles as the *umbrellas,* students will explore the third through observation and the fourth through experimentation. This is not to say that other labs, beyond what are described herein, would not be suitable; the teacher must make use of the resources available to create the most authentic learning experience possible for students.

MP1 The *survival* of a *system* depends upon the successful operation of each of its interdependent parts.

MP2 Change to one part of a *system* results in change to the rest of the system.

MP3 *Systems* strive to achieve and maintain *balance*.

P4 *Conflict* can strengthen or destroy a system.

Skills

Students engage in these intellectual activities with a higher degree of complexity than they did in prior lessons; this is due to the fact that this lesson builds upon all the others.

S1 Analyze systems to determine cause-and-effect relationships within cell structure.

S2 Analyze systems to determine cause-and-effect relationships within and among various biologic systems.

S4 Make/demonstrate connections between systems in English and biology and in the world beyond the classroom.

Standards

Virginia Standards of Learning for Secondary Biology

BI0.4 The student will investigate and understand relationships between cell structure and function. Key concepts include the following:

 a. Characteristics of prokaryotic and eukaryotic cells;
 b. Exploring the diversity and variation of eukaryotes; and
 c. The cell membrane model (diffusion, osmosis, and active transport).

Guiding Questions

These guiding questions are essentially the unit's principles in question form. They refer specifically to the cell's use of cell transport to achieve homeostasis, making them useful for both the planning and the implementation of this biology lesson. Of particular importance, however, is that the guiding questions for the parallel English lesson revolve around the same principles. The English guiding questions refer specifically to the story but seek to uncover the same *relationships* as do the science guiding questions—those set forth in the unit's principles.

1. How does the *survival* of the cell (*system*) depend on the successful function of each of its interdependent parts (cell membrane, receptor protein, carrier proteins, sodium-potassium pump)?

2. What would happen to the *survival* of the cell if any of its interdependent parts quit working?

(Continued)

(Continued)

3. What would happen to the *survival* of the cell if an unwanted element were to be introduced?

4. How does the cell strive to achieve and maintain *balance* (osmosis, diffusion, endocytosis, exocytosis, hypertonic, hypotonic, isotonic)?

5. Does pressure outside a cell strengthen or destroy a *system?*

Unit Sequence—Core Curriculum and Curriculum of Connections	Teacher Reflections
In this lesson, students explore how the cell acts as a system, utilizing cell transport to achieve homeostasis.	
Introduction	
Choose a few of the outstanding illustrations/explanations collected as the formative assessment at the end of the last lesson. Try to choose several examples that took different approaches to demonstrate the same understanding. Ask students to examine them and with a partner come up with one "Ah-ha" (idea the examples clarify) and one question raised by the examples. Use students' responses to conduct a short review of cell "subsystems," correcting any misconceptions revealed by the diagrams. Let students know that they'll be augmenting their own diagrams to reflect what they learn in today's lesson.	It is important that students understand the structure and function of cell parts if they are to build upon that knowledge to grasp the idea of cell transport. This introduction, therefore, serves as a review of prior learning as well as an opportunity for the teacher to correct misconceptions that would block future learning. Finally, students are asked to generate new ideas and questions, tunneling them deeper into the unit's principles as they forge personal connections to the material.
Teaching Strategies and Learning Experiences	
1. Return to the "Offensive Line" group from the previous lesson. Explain that, in the previous lesson, this group presented the "basics" of cell membrane structure and function and explained how the cell membrane works as a whole to keep things in/out of the cell (lipid bilayer, phospholipids). Today the group will take it a step further to show how each part of the cell operates like a different member of the offensive line.	
2. Offensive Line on Football Team—Your subsystem is the cell membrane, and its parts include the following: • Lipid bilayer (phospholipids) • Cell-surface marker • Receptor proteins • Transport proteins • Enzymes	

Unit Sequence—Core Curriculum and Curriculum of Connections	Teacher Reflections

In the previous class, you presented how the cell membrane works as a whole to keep things in/out of the cell (lipid bilayer, phospholipids). Today, I'd like you to be more specific and explain how each part of the cell membrane operates like a different member of the offensive line (quarterback, center, offensive guards and tackles, running backs and fullbacks). Be prepared to demonstrate your "offensive line/cell membrane" in action, to discuss how it helps the cell survive, and to predict what would happen to the rest of the cell if the cell membrane ceased to work (compare this to a faulty offensive line, too).
 	
3. Explain that you'll spend part of this lesson focusing on what the "fullbacks," or transport proteins do. Demonstrate the difference between active (walking) and passive (carrying) transport. Show videos to illustrate each:
 	
  • Passive Transport (diffusion) (http://www.youtube.com/watch?v=s0p1ztrbXPY&NR=1)
  • Active Transport (http://www.youtube.com/watch?v=STzOiRqzzL4&feature=related)
  • Endocytosis and Exocytosis (http://www.youtube.com/watch?v=4gLtk8Yc1Zc&feature=related)
 	
4. Students will be examining each of these functions in more depth in their stations today. They will rotate through three stations, spending 15–20 minutes at each. (Descriptions of these stations are included at the end of this lesson, Appendix 3J.) They should complete their lab packet as they rotate through the stations. At the end of their rotation, or if they have extra time within a rotation, students can work on refining their cell diagrams from last class to: (a) correct errors and (b) design a more detailed, complete version of the cell membrane which shows all its "parts" and indicate what that subsystem would look like "in action."
 	
5. Stations:
 	
Station 1: Diffusion and Osmosis Videos
 	
Watch the following video and answer the questions that follow. You can replay this video, if needed: (http://www.youtube.com/watch?v=H7QsDs8ZRMI&feature=related)
 	
  • Why does diffusion of bromine take less time when it is diffused into a vacuum?
  • Why does nitrogen dioxide diffuse more quickly than bromine?	

(Continued)

Unit Sequence—Core Curriculum and Curriculum of Connections	Teacher Reflections
• Which gas diffuses faster, ammonia or hydrochloric acid? Why? • What affect does temperature have on the rate of diffusion? Why? Next, watch a video depicting diffusion of liquids from an area of high concentration to an area of low concentration (osmosis): (http://www.youtube.com/watch?v=H6N1IiJTmnc&feature=related) • Why does the lettuce behave this way? • How does water behave like the gasses in the other video? What do the two phenomena have in common? Now watch this demonstration of osmosis. The red and blue dots represent water molecules while the green and yellow dots represent sugar molecules: (http://www.youtube.com/watch?v=6Rd2bEp380w&feature=related) • What's the ratio of water molecules from one side to the other at the beginning of the demo? What do you notice about how the water molecules move? Why do you think they do this? • What's the ratio of water molecules from one side to the other at the end of the demo? Why do you think this is so? How is this like the "lettuce demo?" In other words, how does it mirror the process shown with the lettuce and water in the previous video? ***Station 2: Hypertonic, Hypotonic, and Isotonic Solutions*** Conduct a mini lab on hypertonic, hypotonic, and isotonic solutions. Complete the chart in your lab packet and then answer the following questions about solutions and systems: Cells encounter conflict from the outside in the form of 3 different kinds of solutions. They react to each of these change in different ways: • In an isotonic solution, cells will use osmosis to maintain homeostasis • In a hypertonic solution, cells have more water than the solution in which they are placed, so they respond by allowing water "out" and, consequently, "shriveling up." • In a hypotonic solution, cells have less water than the solution in which they are placed. They respond by allowing water into the cell, which causes the cell to swell and often burst.	This is the perfect place for students to see science "in action." Most textbook companies include directions for labs on this very subject; however, if this is not accessible, labs are available on the Internet (e.g., http://www.the-aps.org/education/outreach/outreach/acts-labs/halversn1.htm). In addition to or in place of the lab, students could complete the tutorial, complete with video demonstrations, at the following site: (http://www.linkpublishing.com/video-transport.htm#Elodea_-_Osmosis).

Unit Sequence—Core Curriculum and Curriculum of Connections	Teacher Reflections
Invite students to recall the three ways that systems could respond to change (below) and decide which of the following options describes a cell's reaction to hypertonic, hypotonic, and isotonic solutions. Also, decide if Kino's three systems (self, family, and town) were metaphorically exposed to hypertonic, hypotonic, and isotonic solutions. Your options: a. The system adjusts and adapts its processes to incorporate the change, resulting in a lasting change (and survival) to the system. b. The system expels the addition or change, resulting in survival without change? c. The change results in collapse and destruction of the system. ***Station 3: Creating a Concept Map*** At this station, you should work on creating a concept map that demonstrates how the processes of active and passive transport work in a parallel fashion utilizing cell transport to achieve homeostasis. Terms you should include in this concept map include the following: • Active transport • Concentration gradient • Carrier protein • Cell transport • Diffusion • Endocytosis • Exocytosis • Facilitated diffusion • Homeostasis • Osmosis • Passive transport • Sodium-potassium pump Make sure you show connections and relationships among terms by connecting them with arrows. Remember that the most effective concept maps typically include labels on each arrow.	
Closure	
Gather students together and debrief from the station activities. Ask for both "ah-has" and questions. End with students writing to the following prompt (bulleted lists are acceptable): *What does the cell system do to make sure it survives? What structures and functions does it have/use and how to they contribute to the cell's protection, survival, and well-being?*	Mastery of the content in both academic areas will be measured via student performance on the essay assessment administered at the close of the unit. Use the Postassessment: An Essay About Systems (Appendix 3K) and the included rubric to provide a summative assessment following this unit.

Unit 3 Appendixes

APPENDIX 3A: STORY ELEMENTS PREASSESSMENT

Name: _____

Directions: Read the following fable, and answer the questions below it.

The Shepherd Boy

There was once a young Shepherd Boy who tended his sheep at the foot of a mountain near a dark forest. It was rather lonely for him all day, so he thought upon a plan by which he could get a little company and some excitement. He rushed down towards the village calling out "Wolf, Wolf," and the villagers came out to meet him, and some of them stopped with him for a considerable time. This pleased the boy so much that a few days afterwards he tried the same trick, and again the villagers came to his help. But shortly after this a Wolf actually did come out from the forest, and began to worry the sheep, and the boy of course cried out "Wolf, Wolf," still louder than before. But this time the villagers, who had been fooled twice before, thought the boy was again deceiving them, and nobody stirred to come to his help. So the Wolf made a good meal off the boy's flock, and when the boy complained, the wise man of the village said:

"A liar will not be believed, even when he speaks the truth."

Source: www.AesopFables.com

Questions

Be as thorough as you can in your answers, and use complete sentences. If you don't understand a word from a question, make a hypothesis as to its meaning, and answer the question accordingly.

1. Name and describe the setting of this story.

2. Explain and defend whether or not you think the setting is important to this fable.

3. What is the theme of this story and how do you know?

4. From what point of view is this story written (circle one)?

   a. First Person (Narrator)
   b. Third Person Reporter
   c. Third Person Omniscient

5. Do you think this was a good choice on the author's part? Why or why not? What would be the most effective point of view for this story, in your opinion? Why?

6. Which of the following means of characterization did the author use (circle all that apply)?

   a. Portraying the character in action and speech
   b. Describing the character's appearance

   c. Portraying how other characters respond to the character
   d. Depicting the character's inner thoughts

7. Which means of characterization helps you best understand a character when you're reading a story? Explain.

8. The characters in this story (circle one):

   a. Are well-developed because they seem real; they grow and change
   b. Are not developed because they do not seem real and they do not grow and change

Explain your answer using specifics from the fable.

9. Which of the following types of conflict are central to this story (circle all that apply)?

   a. Person vs. Person
   b. Person vs. Self
   c. Person vs. Society
   d. Person vs. Nature
   e. Person vs. the Supernatural

Explain your choice(s).

10. Draw and label the parts of a plot diagram. Explain what is happening in this story at each point of the diagram. Use the back of the page, if needed.

APPENDIX 3B: STORY ELEMENTS PREASSESSMENT

Answer Key

1. Name and describe the setting of this story.

3 (Expert)	2 (Developing)	1 (Needs Improvement)
Discusses both the time period and the place, making inferences when necessary; references the social atmosphere of the time/place	Discusses both time and place but fails to make inferences or reference social climate	Fails to discuss time and/or place

2. Explain and defend whether or not you think the setting is important to this fable.

3 (Expert)	2 (Developing)	1 (Needs Improvement)
Discusses how both time and place affect two or more of the following: the story's plot, characters, themes, and plausibility	Discusses how time and/or place affect plot, characters, themes, or plausibility	Fails to discuss how time and/or place affect other elements of the story

3. What is the theme of this story and how do you know?

3 (Expert)	2 (Developing)	1 (Needs Improvement)
The student rephrases the moral in a concise yet thorough manner and includes a rationale that references a connection between the theme and what the character learned.	The student repeats or slightly rephrases the moral and includes references to the story.	The student fails to see the connection between the moral, storyline, and theme.

4. From what point of view is this story written?
   a. First Person (Narrator)
   b. Third Person Reporter
   c. Third Person Omniscient

5. Do you think this was a good choice on the author's part? Why or why not? What would be the most effective point of view for this story, in your opinion? Why?

3 (Expert)	2 (Developing)	1 (Needs Improvement)
Student discusses the pros and cons of both first and third person points of view, making specific references to the story in his/her answer. Student asserts and defends opinion with examples from the story and/or other stories. The response makes the reader see the story in a new light.	Student discusses the pros and/or the cons of first and/or third points of view, making specific references to the story in his/her answer. Student asserts and defends an opinion with support.	Student primarily discusses the point of view "as is" in the story and fails to make new connections to other perspectives. Opinion, if present, lacks support.

6. Which of the following means of characterization did the author use (circle all that apply):

    a. Portraying the character in action and speech

    b. Describing the character's appearance

    c. Portraying how other characters respond to the character

    d. Depicting the character's inner thoughts

7. Which means of characterization helps you best understand a character when you're reading a story? Explain.

3 (Expert)	2 (Developing)	1 (Needs Improvement)
Responses will vary, but the strongest answers will discuss that a combination of all methods gives the reader the most well-rounded picture of what characters are like, and that "depicting the character's inner thoughts" helps the reader get to know what a character is *really* like.	Responses will vary, but strong answers will discuss the benefits of the author using more than one method to paint a clear picture of what a character is like.	Student primarily discusses one or more methods of characterization to the exclusion of the others and fails to discuss the benefit of multiple methods.

8. The characters in this story (circle one):

    a. Are well-developed because they seem real; they grow and change

    b. Are not developed because they do not seem real and they do not grow and change

Explain your answer using specifics from the fable.

3 (Expert)	2 (Developing)	1 (Needs Improvement)
Student discusses the surface-level of characterization present in the story, acknowledging the limiting nature of the story's length. Ample use of specifics from the story makes this a well-supported answer.	Student discusses the surface-level of characterization present in the story; he or she may acknowledge the limiting nature of the story's length. Some specifics are included.	Student discusses the surface-level of characterization in the story but fails to either (1) discuss the limiting nature of the story's length and/or (2) use specifics for support.

9. Which of the following types of conflict are central to this story (circle all that apply)?

    a. Person vs. Person

    b. Person vs. Self

    c. Person vs. Society

    d. Person vs. Nature

    e. Person vs. the Supernatural

(Continued)

(Continued)

Explain your choice(s).

3 (Expert)	2 (Developing)	1 (Needs Improvement)
Answer discusses all of the following: Person vs. self—the boy needs to decide whether or not he will call for help when it's not needed Person vs. society—in crying wolf falsely, the boy pitted himself against the townspeople, who, acting as one body, function as "society" in this story. Person vs. nature—the wolf serves as a force of nature, not a characterized animal or person	Answer discusses two of the conflicts described to the left.	Answer discusses one or fewer of the conflicts described to the left.

10. Draw and label the parts of a plot diagram. Explain what is happening in this story at each point of the diagram. Use the back of the page, if needed.

Figure 3.1

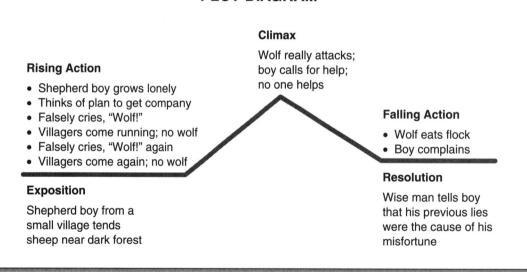

PLOT DIAGRAM

Climax

Wolf really attacks; boy calls for help; no one helps

Rising Action

- Shepherd boy grows lonely
- Thinks of plan to get company
- Falsely cries, "Wolf!"
- Villagers come running; no wolf
- Falsely cries, "Wolf!" again
- Villagers come again; no wolf

Falling Action

- Wolf eats flock
- Boy complains

Exposition

Shepherd boy from a small village tends sheep near dark forest

Resolution

Wise man tells boy that his previous lies were the cause of his misfortune

APPENDIX 3C: CELL BUILDING BLOCKS PREASSESSMENT

Name: _____

In addition to water, our bodies are composed of the following organic compounds:

- Carbohydrates
- Lipids
- Proteins
- Nucleic Acids

These compounds are essential to the proper functioning and survival of cells.

Directions: Read each question and answer to the best of your ability. If you can't remember specific terms, that's OK; paraphrase or describe those terms instead.

Carbohydrates are made of carbon, hydrogen, and oxygen atoms in the proportion 1:2:1. They are soluble in water and are found in many foods.

1. Which of the following are considered carbohydrates (circle all that apply)?
   a. Sugars
   b. Fats
   c. Steroids
   d. Waxes

2. Which of the following food groups are rich in carbohydrates (circle all that apply)?
   a. Vegetables
   b. Meats
   c. Breads and Pastas
   d. Eggs
   e. Butter and Oils

3. Why is it important that our cells and our bodies have carbohydrates (circle all that apply)?
   a. Some promote needed chemical reactions in the cell.
   b. They are a key source of energy.
   c. Some promote necessary functions in our organs and tissues.
   d. They store energy.
   e. Some contain genetic information.
   f. They play a key role in cell membrane function.
   g. Some manufacture proteins.

Lipids are nonpolar molecules that are not soluble in water. They are also found in many foods.

1. Which of the following are considered lipids (circle all that apply):
   a. Sugars
   b. Fats
   c. Steroids
   d. Waxes

2. Which of the following foods are composed of lipids (circle all that apply)?
   a. Vegetables
   b. Meats
   c. Breads and Pastas
   d. Eggs
   e. Butter and Oils

(Continued)

(Continued)

3. Why is it important that our cells and our bodies have lipids (circle all that apply)?

    a. Some promote needed chemical reactions in the cell.
    b. They are a key source of energy.
    c. Some promote necessary functions in our organs and tissues.
    d. They store energy.
    e. Some contain genetic information.
    f. They play a key role in cell membrane function.
    g. Some manufacture proteins.

Proteins are large molecules formed by linked smaller molecules called amino acids. They perform necessary cell functions and are found in many foods.

1. Which of the following food groups are rich in protein (circle all that apply)?

    a. Vegetables
    b. Meats
    c. Breads and Pastas
    d. Eggs
    e. Butter and Oils

2. Why is it important that our cells and our bodies have protein (circle all that apply)?

    a. Some promote needed chemical reactions in the cell.
    b. They are a key source of energy.
    c. Some promote necessary functions in our organs and tissues.
    d. They store energy.
    e. Some contain genetic information.
    f. They play a key role in cell membrane function.
    g. Some manufacture proteins.

Nucleic acids are long chains of smaller molecules called nucleotides. Each cell contains nucleic acids, and there are two major types: RNA and DNA.

1. Why is it important that our cells and our bodies have nucleic acids (circle all that apply)?

    a. Some promote needed chemical reactions in the cell.
    b. They are a key source of energy.
    c. Some promote necessary functions in our organs and tissues.
    d. They store energy.
    e. Some contain genetic information.
    f. They play a key role in cell membrane function.
    g. Some manufacture proteins.

2. ATP is a single nucleotide with two extra phosphate groups that serve as a kind of "reservoir." This structure allows ATP to perform a specialized function. What is this important function?

    a. Promotes needed chemical reactions in the cell.
    b. Serves as a key source of energy.
    c. Promotes necessary functions in our organs and tissues.
    d. They store energy.
    e. Contains genetic information.
    f. Play a key role in cell membrane function.
    g. Manufacture proteins.

Use the rest of this space to answer the following question.

What questions do you have about cell makeup and organic compounds?

APPENDIX 3D: CELL BUILDING BLOCKS PREASSESSMENT

Answer Key

Carbohydrates are made of carbon, hydrogen, and oxygen atoms in the proportion 1:2:1. They are soluble in water and are found in many foods.

1. Which of the following are considered carbohydrates (circle all that apply)?

   a. Sugars
   b. Fats
   c. Steroids
   d. Waxes

2. Which of the following food groups are rich in carbohydrates (circle all that apply)?

   a. Vegetables
   b. Meats
   c. Breads and Pastas
   d. Eggs
   e. Butter and Oils

3. Why is it important that our cells and our bodies have carbohydrates (circle all that apply)?

   a. Some promote needed chemical reactions in the cell.
   b. They are a key source of energy.
   c. Some promote necessary functions in our organs and tissues.
   d. They store energy.
   e. Some contain genetic information.
   f. They play a key role in cell membrane function.
   g. Some manufacture proteins.

Lipids are nonpolar molecules that are not soluble in water. They are also found in many foods.

1. Which of the following are considered lipids (circle all that apply):

   a. Sugars
   b. Fats
   c. Steroids
   d. Waxes

2. Which of the following foods are composed of lipids (circle all that apply)?

   a. Vegetables
   b. Meats
   c. Breads and Pastas
   d. Eggs
   e. Butter and Oils

3. Why is it important that our cells and our bodies have lipids (circle all that apply)?

   a. Some promote needed chemical reactions in the cell.
   b. They are a key source of energy.
   c. Some promote necessary functions in our organs and tissues.
   d. They store energy.
   e. Some contain genetic information.
   f. They play a key role in cell membrane function.
   g. Some manufacture proteins.

(Continued)

(Continued)

Proteins are large molecules formed by linked smaller molecules called amino acids. They perform necessary cell functions and are found in many foods.

1. Which of the following food groups are rich in protein (circle all that apply)?

    a. Vegetables

    b. Meats

    c. Breads and Pastas

    d. Eggs

    e. Butter and Oils

2. Why is it important that our cells and our bodies have protein (circle all that apply)?

    a. Some promote needed chemical reactions in the cell.

    b. They are a key source of energy.

    c. Some promote necessary functions in our organs and tissues.

    d. They store energy.

    e. Some contain genetic information.

    f. They play a key role in cell membrane function.

    g. Some manufacture proteins.

Nucleic acids are long chains of smaller molecules called nucleotides. Each cell contains nucleic acids, and there are two major types: RNA and DNA.

1. Why is it important that our cells and our bodies have nucleic acids (circle all that apply)?

    a. Some promote needed chemical reactions in the cell.

    b. They are a key source of energy.

    c. Some promote necessary functions in our organs and tissues.

    d. They store energy.

    e. Some contain genetic information.

    f. They play a key role in cell membrane function.

    g. Some manufacture proteins.

2. ATP is a single nucleotide with two extra phosphate groups that serve as a kind of "reservoir." This structure allows ATP to perform a specialized function. What is this important function?

    a. Promotes needed chemical reactions in the cell.

    b. Serves as a key source of energy.

    c. Promotes necessary functions in our organs and tissues.

    d. They store energy.

    e. Contains genetic information.

    f. Play a key role in cell membrane function.

    g. Manufacture proteins.

APPENDIX 3E: CELL STRUCTURE AND FUNCTION PREASSESSMENT

Name: _____

1. Briefly explain the difference between a eukaryotic cell and a prokaryotic cell:

2. Match the following eukaryotic animal cell organelles and materials to their functions in the boxes to the right of the terms:

   a. ATP

   b. Cell membrane

   c. Cell-surface marker

   d. Cytoplasm

   e. Cytoskeleton

   1. _____ Allows required material to enter/exit cell while denying access to unwanted material.

   2. _____ The portion of the cell enclosed within the cell membrane that contains the cell's organelles.

   3. _____ Scaffolding within the cytoplasm.

   4. _____ Communicates the type of cell.

   5. _____ Transports chemical energy within the cells for metabolism.

   f. Enzymes

   g. Endoplasmic Reticulum

   h. Golgi Apparatus

   i. Lipid Bilayer

   j. Lysosomes

   1. _____ The "rough" variety produces proteins in the ribosomes on its surface.

   2. _____ Made of phospholipids that arrange themselves in such a way that the polarized heads face in opposite directions. In the cell membrane.

   3. _____ Contains digestive enzymes.

   4. _____ Processes and packages proteins.

   5. _____ Facilitate a variety of chemical reactions.

   k. Mitochondria

   l. Nucleus

   m. Ribosomes

   n. Specialized Proteins

   o. Vesicles

   1. _____ Contains most of the cell's genetic material.

   2. _____ Store, transport, and digest cellular products and waste.

   3. _____ Generates the majority of the cell's energy.

   4. _____ Some lie on the surface of the ER and manufacture proteins.

   5. _____ Imbedded in the cell membrane, their jobs include receiving signals and transporting materials.

3. What three cell structures do plant cells have that animal cells do not?

(Continued)

(Continued)

4. Explain the difference between active and passive transport. Include in your discussion the phospholipid bilayer, specialized proteins, osmosis, and diffusion.

5. Label the diagrams below as to whether they represent an isotonic, hypotonic, or hypertonic solution. There is one of each. Explain your reasoning.

Figure 3.2

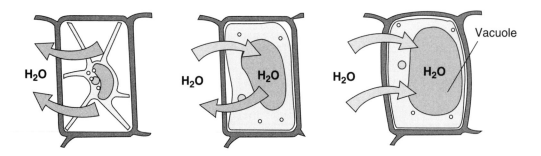

Vacuole

H_2O H_2O H_2O H_2O H_2O H_2O

Source: Wikimedia Commons (http://en.wikipedia.org/wiki/File:Turgor_pressure_on_plant_cells_diagram.svg)

APPENDIX 3F: CELL STRUCTURE AND FUNCTION PREASSESSMENT

Answer Key

1. Briefly explain the difference between a eukaryotic cell and a prokaryotic cell:

3	2	1
Answers discuss 3 to 5 of the following: 1. Eukaryotic cells are those we typically discuss when studying animal and plant cells. 2. They have a nucleus, cell membrane, and several organelles such as mitochondria and Golgi apparatuses. 3. Prokaryotic cells do not have a cell nucleus, nor do they have most of the organelles that eukaryotic cells possess, 4. although they do have ribosomes, which manufacture proteins, and cytoskeletons. 5. Prokaryotic cells have appendages called flagella, which help them move. 6. They can be classified as either bacteria or archaea.	Answers discuss 2–3 of the points at left. If only 2 are discussed, they are discussed thoroughly.	Answers discuss 0–1 of the points in the left column.

2. Match the following eukaryotic animal cell organelles and materials to their functions in the boxes to the right of the terms:

a. ATP

b. Cell Membrane

c. Cell-Surface Marker

d. Cytoplasm

e. Cytoskeleton

f. Enzymes

g. Endoplasmic reticulum

h. Golgi Apparatus

i. Lipid Bilayer

j. Lysosomes

1. *b* Allows required material to enter/exit cell while denying access to unwanted material.
2. *d* The portion of the cell enclosed within the cell membrane that contains the cell's organelles.
3. *e* Scaffolding within the cytoplasm.
4. *c* Communicates the type of cell.
5. *a* Transports chemical energy within the cells for metabolism.

1. *g* The "rough" variety produces proteins in the ribosomes on its surface.
2. *i* Made of phospholipids that arrange themselves in such a way that the polarized heads face in opposite directions. In the cell membrane.
3. *j* Contains digestive enzymes.
4. *h* Processes and packages proteins.
5. *f* Facilitate a variety of chemical reactions.

(Continued)

(Continued)

k. Mitochondria

l. Nucleus

m. Ribosomes

n. Specialized Proteins

o. Vesicles

1. *l* Contains most of the cell's genetic material.
2. *o* Store, transport, and digest cellular products and waste.
3. *k* Generates the majority of the cell's energy.
4. *m* Some lie on the surface of the ER and manufacture proteins.
5. *n* Imbedded in the cell membrane, their jobs include receiving signals and transporting materials.

3. What three cell structures do plant cells have that animal cells do not?

Cell Wall

Chloroplasts

Vacuoles

4. Explain the difference between active and passive transport. Include in your discussion the phospholipid bilayer, specialized proteins, osmosis, and diffusion.

3	2	1
Answers discuss each of the following including each of the **bold** terms: In passive transport, or **osmosis**, **no energy is used**. Specialized proteins, located in the **phospholipid bilayer** of the **cell membrane**, act as **channels** and allow molecules to flow, or **diffuse**, from an area of greater concentration to an area of lesser concentration. Active transport **requires energy** to cause the specialized **transport proteins**, also located in the **phospholipid bilayer** of the **cell membrane**, **to pump** molecules from an area of greater concentration to an area of lower concentration.	Answers discuss both active and passive transport but lack the detail/inclusion of bolded terms in the "3" column. OR Answers discuss either passive or active transport in the detail/ with the terms present in the left-hand column's descriptions.	Answers discuss one or both types of transport but with few details and terms present in the "3" column.

5. Label the diagrams below as to whether they represent an isotonic, hypotonic, or hypertonic solution. There is one of each. Explain your reasoning.

Figure 3.3

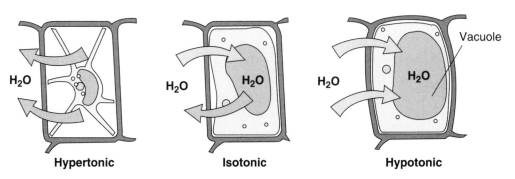

Hypertonic   **Isotonic**   **Hypotonic**

Source: Wikimedia Commons (http://en.wikipedia.org/wiki/File:Turgor_pressure_on_plant_cells_diagram.svg)

3	2	1
Answers include all three of the following explanations: 1. A hypertonic solution is made up of less water than is the cell. When the cell is placed in a hypertonic solution, water diffuses out of the cell; hence, the cell shrinks. 2. A hypotonic solution contains more water than does the cytoplasm of the cells. Thus, when a cell is placed into a hypotonic solution, water moves into of the cells; hence, the cells swell. 3. Isotonic solutions contain the same concentration of water as the cells they surround; thus, there is no movement of water into or out of the cell.	Student discusses two out of the three solutions or discuss all three but in less detail than is presented in the "3" column.	Student discusses only one of the solutions in the "3" column correctly or two in little detail.

APPENDIX 3G: STRUCTURED ACADEMIC CONTROVERSY

The Pearl

"Kino made a wise decision to reject the pearl-seller's offer."

Step 1: Prepare your position. Meet with your partner(s) and plan how to argue effectively for your position, be it PRO or CON. Once you have a fairly specific and complete position prepared, compare positions with other groups preparing the same position.

To prepare the best case for your position, gather evidence to support your assigned position. Gather all relevant examples from the story's plot along with quotations and page numbers. Organize what you know into a reasoned position and persuasive argument by:

1. Arranging the information into a thesis statement or claim that asserts something is "true."
2. Arranging the supporting facts, information, experiences, and other evidence into a coherent, reasoned, valid, and logical rationale.
3. Making the conclusion that your claim is true (back to original thesis).

Your aim is to lead listeners step-by-step from a lack of knowledge to an informed conclusion that agrees with your thesis statement.

Step 2: Present and advocate your position. Find a matching opposing pair or small group with whom to work. Meet with this group and present your position. Each member of the group has to participate in the presentation.

Some guidelines for helping present the best case:

- Begin and end with a strong, sincere, and enthusiastic appeal for the listeners to agree with your position.
- Present several points of evidence organized in a logical way.
- Select four or five major points during the initial presentation.
- Expand on these points by using examples, stories, and anecdotes.
- Restate important points.
- Make eye contact with audience.
- Keep presentation to time limit.

As you listen to the opposing presentation, you need to learn that view so that you can argue it in the next step. Also, you will be better able to refute the argument if you understand it. Listen carefully to the opposing position and analyze the points in the argument as being strong or weak. Make certain that the opposing team clarifies any muddy points. Take notes of what your opponent says (in right-hand portion of web) so that you can use those points in the next steps.

Step 3: Engage in an open discussion in which you refute the opposing position and rebut attacks on your own position. Continue to advocate your position by emphasizing facts, evidence, and rationale. Refute the evidence of the opposition. Refute the reasoning of the opposition based on errors of perception and judgment. Rebut the arguments of the opposition by presenting counter arguments, clarifications, and extensions.

Step 4: Reverse positions. Rotate to find a new opposing pair who argued the other side of the issue in the previous three steps. You will now reverse positions: those who were CON are now PRO, those who were PRO are now CON. You will repeat Steps 1–3 but now arguing from the opposite side. Caucus briefly with your partner and plan your presentation. Use the points and insights you gleaned from your former opponents to help you formulate your new position statement. As you present the opposing position be forceful and persuasive and, if possible, add new facts and evidence. When responding to the opposition, present new points, correct errors, and note omissions.

Step 5: Synthesize and integrate the best evidence and reasoning into a joint position. The four or five members of your final group drop all advocacy and synthesize and integrate what is known into a factual and judgmental joint position on which both sides can agree.

To do this:

1. Step back and look at the issue from a variety of perspectives.

2. Synthesize the best evidence from all sides of the issue.

3. Synthesis occurs when a new position is created that subsumes the previous two—a new position that unifies the previous ones, brings them to harmony, and unites their best features on a higher level. In trying to create a synthesis, it is helpful to summarize the two original positions into a few words. Organizing large blocks of information into an abbreviated form often clarifies the underlying nature of the positions and illuminates the relationships and patterns in the evidence gathered by both sides. This will help to generate the create insights necessary to synthesize the two positions.

Step 6: Write a bulleted list that shows the major points of the group synthesis. Put this list on poster paper and post it somewhere in the room. All group members must be involved in the creation of this statement, but you may assign roles as follows: Choose one of your groupmates to dictate, another to write, another to edit/check quality, and another to present to the rest of the class.

Step 7: Present your joint position statement to the class.

Step 8: Listen, take notes, and respond individually. Each class member must take notes on other classmates' presentations; you will be asked to compose and submit a personal statement about if/how your original views have changed and what particular pieces of information were most influential in solidifying or swaying your views.

Adapted from *For Teachers: Academic Controversy Primer.* Retrieved December 19, 2010, from http://www.pbs.org/wnet/wideangle/classroom/controversy.html

The Pearl, Chapters 4–6

Kino's decision to reject the pearl seller's offers was _____wise _____unwise. Textual support of this can be found by examining the following (include notes, quotes, and page numbers):

Kino's Psyche (his Desire to Be a Man and His Dreams for His Son)	Kino's Relationships With His Immediate Family and Extended Family (Villagers)

Kino's "Place" Within the Town System	Kino's Need to Survive

APPENDIX 3I: STRUCTURED ACADEMIC CONTROVERSY DISCUSSION WEB

Figure 3.4

STRUCTURED ACADEMIC CONTROVERSY DISCUSSION WEB

Reasons why our position is right (arguments with quotes and page numbers)		*Reasons why our position might be wrong (arguments with quotes and page numbers)*
_____		_____
_____		_____
_____		_____
_____	**PRO**	_____
_____	*Kino made a wise decision to reject the pearl-seller's offer.*	_____
_____		_____
_____		_____
_____		_____
_____		_____

Conclusion: _____

_____

_____

_____

_____

_____

_____

APPENDIX 3J: STATIONS FOR LESSON 3.5

Station 1: Diffusion and Osmosis Videos

Watch the following video and answer the questions that follow. You can replay this video as many times as needed: http://www.youtube.com/watch?v=H7QsDs8ZRMI&feature=related
Why does diffusion of bromine take less time when it is diffused into a vacuum?

Why does nitrogen dioxide diffuse more quickly than bromine?

Which gas diffuses faster, ammonia or hydrochloric acid? Why?

What effect does temperature have on the rate of diffusion? Why?

Next, watch this video depicting diffusion of liquids from an area of high concentration to an area of low concentration (osmosis): http://www.youtube.com/watch?v=H6N1IiJTmnc&feature=related
Why does the lettuce behave this way?

How does water behave like the gasses in the other video? What do the two phenomena have in common?

Now watch this demonstration of osmosis. The red and blue dots represent water molecules while the green and yellow dots represent sugar molecules: http://www.youtube.com/watch?v=6Rd2bEp380w&feature=related
What's the ratio of water molecules from one side to the other at the beginning of the demo? What do you notice about how the water molecules move? Why do you think they do this?

What's the ratio of water molecules from one side to the other at the end of the demo? Why do you think this is so? How is this like the "lettuce demo"; in other words, how does it mirror the process shown with the lettuce and water in the previous video?

Station 2: Hypertonic, Hypotonic, and Isotonic Solutions

Conduct a mini lab on Hypertonic, Hypotonic, and Isotonic Solutions (attached) or complete the video tutorial at the following site (see your teacher to determine which option to pursue): http://www.linkpublishing.com/video-transport.htm#Elodea_-_Osmosis
Use your findings and your readings to complete the following chart:

	Conditions: Inside the Cell vs. Outside the Cell	Movement: Endocytosis or Exocytosis (In to or Out of Cell)	Result: How does the cell react? What happens to it?
Isotonic			
Hypertonic			
Hypotonic			

Now answer the following question about solutions and systems.

Cells encounter conflict from the outside in the form of three different kinds of solutions: isotonic, hypertonic, and hypotonic. They react to each of these conditions in different ways:

- In an isotonic solution, cells will use osmosis to maintain homeostasis.
- In a hypertonic solution, cells have more water than the solution in which they are placed, so they respond by allowing water "out" and, consequently, "shriveling up."
- In a hypotonic solution, cells have less water than the solution in which they are placed. They respond by allowing water into the cell, which causes the cell to swell and often burst.

Think back to the three ways we discussed that systems could respond to change:

1. The system adjusts and adapts its processes to incorporate the change, resulting in a lasting change (and survival) to the system.

2. The system expels the addition or change, resulting in survival without change.

3. The change results in collapse and destruction of the system.

Which of these options best describes a cell's reaction to hypertonic, hypotonic, and isotonic solutions? You do not have to use all three if you believe they don't fit. Explain your answers.

Now "flip" your thinking, and decide if Kino's three systems (self, family, and town) were metaphorically exposed to hypertonic, hypotonic, and isotonic solutions. Defend your answers with examples from both the story and from what you learned in your lab/video tutorial.

Station 3: Creating a Concept Map

At this station, you should work on creating a concept map that demonstrates how the processes of active and passive transport work in a parallel fashion, utilizing cell transport to achieve homeostasis. Terms you should include in this concept map include the following:

- Active transport
- Concentration gradient
- Carrier protein
- Cell transport
- Diffusion
- Encocytosis
- Exocytosis
- Facilitated diffusion
- Homeostasis
- Osmosis
- Passive transport
- Sodium-potassium pump

Make sure you show connections and relationships among terms by connecting them with arrows. Remember that the most effective concept maps typically include labels on each arrow.

APPENDIX 3K: POSTASSESSMENT

An Essay About Systems

1. For this assignment, you will choose one or more systems from *The Pearl* and compare its/their parts and functions to those of a eukaryotic cell system. You will be able to choose (1) the system(s) from *The Pearl* on which you'd like to focus, and (2) the three unit principles that will serve as your points of comparison between the novella and eukaryotic cell structure and functioning.

2. Your *Pearl* system choices include the following:
   a. The self/psyche
   b. The family (immediate and fellow fishermen's families)
   c. The larger community (the town)

   Circle the system(s) on which you'd like to focus in this essay assignment, then record them in the graphic organizer provided.

3. Your principle choices include the following:
   a. The **survival** of a **system** depends upon the successful operation of each of its interdependent parts.
   b. Change to one part of a **system** results in change to the rest of the **system**.
   c. **Systems** strive to achieve and maintain **balance**.
      Function/identity reflects the environment in which it operates.
   d. **Function** dictates structure.
   e. **Conflict** can strengthen or destroy a **system**.

   Circle the three principles you'd like to use as your main points of comparison in this essay. Record your chosen principles in the graphic organizer provided.

4. You will consider the cell system in terms of its structure and functions, and explain how it, like your chosen system(s) in *The Pearl*, illustrates the *three* principles of systems you've selected. Make sure your essay accomplishes the following:

   - Thoroughly and accurately discusses the cell's (eukaryotic) interdependent structures and operations (cell membrane [marker, receptor, and transport proteins], cytoplasm, cytoskeleton, nucleus, ribosomes, ER, vesicles, lysosomes, Golgi apparatus, mitochondria, DNA, RNA, enzymes, cell wall, chloroplasts, and central vacuole).
   - Thoroughly and accurately discusses active and passive transport (osmosis, diffusion, hypotonic, hypertonic, sodium-potassium pump, movement against a concentration gradient, endocytosis, exocytosis, signal molecule, ATP).
   - Thoroughly discusses one or more of the following systems from *The Pearl*—the self/psyche; the family (immediate and fishermen's village); and the larger community (town)—in terms of their interdependent parts and their relationships.
   - Demonstrates a thorough understanding of the characters' identities, conflicts, and perspectives, and discusses how setting impacts them as well as how they work together to shape theme.
   - Makes genuine connections between the purpose and relationships in literature and cell structure and function.

   You may use illustrations and/or diagrams within your essay (Figure 1, 2, etc.) or at the conclusion of (Appendix 1, 2, etc.). Make sure your illustrations supplement your written discussion; they cannot replace written discussion.

   Use this template to plan your essay. Begin by listing your chosen principles and systems. Then, in the empty sections where they intersect, record information that shows these principles in action in biology and English.

Helpful Hints

- Use specific explanations and vocabulary concerning cell structure and function.
- Use specific details/quotes and vocabulary from the story.
- Check your details against the criteria in Step 4 above to ensure you've included all required material.
- Order your details before you begin writing.
- Plan for and indicate where you think you might need to incorporate a figure or an appendix.

Principle (list your selected principles in the blocks provided)	Its Application to a Eukaryotic Cell's Structure and Function	Its Application to The Pearl System(s)

Name: _____

System(s): _____

Principle Number(s): _____

(Continued)

(Continued)

	Expert	Well Developed	Needs Improvement
Organization	You meet all organizational requirements:	All five parts are included but are difficult to distinguish from one another (circled):	You are missing one or more parts of this essay (circled):
	You introduce your *Pearl* system(s) and chosen principles at the outset.	Introduction	Introduction
	You discuss how each of your chosen principles is illustrated by your chosen system(s) in *The Pearl*.	Discussion of each principle in terms of *The Pearl*	Discussion of each principle in terms of *The Pearl*
	You discuss how each of your chosen principles is illustrated by the structure and function of a eukaryotic cell.	Discussion of each principle in terms of a eukaryotic cell	Discussion of each principle in terms of a eukaryotic cell
	You end by sharing the lesson you learned from and/or the importance of the overlap between interdisciplinary systems.	Conclusion with interdisciplinary insight	Conclusion with interdisciplinary insight
Details and Support		Missing 1 or 2 (Well-Developed) or more (Needs Improvement) of the following required pieces of information	
	Thoroughly and accurately discusses all aspects of the cell's (eukaryotic) interdependent structures and operations	Structures and their operations: cell membrane (marker, receptor, and transport proteins), cytoplasm, cytoskeleton, nucleus, ribosomes, ER, vesicles, lysosomes, Golgi apparatus, mitochondria, DNA, RNA, enzymes, cell wall, chloroplasts, and central vacuole	
	Thoroughly and accurately discusses all aspects of active and passive transport	Active and passive transport: osmosis, diffusion, hypotonic, hypertonic, sodium-potassium pump, movement against a concentration gradient, endocytosis, exocytosis, signal molecule, ATP	
	Thoroughly and specifically discusses one or more of the systems from *The Pearl* in terms of its interdependent parts and their relationships.	Specifics from *The Pearl:* details/quotes pertaining to system	
	Uses specific details and quotes to demonstrate understanding of the interdependence of story elements	Interdependence of story elements: characters' identities, conflicts, and perspectives, and discuss how setting impacts them as well as how they work together to shape theme	

	Expert	*Well Developed*	*Needs Improvement*
Quality of Discussion	You make genuine connections between the story and cell structure and function. These connections help the reader understand the story and cell structure and function. Illustrations enhance meaning.	Your connections and/or illustrations seemed forced, AND/OR they do not clarify the meaning of the story and/or cell structure and function.	You fail to make connections that clarify *The Pearl* and/or cell structure and function. Your discussion and illustrations remain at the surface level.
Formatting	Your spelling, punctuation, and grammar are error-free. Your essay reads smoothly and shows ample evidence of being read aloud, proofread, and rewritten (e.g., drafts).	You make minor errors in spelling and punctuation that don't distract from your point. Your essay is "bumpy" but shows some evidence of being read aloud, proofread, and rewritten (e.g., drafts).	Your essay contains distracting errors in spelling, punctuation, and/or grammar. Little evidence of proofreading/editing exists (e.g., drafts).

REFERENCES

Johnson, D. W., & Johnson, R. T. (1999). Structuring academic controversy. In S. Sharan (Ed.), *Handbook of cooperative learning methods* (pp. 66–81). Westport, CT: Praeger Publications.

Johnson, G. B., & Raven, P. H. (2004). *Holt biology.* Austin, TX: Holt, Rineheart & Winston.

Steinbeck, J. (1945). *The pearl.* New York, NY: Penguin Books.

Wiggins, G., & McTighe, J. (2006). *Understanding by design* (2nd Expanded ed.). Alexandria, VA: Association for Supervision & Curriculum Development.

HELPFUL WEBSITES/VIDEOS

PASSIVE TRANSPORT (DIFFUSION)

http://www.youtube.com/watch?v=s0p1ztrbXPY&NR=1

ACTIVE TRANSPORT

http://www.youtube.com/watch?v=STzOiRqzzL4&feature=related

ENDOCYTOSIS AND EXOCYTOSIS

http://www.youtube.com/watch?v=4gLtk8Yc1Zc&feature=related

HYPERTONIC, HYPOTONIC, ISOTONIC LAB

http://www.the-aps.org/education/outreach/outreach/acts-labs/halversn1.htm

HYPERTONIC, HYPOTONIC, ISOTONIC VIDEO TUTORIAL

http://www.linkpublishing.com/video-transport.htm#Elodea_-_Osmosis

The Periodic Table

Getting To Know and Appreciate the Elements and Their Families, Grade 10

Fie Budzinsky

BACKGROUND TO THE UNIT

This set of lessons focuses on the work of the scientist and critical understandings about the periodic table. These lessons are part of a much larger unit about reactions and interactions that was developed and is available on the Connecticut State Department of Education website: http://www.sde.ct.gov/sde/cwp/view .asp?a=2618&q=320852

These lessons are a companion piece to a high school science class's study of reactions and interactions. The examples, activities, and projects in the lessons are linked to the elements and their arrangements in the periodic table. The lessons are designed and organized to deepen students' understandings of the relationships among elements and their compounds. However, the unit is not a comprehensive study of reactions and interactions and would need to be accompanied by other instruction to ensure content coverage.

Within the Parallel Curriculum Model, the unit reflects the Core Curriculum, the Parallel of Practice and the Curriculum of Connections. With respect to the Curriculum of Practice, the learning activities invite students to engage in the thinking required of scientists: observation, analysis, comparing and contrasting, and identify patterns, for example. Students who complete these lessons will find themselves asking questions such as: How does a scientist approach problems? How does he or she draw conclusions about data? How do I know that conclusions are valid?

The Core Parallel is also addressed through the content of the concepts and principles. The lessons help students answer general questions such as: What does this information mean? Why do these ideas make sense in my life? Further, they are organized in such a way that helps students to understand, make meaning, and use what they know as they move forward in science.

Finally, opportunities exist for students to see connections between the disciplines of science and English/language arts. Several of the later lessons require students to research and write creatively and in authentic ways about elements. Students will find themselves asking questions like the following: In what other contexts can I use this information? How does looking at one thing help me to understand another? How are perspectives shaped by time, place, culture, events, and circumstances?

Several strategies have been incorporated to differentiate for the range of learners. Some of the learning activities have been differentiated to respond to student readiness. Others have been designed to address differences in student interest.

How This Unit Differs From Other More Traditional Approaches

The more traditional approaches about chemical elements are textbook based and lecture driven. The lessons included here are different because they are constructivist. Students are required to explore the concepts and principles in multiple ways: lab explorations, kinesthetic activities, research that requires an understanding of the multiple influences that shape science understandings, and creative writing. The drawback to this approach, of course, is that it takes more time than the traditional approaches. The time invested, however, is worthwhile because it ensures deep learning, not just temporary memorization.

What the Teacher Needs to Know Before Starting

The expectation is that students will enter these lessons with some background in chemistry and scientific inquiry. With regard to chemistry, students should understand the properties of matter and their related behaviors. They should understand the difference between pure substances and mixtures. Finally, they should be able to describe the properties of common elements, such as oxygen, hydrogen, and carbon and of simple compounds, such as water and table salt.

With respect to scientific inquiry, students should be able to identify questions that can be answered through scientific investigation, design and conduct appropriate scientific investigations, and use appropriate tools and techniques to make observations and gather data. They should also be able to provide explanations to investigated problems or questions. Lastly, they should be able to communicate about science in different formats, using relevant science vocabulary, supporting evidence, and clear logic.

CONTENT FRAMEWORK

Organizing Concept

Macroconcept

M1   System

Discipline-Specific Concepts

C1   Reactant

C2   Product

C3   Acid

C4   Base

C5   Chemical properties

C6   Physical properties

C7   Chemical reactivity

C8   Chemical change

C9   Element

C10 Compound

C11 Chemical change

C12 Metal

C13 Semimetal

C14 Nonmetal

C15 Nobel gas

C16 Reactive gas

C17 "Families" of elements

C18 Periodicity

C19 Scientific investigation

C20 Intended consequences

C21 Unintended consequences

C22 Social context

C23 Historical context

Principles

P1   Matter is made of elements that can be by themselves or joined to form compounds.

P2   Although substances may look physically the same, they can be distinguished by their reactivity with other elements.

P3   Compounds are made from combining different elements in different arrangements.

P4   Many compounds can be produced from a much smaller number of basic kinds of materials called elements.

P5   Matter can be acidic, basic, or neutral.

P6   Different elements have different physical and chemical properties.

P7   Different compounds have different physical and chemical properties.

P8   Elements can be grouped together depending on their physical and chemical properties.

P9   Reactivity is an example of a chemical property of elements that varies from one element to another.

P10   Elements can be categorized into metals, nonmetals, and semimetals (metalloids).

P11   Tables can be used to organize large amounts of information and therefore make data more manageable.

P12   Matter varies in its ability to chemically react with other matter.

P13   The nature of matter can be explored through scientific investigations.

P14   Elements can be grouped together depending on their physical and chemical properties.

P15   Elements vary in their chemical reactivity.

P16   Scientists communicate knowledge about matter in clear and varied ways.

P17   Groups of elements have similarities, much like families.

P18   The study of matter and the subsequent technology and the social and historical context in which this study takes place are interdependent.

P19   Scientific discoveries and interventions have beneficial and detrimental consequences.

Skills

S1   Identify characteristics

S2   Describe characteristics

S3   Analyze

S4   Compare and contrast

S5   Draw conclusions

S6   Describe characteristics

S7   Identify patterns

S8   Categorize

S9   Write creatively

S10   Use analogies and metaphors

S11   (Optional) Use computer technology to enhance communication

S12   See relationships

S13   Brainstorm

S14   Plan

S15   Organize

S16   Write

S17   Demonstrate originality

National Standards (from National Science Education Standards, Grades 9–12)

SD1   Students will develop an understanding about the structures and properties of matter and chemical reactions.

SD2   Students will develop an understanding of science and technology in local, national, or global challenges.

SD3   Students will develop an understanding of science as a human endeavor, the nature of scientific knowledge, and the historical perspectives about science.

Unit Assessments

The unit incorporates a variety of formative assessment opportunities throughout that teachers can use to tailor their instruction. These assessments are included because they have been field-tested and found to be sensitive to student misunderstandings related to elements, compounds, and their organization in the periodic table. Teachers who use these assessments, including the accompanying rubrics, should be particularly attuned to student errors, whether in written or verbal format. Furthermore, teachers need to modify their instruction to address the misconceptions that have surfaced.

OVERVIEW OF KEY LESSON IDEAS/PURPOSES

Lesson 4.1, Getting to Know You, is an introduction to the connection between chemical reactions (the whole), and the elements and compounds that make them up (the parts). The focus is on one important idea: chemical reactions involve elements, compounds, and change. Several demonstrations illustrate this idea, and a poster project extends it by linking elements, compounds, and their reactions to an historical context (3–5 class periods).

Lesson 4.2, The Elements: Up Close and Personal, includes a lab and small group work in which students peer review each other's posters. The small group work about the posters extends students' understanding of *all* the elements, not just the one they researched (2–3 days).

In Lesson 4.3, We Are Family!, students will discover that elements can be grouped by similarities into *families*. Through kinesthetic activities that extend over two class periods, they will become familiar with the concept of periodicity and the periodic table, which scientists use as a tool for prediction and explanation (2–3 days).

Lessons 4.4, The Elements in Action, focuses on the Curriculum of Connections because students are invited to write a story about an element that becomes a hero. In their creative stories, they have to integrate aspects of heroism and the characteristics of tragic or romantic heroes and the facts they have learned about their particular element's "personality" and "family" (2–3 days).

Like Lesson 4.4, Lesson 4.5, Breaking News, also focuses on the Curriculum of Connections. Students are invited to create a newspaper front page in which they feature a historical event associated with one of the elements or its important compounds. This project provides student with an opportunity to link the information regarding the properties and behaviors of an element/compound to its historical and social context (3–5 days).

Lesson 4.1: The Elements: Getting to Know You

Time allocation: 3–5 class periods, depending on the amount of in-class time dedicated to student research

Concepts

C9 Element
C10 Compound
C19 Scientific investigation

Principles

P1 Matter is made up of elements that can be by themselves or joined to form compounds.

P6 Different elements have different physical and chemical properties.

P8 Elements can be grouped together depending on their physical and chemical properties.

P9 Reactivity is an example of a chemical property of elements that varies from one element to another.

P10 Elements can be categorized into metals, nonmetals, and semimetals (metalloids).

P15 Elements vary in their chemical reactivity.

Skills

S1 Identify characteristics
S2 Describe characteristics
S3 Analyze
S4 Compare and contrast
S7 Identify patterns
S8 Categorize

Standards

SD1 Students will develop an understanding about the structures and properties of matter and chemical reactions.

Guiding Questions

1. What are elements?
2. What are they good for?

Unit Sequence—Core Curriculum	Teacher Reflections
Preparation	
Gather materials for this introductory lesson on elements. • An iron nail that has been sanded so that it shows no evidence of rust and a nail that is rusted. • Magnesium metal, metal tongs, wire gauze that can be obtained from most high school science departments or offered from Frey Scientific, P.O. Box 8101, Mansfield, Ohio 44901-8101, or ordered via the Web at www.freyscientific.com. The item numbers, at the time of this writing, are as follows: magnesium ribbon (hazardous material), #15573162 at $10.35, stainless steel tongs, #15574149, and ceramic gauze (6″ by 6″) #15584325, $9.75, plus 8% shipping and handling. • Matches • Internet sites to assist students in their research on the elements such as http://web.buddyproject.org/web017/web017/. Many Web quests about elements are available for teachers. Simply type in "elements web quests" into your Internet browser to search for sites. • Poster board • Markers • Scissors • Glue • Rulers • Stencils Prepare a poster on the element carbon (Family IV) as an exemplar for the element project, if time allows. It will show students how to depict the information they gather in their research. The benchmark will serve as an illustration of the quality expected.	

(Continued)

(Continued)

Unit Sequence—Core Curriculum	Teacher Reflections
Introduction	
Introductory Activities (15 minutes) 1. Brainstorm with the class what they already know about the elements by inviting student reflection on such questions as: What is an element? Where are they found? Why are they important? Are there different elements? How might they differ from one another? What are elements made of? What are they good for? 2. You can use video clips to engage students in a discussion of the nature and discovery of elements. Many interactive sites are available with an Internet search (http://www.rsc.org/chemsoc/visualelements/pages/pertable_j.htm).	Be listening to students for those who seem to have a rich knowledge of chemistry and/or deeper insight into the nature of elements. Look to the extension activity for those students ready and interested in further exploration of the elements or organic chemistry.
Teaching Strategies and Learning Experiences (25 minutes)	
1. Hold up the iron nail that has been sanded so that it shows no sign of rust and a nail that is rusted. Share with students that the iron nail is pure iron, an element, and the other nail has a compound, rust on its surface. Ask students how the rust formed? They should be able to hypothesize that the rust is composed of two elements: iron and oxygen. 2. Take the strip of magnesium and hold it in a pair of tongs. Light the free end with a match. A white powder should drop to the table. As it burns, discuss the fact that magnesium is an element that is shiny and malleable. It combines with another element in the air, oxygen, to form the white powder they see falling, which is magnesium oxide. Ask students how the reactants and products are different physically (e.g., silver, flexible, metallic, versus white and powdery). Invite students to think about the product. Would it burn like the original? 3. Instruct students that they will be doing a research project for the purpose of "getting to know and appreciate the elements and their families."	Provide students with time to think together in small groups. These conversations reflect the ways scientists work. As scientists learn from each other, so, too, will students. Students should recognize that they cannot predict the chemical properties (e.g., flammability) of a new product based on the chemical properties of the reactants. **Extension Activity** If you anticipate that some students will complete the assignment more

Unit Sequence—Core Curriculum	Teacher Reflections
4. Assign each student one of the following 24 elements: lithium; sodium potassium (from Family I); beryllium, magnesium, calcium (from Family II); copper, silver, gold (from Transition Metals); boron, aluminum, gallium (from Family III); silicon, germanium (from Family IV); nitrogen, phosphorous, arsenic (from Family V); sulfur, selenium (from Family VI); fluorine, chlorine, bromine (from Family VII); helium, neon (from Family VIII). If you do not have 24 students, you can eliminate gold, arsenic, or bromine in any order. If you have more than 24 students, you can add elements from each of these families. It is important for later activities that you assign at least two elements, preferably three, from each of the nine groups/families of elements, Families 1–8 and the Transition Metals.	quickly than others, assign these students one of the three most important elements in living things: oxygen (from Family VI), hydrogen (characteristics of Family I and Family VII), or carbon (from Family IV) (Note: A student can complete the carbon poster if the teacher has not already done so. See Preparation notes.). These three elements are more complex and will require more in-depth research.
5. Apprise students that a poster presentation will be the assessment tool that is used to evaluate their understandings and research efforts.	Students who have access to home computers and the support of significant adults will require less in-class time on their posters. Students who lack these resources will need more in-class time.
6. Inform students they can start their posters at home and that they are due in 4 days. They will have some class time in the next few days to work on the poster after they have gathered some of their research information.	
7. Advise students that they can sign out some of the supplies they need to work on their posters, if necessary.	
8. Distribute and review the Instructions for the Poster Project, What's My Element's Story (Appendix 4A).	
9. Circulate and go over the Poster Rubric (Appendix 4B).	
10. Instruct students that for homework each student is to look up the symbol for his or her element and make a neck tag (oak tag or construction paper, with string and reinforcement tabs for the holes). It should be 8″ by 8″ in size and sturdy enough to be worn for several activities in future.	

Closure (10 minutes)

Ask students to summarize their learning for the day. Invite students to list one thing they already knew about elements. Invite them to write down two new ideas about elements that they want to explore further. Have them share their thinking in a small group and then debrief with the whole class	This is a perfect opportunity for the teacher to listen carefully to students' conceptions, misconceptions, and what they believe their new learning to be. Based upon the data gathered during closure activity, the teacher should review any misconceptions about elements or move ahead with the next lab.

Lesson 4.2: The Elements: Up Close and Personal

Time allocation: 2–3 class periods

Concepts

C5	Chemical properties	C10	Compound
C7	Chemical reactivity	C19	Scientific investigation
C9	Element		

Principles

P6   Different elements have different physical and chemical properties.

P8   Elements can be grouped together depending on their physical and chemical properties.

P9   Reactivity is an example of a chemical property of elements that varies from one element to another.

P10   Elements can be categorized into metals, nonmetals, and semimetals (metalloids).

P12   Matter varies in its ability to chemically react with other matter.

P13   The nature of matter can be explored through scientific investigations.

P15   Elements vary in their chemical reactivity.

Skills

S1   Identify characteristics

S2   Describe characteristics

S3   Analyze

S4   Compare and contrast

S7   Identify patterns

S8   Categorize

Standard

SD1   Students will develop an understanding about the structures and properties of matter and chemical reactions.

Guiding Question

1. Can chemical reactivity between elements be used to differentiate groups of elements?

Unit Sequence—Core Curriculum	Teacher Reflections
Introduction	
Introductory Activities (25 minutes) 1. Distribute and review **Instructions for Reactivity of Substances Lab** (Appendix 4D). 2. Distribute and review the **Data Collection Table** (Appendix 4E). 3. Distribute and review the **Questions for Reactivity of Substances Lab** (Appendix 4F).	In previous lessons students might have been introduced to the concept of periodicity, as evidenced by the change in state of matter at room temperature as you go **across a row (period).** This lesson explores another aspect of periodicity; that is, chemical reactivity occurs across rows, too. In a think-pair-share, invite students to reflect on their earlier work with elements and compounds and define "element." In large group discussion, record answers on flip chart paper. In a second think-pair-share, ask students to brainstorm a list of things they know about chemical changes. Once again, record responses on flip chart paper. Share with students that they are beginning the next two to three lessons that will help them understand elements and their families. Share a metaphor if you like with the notion of families. Elements are grouped into families because they share certain properties. At the same time, they are slightly different from each of their family members. Their job as scientists will be to list some of the similarities and differences among the elements in their family. Save the flip chart paper in front of the room, and use the responses as formative data. In addition, return to the items on the flip chart paper to underscore accurate understandings, correct misconceptions, and elaborate on understandings.
Preparation	
Gather materials for the lab. • Copy Instructions for Reactivity of Substances Lab for all students. • Copy Questions for Reactivity of Substances Lab for all students. • Iron nail (make sure it is not a stainless steel nail) • Sandpaper (to shine up the nail before the experiment) • Penny • Graphite (break a pencil tip or buy some replacement sticks for a graphite pencil) • Vinegar	

(Continued)

(Continued)

Unit Sequence—Core Curriculum	Teacher Reflections
Teaching Strategies and Learning Experiences (50–55 minutes)	
1. Direct students to conduct the lab (Class Session 1). 2. Advise students that there will be a class discussion the next day, as the lab materials must sit overnight (Class Session 1). 3. While students are conducting the lab activity, collect the posters, put their posters around the room, grouping the posters in families, so that you end up with a partial periodic table of element posters. 4. Instruct students to examine their peers' posters after they finish their lab work (Class Session 1).	
	Prepare some sort of accountability process for students to ensure they appreciated or learned something from the work of others. "Exit Slips" are a good way to capture this information and hold students accountable (see examples at the end of this lesson, **Lesson 2 Exit Slip** (Appendix 4C). Collect these slips as students exit your class.
5. As an introduction to the second day of this lesson, randomly select elements from each of the eight major families. Invite the students who did the posters for those elements to review their posters, emphasizing similar properties that elements have within a family (Class Session 2).	It is important in teaching to provide frequent opportunities to paraphrase, summarize, draw interconnections, and review. It is always better if students actually take responsibility for these aspects of the learning process. In addition, it is important for students to think critically and, therefore, students should be asked to demonstrate their abilities to compare and contrast properties between families. An example of what you might expect a student who represents an element from Family 1A to conclude is that all of its group's elements react violently with water. On the contrary a member of Group VIIA would conclude its family members are unreactive with water. Students should be directed to compare and contrast trends in melting and boiling points of elements for these same two families (e.g., Family IA elements have higher melting and boiling points than those of Family VIIA). This review discussion will lay the groundwork for student analysis and discussion of the lab results.

Unit Sequence—Core Curriculum	Teacher Reflections
6. Discuss the results of the experiment by bringing together two sets of lab groups to make foursomes. The groups of four will compare results and begin to answer the questions for the lab (Class Session 2).	It is critical that students share their data with peers, as this process is analogous to what scientists do when they share data at meetings. Students need to recognize that it is important to compare results to ensure their validity. Circulate to each group assisting them with the analysis and conclusions.
7. Have the larger groups of four put their agreed upon (individually revised if necessary) results on the board (Class Session 2 or 3).	
8. Check to make sure that their results show that three of the elements had high reactivity, copper, iron, and silver, and carbon in its graphite and diamond forms is unreactive (Class Session 2 or 3).	Students should recognize copper, iron, and silver as metals and carbon as a nonmetal because of its lack of reactivity.
9. Invite students to suggest into what group, metal or nonmetal, they would put each of these elements based only on its chemical reactivity (Class Session 2 or 3).	The latter discussion serves to distinguish between the two major property categories, physical versus chemical. They should realize that most nonmetals are nonreactive with the exceptions of the halogen family, which consists of reactive gases. This
10. To summarize, have students discuss how they can differentiate between metals and nonmetals using physical and chemical properties.	question brings them back to the entire periodic table and forces them to realize that they must be careful with generalizations.
11. Ask students, "Why is the statement, all nonmetals are nonreactive, incorrect?" (Class Session 2 or 3)	
12. Collect students' answers to the lab questions (Class Session 2 or 3).	

Closure (10–15 minutes)

Review the fact that elements as well as families of elements can vary in their chemical properties, such as reactivity.	It is important that students take a "step back" and look at the "Periodic forest" without being blinded by the "trees of elements." Ask students for some generalizations they can make about the table, including trends within families and those across periods. Write these on the board as they will serve as the summary of how the structure of the periodic table can be so useful.
Instructions for Reactivity of Substance Lab	
1. Each student will wear safety glasses throughout this lab.	
2. Each group will go to the stations around the room and carry out the reactions as instructed at the site.	

(Continued)

(Continued)

Unit Sequence—Core Curriculum	Teacher Reflections
3. Each student will identify the states of matter included in the reaction and record and discuss his or her observations. Each station is equipped with a thermometer except for the match and soda stations. 4. Each student will think and discuss whether what he or she saw was a chemical or physical change and why. 5. The lab partners will discuss all the questions at the end of the lab sheet, and then each partner will answer the questions on his or her own lab sheet.	

Lesson 4.3: We Are Family!

Time allocation: 2–3 class periods

Concepts

C1	Reactant	C12	Metal
C2	Product	C13	Semimetal
C5	Chemical properties	C14	Nonmetal
C6	Physical properties	C15	Noble gas
C7	Chemical reactivity	C16	Reactive gas
C9	Element	C17	"Families" of elements
C10	Compound	C18	Periodicity

Principles

P1   Matter is made of elements that can be by themselves or joined to form compounds.

P6   Different elements have different physical and chemical properties.

P8   Elements can be grouped by their chemical properties.

P9   Reactivity is an example of a chemical property of elements.

P10   Elements can be categorized into metals, nonmetals, and semimetals.

P11   Tables can be used to organize large amounts of information and therefore make data more manageable.

P17   Groups of elements have similarities, much like families.

Skills

S1   Identify characteristics

S2   Describe characteristics

S3   Analyze

S4   Compare and contrast

S7   Identify patterns

S8   Categorize

Standard

SD1   Students will develop an understanding about the structures and properties of matter and chemical reactions.

Guiding Questions

1. How can so many compounds be made from so few elements?
2. How do scientists learn about elements and their compounds?
3. Why do scientists group elements based on their chemical properties?

Unit Sequence—Curriculum of Practice	Teacher Reflections
Preparation	
Teacher Information • Most metals are ductile. • Most metals have luster or shininess. • Most metals conduct electricity. • Most metals are heavy for their size (have a high density). • Most metals are malleable, which means they can be hammered into sheets. • Selenium exists in several allotropic forms (elements that exist in different structures and as a result have different physical and chemical properties). • The work "period" as it is used in reference to the periodic table means a completion of a cycle. • The work "periodicity" as it is used in reference to the periodic table means the quality of re-occurring. "Google" for a copy of the periodic table if the chart is not readily available to students. The following web site contains multiple versions of frequently used images that can be downloaded with ease (http://search.live.com/images/results.aspx?q=periodic+Table&form=IIRE0#).	

(Continued)

Unit Sequence—Curriculum of Practice	Teacher Reflections
Introduction	
Introductory Activities (5 minutes) Explain to students that they will be participating in an activity that requires them to wear their element name tag and complete a series of activities. While they are moving about the room, they are to be thinking about how their movement reveals information about chemical elements and the way they react and interact with other elements.	
Teaching Strategies and Learning Experiences (2 class periods)	
1. Put the students in small groups of elements that are from the same family or group on the periodic table, which means groups of three or four (see Lesson 1 for the families/groups) (Class Session 1). 2. Instruct the student who researched hydrogen that he or she is to spend half of his or her time in two groups (make sure he or she goes to the group of elements from Family I and Family VII). 3. In these groups students will discuss their research finding and derive a list of similar attributes that all their elements share (e.g., tin and lead are both solids at room temperature; tin and lead are found in ores) (Class Session 1). 4. As part of a class discussion, generate a list of similarities from each group of students and put them on the board under columns labeled Group 1, Group 2, etc., starting with the lithium, sodium, and potassium group, thus mirroring the families in the periodic table. 5. Bring up representatives from each of the major families and have each member of the group identify one or two major characteristics of that group (e.g., the alkali metals would say they react vigorously with water and are solid at room temperature) (Class Session 1). 6. Direct students to copy this information into their notebooks (Class Session 1). 7. Select two groups for comparison: e.g., Group 1, alkali metals, lithium, sodium, and potassium; and Group 2, another metal group, copper, gold, and silver, and compare and contrast their characteristics, encouraging students to realize that there are more similarities within a group than between groups (Class Session 1).	Do not tell the students how you are grouping them. They will discover this on their own. Circulate among the groups of students, listening carefully to their conversation. Use differentiated questioning strategies to probe student understanding. For groups that appear to be puzzling over the characteristics of the elements, ask more leading questions that require "smaller bites" of knowledge from students. For students who appear to be moving ahead with easy, ask fewer leading questions that require greater synthesis on their part.

Unit Sequence—Curriculum of Practice	Teacher Reflections

Ask the students from Family I, "Why do you think you were put together as a Family I?" They should indicate that they have similar physical and/or chemical properties by giving examples of these properties (Class Session 1).
 	
    8. Question the students from the Transition Metals, "Why do you think you were put together as a group?" (Class Session 1)
 	
Inform students that these groups are called "families" in the science field, except for a group of substances that have a special name, "Transition Metal" and that there are reasons for this distinction that they will learn about in later years, as they study the actual make-up/parts of the elements themselves. Thank students and invite them to sit (Class Session 1).
 	
    9. Point out that the student groups were formed based on the fact that the members of each group have similar properties (Class Session 1).
 	
  10. Direct Families I, VII, and hydrogen to come to the front of the room (Class Session 1).
 	
  11. Ask hydrogen to explain why he or she was called to the front of the room (Class Session 1).
 	
  12. Instruct students to order themselves so that the heaviest element is facing the students seated in the class with lighter ones lined up behind them. Hydrogen can stand between both families but farthest back, as he or she is the lightest member of either family (Class Session 1).
 	
  13. Show them a copy of the periodic table (Class Session 1).
 	
  14. Invite students to share what they think the periodic table does for scientists (Class Session 1).
 	
  15. Point out the location of the eight groups or families and the Transition Metals (Class Session 1).
 	
Continue to remind students that families have similar physical and chemical properties and this reality is reflected in the organization structure of the periodic table (Class Session 1).
	Once again, listen intently to students to ensure that they are providing the correct responses. When student comments reveal misunderstandings, offer probing questions that lead students to the correct understandings about the characteristics of each family.
	
	    They should indicate that they have similar physical and/or chemical properties by giving examples of these properties.
	
	That student should realize that he has properties of both families.
	
	A graphic organizer like the periodic table is a tool that scientists use to organize a large amount of information in a logical way that allows scientists to predict properties and reactions because of its organizational structure. This visual representation may help many students who are visual learners to understand the concepts such as family and reactivity.

(Continued)

Unit Sequence—Curriculum of Practice	Teacher Reflections
16. Ask the three students who research lithium, sodium, and potassium, "In Family I, what did you discover about your reactivity? Who is most reactive and who is the least?"	Potassium should answer that he or she is the most reactive, and lithium should answer that he or she is the least reactive.
17. Ask, "In Family VII, who is most reactive and who is the least?" (Class Session 1).	Fluorine should know he or she is the most reactive element of the three, and bromine should respond as being the least.
18. Referring to the periodic table, while the students stand one in front of the other in their respective families in the front of the room, thus mirroring its structure, as the class, "What is the trend in reactivity as you go down Family I?" (Class Session 1).	Students should realize that as you get larger and go down the family, reactivity goes up.
19. Ask students, "What is the trend in reactivity as you go down Family VII?" (Class Session 1).	Students should recognize that as you get larger and down the family, reactivity goes down.
20. Inform students that the periodic table can be used to examine trends and then the trends can be used to predict the characteristics of the elements without looking up the specifics of the element. For instance, tell students if in fact the most reactive solid is found in Family I, which element would it be? Have one student volunteer come up to the periodic table and identify it (Class Session 1).	Francium is the element at the bottom of Family I, as the trend dictated that the heavier the element, the more reactive it was.
21. Ask students, "What is the least reactive element from Family VII?" Have one student volunteer come up to the periodic table and identify it (Class Session 1).	Astatine should be identified as it again follows the trend for that family, reactivity falls as you go down Family VII, which is opposite to the trend seen in Family I.
22. Have the class members carry out the following activities by moving to certain parts of the room depending on the characteristics of their respective elements. All students must be wearing their element nametags (Class Session 2).	
a. Explain that all the elements that are solids at room temperature should go to the left side of the room. Record the results on the board. Instruct students to record this information in their science notebooks when they return to their seats.	

Unit Sequence—Curriculum of Practice	Teacher Reflections
b. Inform students that whoever is a gas at room temperature should go to the right side of the room. Record the results on the board.	
c. Summon students to return to their seats, and instruct them to record this information in their science notebooks.	
d. Using the periodic table, show students that the solids are located on the left-hand side of the periodic table and the gases seem to be mostly found on the right-hand side of the table.	
e. Invite the class to describe a metal. Put their descriptors (e.g., solid at room temperature, shiny, malleable, ductile, conducts electricity) on the board. Record the results on the board.	
f. Instruct students to record this information in their science notebooks.	
g. Invite the class members who have most of the characteristics of a metal to stand on the left side of the front of the room in family groups lined one behind another (lithium, sodium, potassium [Family I], beryllium, magnesium, and calcium [Family II], copper, silver, and gold [Transition Metals], aluminum and gallium [Family III]) should come forward.	
h. Record the results on the board. Tell students to record this information in their science notebooks, making sure they describe this group as "metals."	
i. Tell students that the names of Family I and II are called the "Alkali Metals" and the "Alkaline Earth Metals," respectively. Change the Group 1 and 2 names on the board to reflect these new identities.	
j. Instruct students to add this name above the group heading in their notebooks.	
k. Inform students that aluminum and gallium are from what is called the "Boron Family." Change Group 3's name to "Boron Family."	Boron, silicon, germanium, arsenic, and selenium should come to the middle of the room.
l. Tell students to add this name above the group heading in their notebooks.	
m. Direct the students that have characteristics of nonmetals to go to the right side of the room (the members of Families VII and VIII and carbon, nitrogen, phosphorous, oxygen, and sulfur should move to the right).	

(Continued)

(Continued)

Unit Sequence—Curriculum of Practice	Teacher Reflections
n. Note the results on the board. Tell students to record this information in their science notebooks, making sure they describe this group as "nonmetals." o. Inform students that carbon heads Group 4 and the name of the family is referred to as the "Carbon Family." Change Group 4's name to "Carbon Family." p. Instruct student to add this name above the group heading in their notebooks. q. Call upon any of the remaining elements that are unsure of their "identity" to stand in the middle of the room, even if they are from families that have elements that are sure of their metallic or nonmetallic nature. r. Make sure that the students who are representing phosphorous and sulfur recognize that they have properties more like nonmetals than metals.	Point out that they have little luster, no malleability, and no ductility and do not conduct electricity or heat well. They should not be standing with these elements, metalloids, that have some of the properties of metals (e.g., metalloids conduct heat and electricity better than nonmetals; germanium is used in transistors, and silicon is used in solar cells; selenium and silicon can be shiny, depending on the allotropic form; selenium and silicon are semiconductors).
s. Copy the results on the board. Remind students to record this information in their science notebooks. t. Inform students that this group is called the "metalloids" and they come from Families III, IV, and V. u. From the nonmetal group, ask all the non-reactive gases at room temperature to step to the furthest right of the front of the room. This group will consist of helium and neon. v. Note the results on the board and have students record this information in their science notebooks. w. Point out to students that these two elements are from the same family. Describe this group as the "noble gases," (in some texts they are called "rare gases"). Tell student this is Group 8. Change the name of Group B on the board to	

Unit Sequence—Curriculum of Practice	Teacher Reflections
"Noble Gases" and have students add this name above the group heading in their notebooks. x. Direct the remaining elements (hydrogen, oxygen, nitrogen, phosphorous, fluorine, chlorine, and bromine) to separate into families based on similar properties and behaviors found during their research. y. Apprise students that through examination of other properties we find that fluorine, chlorine, and bromine, a liquid at room temperature, are more closely related to each other than to other gases included in this larger group of nonmetal gases at room temperature. Inform them that this group is called the "Halogen Family." Change the name of Group 7 on the board to "Halogen Family" and advise students to add this name above the group heading in their notebooks. z. Remind students that hydrogen reacts in ways that are similar to both families, and as a result, it is separated on the periodic table. Point this out on the table itself. Hydrogen has already been discussed as an element with a unique combination of Family I and Family VII, metal and nonmetal families, yet as a gas, it does not fall into the "metalloid" group. Advise students that nitrogen heads Group 5, and thus, this family, which included phosphorous, is called the "Nitrogen Family." Change the name of Group 5 on the board to "Nitrogen Family." Instruct them to add this name above the group heading in their notebooks.	
• Share with students that oxygen heads Group 6, and thus, this family, which included sulfur, is called the "Oxygen Family." Change the name of Group 6 on the board to "Oxygen Family." Instruct students to add this name above the group heading in their notebooks.	In case students ask why some families do not have special names, you can tell them that they some do, but they are not commonly used in most textbooks (e.g., the oxygen family is also known as the "Chalcogen Family." The name comes from the Greek word *chalkos* meaning "ore." Both oxygen and sulfur are found in most ores.
Invite students to look at the elements from the point of view of state of matter at room temperature going across the periodic table. Ask them how things change (Class Session 2).	They should see that the elements go from active solids to inactive gases in each row.

(Continued)

Unit Sequence—Curriculum of Practice	Teacher Reflections
23. Point out that at the end of every row, we come back to a solid which starts the next row. We have a pattern here that is referred to as a period. The word "period" means a completion of a cycle. Tell students it is similar to using a "period" at the end of a sentence as it signals that another sentence is coming. In the periodic table the end of a row is a period because a new row or period will start (Class Session 2).	If students encounter difficulty with this concept of cycles in the periodic table, invite them to generate other cycles that they know. Discuss with students the similarities among the cycles they have generated and then crosswalk them to the cycles in the periodic table.
24. Inform students this periodicity, the quality of re-occurring (which can be seen as you go down from one period to the next, you find an element similar to the one above it in the previous period) is the reason they call this table the "periodic table" (Class Session 2).	
25. Discuss the fact that as we go through the table, going from heavy element to heavier element, the numbers 1–109 are used as the identifier for each element.	It is not necessary to tell students at this time that this number represents the number of protons in the element's nucleus.

Closure (10 minutes)

As a whole group, invite students to share their new understandings about chemical elements and their families. Share that they have covered a great deal of material over the last 2–3 days and that they will be revisiting some of it over the next week or so. The upcoming assignments and activities will help them to deepen their understandings about the elements, their characteristics and their families. Ask students to complete a **Lesson 3 Exit Slip** (see the end of this lesson; Appendix 4G). Explain that the information they provide will help you tailor the lessons over the next few days.	Use the formative assessment data from the **Exit Slips** to gauge how well the class members understood the content about elements and their organization in the periodic table. The whole class may need to spend more time on some topics. At the same time, the formative data may reveal that only some groups of students need more time on the topics. 3" by 5" note cards will work just as well as the exit slip template provided in Appendix 4G.

Lesson 4.4: The Elements in Action

Time allocation: 1 hour, 30 minutes, 2–3 days

Concepts

C5	Chemical properties	C10	Compound
C6	Physical properties	C17	"Families" of elements
C9	Element		

Principles

P1   Matter is made of elements that can be used by themselves or joined to form compounds.

P3   Compounds are made from combining different elements in different arrangements.

P6   Different elements have different physical and chemical properties.

P7   Different compounds have different physical and chemical properties.

P16 Scientists communicate knowledge about matter in clear and varied ways.

P17 Groups of elements have similarities, much like families.

Skills

S2   Describe characteristics

S4   Compare and contrast

S9   Write creatively

S10 Use analogies or metaphors

S11 (Optional) Use computer technology to enhance communication

Standard

SD1 Students will develop an understanding about the structures and properties of matter and chemical reactions.

Guiding Question

1. Can my perception of heroes be used to convey my understanding of the nature of some element?

Unit Sequence—Curriculum of Connections	Teacher Reflections
Introduction (35 minutes)	
1. Share with students that they will be writing a story about an element that is a hero. In their creative stories, they will have to integrate the aspects of heroism and characteristics of tragic or romantic heroes/ heroines with the facts they have learned about their particular element's "personality" and "family" (Class Session 1). 2. Advise students to make sure to include characters (in addition to the hero/ heroine), setting, and plot (Class Session 1).	Writing is seen as a mode of self-expression and communication and as an aid to thought and reflection. Writing can serve as a tool to improve the quality of teaching as well as to promote deeper and more meaningful student learning. Students are usually asked to write lab reports in science classes, but are not often asked to apply knowledge in a creative way. The novelty of this activity should increase student engagement. Furthermore, the novelty may reveal latent student strengths.

(Continued)

(Continued)

Unit Sequence—Curriculum of Connections	Teacher Reflections

3. Inform students that their story should include a beginning, middle, and ending.
 	
   • The beginning establishes the setting, introduces the hero/heroine, and sets up the conflict. Remind them that a conflict is a problem or opposing force that must be confronted. Depending upon the type of hero/heroine, the hero/heroine either solves the conflict or the conflict overcomes the hero/heroine. Remember, without a conflict, there is no story.
 	
   • The body or middle of the story is the main section, and here the student should develop the conflict as well as the character of the hero/heroine. In this section the plot or action reaches its highest point, and we begin to see how the hero/heroine will fare. The hero's/heroine's qualities will be reflected by his/her actions, as well as how he or she interacts with other characters.
 	
The ending or conclusion should explain the conflict's resolution one way or another and clarify how its resolution affected the hero/heroine and any other important characters.
	Teacher-directed instruction reflects the teacher's thinking and organization of the science content. Through the use of student writing assignments, students are given opportunities to put science information into their own words, thus coming to "own it." Thus, these writing assignments not only help students construct their own knowledge of the content, but also act as a formative assessment. The data revealed in this embedded assessment can be used by the teacher to detect—and address—student misconceptions.

4. Ask students what makes someone a hero/heroine. A hero or heroine has to face various adversities. Students should talk about self-sacrifice for the sake of others or for causes (Class Session 1).
 	
5. Remind students about the two types of heroes/heroines, tragic and romantic. Give examples of both. Romeo in *Romeo and Juliet*, the Wizard in *Wizard of Oz*, Mufasa in *The Lion King*, and the Beast in *Beauty and the Beast* were tragic heroes, where as the Spaniard in the *Gladiator* and Frodo Baggins in *Lord of the Rings* are romantic heroes. Ask them to explain the difference between a romantic and a tragic hero (Class Session 1).
	In many English classes, as a result of the literature that is explored, the concepts of heroes/heroines and heroism are examined in detail. This assignment can be a collaborative effort between English department members and the science teachers to support curriculum in both disciplines.
	
	   The *romantic* hero is a character that rejects established norms and conventions, has been rejected by society, and has the self as the center of his or her own existence. The romantic hero is often the main protagonist in the literary work and there is a primary focus on the character's thoughts rather than his or her actions. Literary critic Northrop Frye noted that the Romantic hero is often "placed outside the structure of civilization and therefore represents the force of physical nature, amoral or ruthless, yet with a sense of power, and often leadership."
	
	   A *tragic hero* is a literary character who makes errors in judgment, usually in their actions, that inevitably leads to his/her own demise (death).

Unit Sequence—Curriculum of Connections	Teacher Reflections
Preparation	
If possible, work with a teacher of literature who has taught about tragic and romantic heroes and heroines.	In these discussions, it is important for teachers to emphasize the common ideas in their respective lessons. By emphasizing commonalities, students are more likely to see the connections between the disciplines of science and literature. It is also important for teachers to have some idea *when* each will present the overlapping content. With this in mind, each teacher can refer to the common content with statements to students such as: • Do you remember last month in English class when you were discussing tragic and romantic heroes? • What character was romantic? Which tragic? • How might these concepts apply to this assignment?
Teaching Strategies and Learning Experiences	
1. Distribute and review instructions for the creative story, Elements of Heroism Instructions, Appendix 4H (Class Session 1). 2. Circulate and go over the Elements of Heroism Rubric (Appendix 4I) (Class Session 1). 3. Instruct students to begin writing their creative story, the Elements of Heroism (Class Session 1). 4. If computers are available, save and print out each student's work at the end of the day (Class Session 1). 5. Direct students to work on their creative stories for homework. They must complete at least one new paragraph (mark student papers as they leave the class) (Class Session 1). 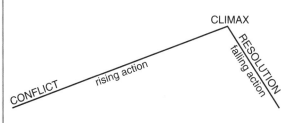	1. A tragic hero/heroine has the following characteristics: • A position of authority • A tragic flaw that leads to his or her demise • A goal • Freedom to make choices 2. A tragic hero/heroine is a sympathetic character. 3. The audience must be able to see the tragic hero's/heroine's future before the hero/heroine dies. 4. The romantic hero or heroine has the following characteristics: • He or she has rejected the norms of society. • May find himself or herself rejected by society. • He or she holds a position of power.

(Continued)

(Continued)

Unit Sequence—Curriculum of Connections	Teacher Reflections
6. Advise students to work in pairs, exchange their creative stories, and do some peer editing (Class Session 2). 7. Instruct students to finish their stories using the rest of the second day (Class Session 2). 8. Circulate from group to group assisting students in the editing process (Class Session 2). 9. Instruct students to write their final drafts of the creative stories for homework (Class Session 2). Advise students to take their stories home for homework. Have a parent read the story and work with them on editing and/or clarifying the story if necessary (Class Session 2).	One of the advantages of this assignment is that it challenges students to personify their elements and to demonstrate their understandings of an element's characteristics and behaviors in a creative way. The quality of thinking required to produce an essay of this nature is significant. If a student does not have clear understanding of the science, the essay will reveal clearly the nature of the students' misunderstandings and provide a starting point for a remedial discussion with the teacher.
Closure	
1. After assessing the students' work, ask permission to display the stories around the room so that the rest of the class members have the benefit of reading each other's work. 2. Provide time for students to conduct a "gallery walk." The structure of this can be dictated by the amount of time you have for this closure activity. 3. Ensure there is some form of accountability for the time spent examining each other's	Students need authentic audiences for their work. In addition, this activity will support peer-to-peer learning.

Unit Sequence—Curriculum of Connections	Teacher Reflections
stories, such as a brief whole class discussion at the end of the walk using some lead questions, such as: Which story did you enjoy the most and why? Which story had used the science content the most? Was it effective? **Products and Assignments** Collect and assess the creative story assignment, using the **Elements of Heroism Rubric** (Appendix 4I), and work with a teacher of literature to assess those categories that pertain to understandings aspects of romantic or tragic heroes, creativity, writing style and grammar. It will also be an assessment for the accuracy and thoroughness of its science content (Class Session 2). **Differentiation** After assessing the stories, invite students who demonstrated the deepest understanding of both the science and English content, and whose work exhibited exceptional creativity, elaboration, or connections, to consider one of the following: Option 1: Arrange for these students to go to another classroom (e.g., lower grade, a class that is studying creative writing, even at the high school level) and read their story. Option 2: Arrange for these students to have their stories published in a town or district newspaper. Option 3: For students who have artistic aptitude, tell them to create a visual representation of their story. Work with an art teacher to assist the students in conveying the overall heroic aspect of the story in their artwork. Again, find an authentic audience to display both the story and the art piece.	The rapid increase in Internet media resources, such as video sharing websites, and audio and video podcasts, as communication tools clearly demonstrates the desire to share. Students are part of a growing, participatory culture that encourages and supports sharing. Providing authentic opportunities for students to share their science understandings in a creative written fashion is important to their self-esteem and their desire to continue to learn and create. The community of learners will be enlarged as a result of the students sharing their creative products with others outside of school.

Lesson 4.5: Breaking News

Time allocation: 3 hours

Concepts

C5	Chemical properties	C20	Intended consequences
C6	Physical properties	C21	Unintended consequences
C9	Element	C22	Social context
C10	Compound	C23	Historical context

Principles

P1   Matter is made of elements that can be by themselves or joined to form compounds.

P6   Different elements have different physical and chemical properties.

P7   Different compounds have different physical and chemical properties.

P18   The study of matter and the subsequent technology and the social and historical context in which this study takes place are interdependent.

P19   Scientific discoveries and inventions have beneficial and detrimental consequences.

Skills

S1   Identify characteristics

S4   Compare and contrast

S11   (Optional) Use computer technology to enhance communication

S12   See relationships

S13   Brainstorm

S14   Plan

S15   Organize

S16   Write

S17   Demonstrate originality

Standards

SD1   Students will develop an understanding about the structures and properties of matter and chemical reactions.

SD2   Students will develop an understanding of science and technology in local, national, or global challenges.

SD3   Students will develop an understanding of science as a human endeavor, the nature of scientific knowledge, and the historical perspectives about science.

Guiding Questions

1. What is an element's story?
2. Are scientific discoveries and innovations influenced by the historical and social context in which they occur?

Unit Sequence—Curriculum of Connections	Teacher Reflections
Preparation	

Teacher Information

1. In the journalism field "copy" is the term used for the material that will be set up for printing.
2. In the journalism field "byline" is the second line under a newspaper article's title or main heading that includes the writer's name.
3. Sodium tripolyphosphate ($Na_5P_3O_{10}$) is found in detergents.
4. Sodium metaborate ($NaBO_2$) is used in herbicides.

Material and Resources

- Collect resources related to journalism (e.g., copies of different newspaper front pages, list of terms used in the newspaper industry, such as "copy" and "byline") for students to use in their efforts to simulate the front page of a newspaper.
- Collect resources on the elements/compounds that the students will be researching containing information about their discovery, history, and uses. The following three volumes would supply all the initial information students would need about the uses of the element, especially the useful compounds it forms. [Newton, D. (1999). *Chemical elements from carbon to krypton* (Vols. 1, 2, and 3). Detroit, MI: UXL].
- Stencils
- Rulers
- Magic markers
- Scissors
- White paper
- (Optional) Computers
- (Optional) Publishing software (e.g., Microsoft Publisher, Adobe Creative Suite). If this software is not available, the articles can be typed using regular word processing software and made into columnar format.

Universal Themes

- System
- Cause and effect

(Continued)

(Continued)

Unit Sequence—Curriculum of Connections	Teacher Reflections
Preparation Activities 1. Gather the information resources for the list of possible elements from which students can choose. These elements are ones that students have already researched. Include an important compound for each element in case students would rather write about the history of the compound's discovery or significant use (see **Element and Compound List for Featured Article, Appendix 4J**). The list contains only a few examples of compounds, and students can choose any compound that contains one of their elements but it cannot be a compound that was already discussed in class (e.g., magnesium hydroxide, iron oxide (rust), magnesium sulfate (milk of magnesia), acetic acid (vinegar), potassium bitartrate (cream of tartar), etc.). This list should help constrain the amount of informational resources you must provide for students (Class Session 1). 2. Collect multiple copies of front-pages from newspapers. 3. Make copies of the following handouts: **Element and Compound List for Featured Article (**Appendix 4J**), **Instructions for the Worthy Elements of News Project** (Appendix 4K), **Tips for Journalistic Writing** (Appendix 4L), **Newspaper Front Page Self-Assessment Rubric** (Appendix 4M), **Newspaper Front Page Teacher Assessment Rubric** (Appendix 4N), and the **Grade Evaluation Format** (Appendix 4O). 4. Secure poster boards for each student or have students purchase them ahead of time (Class Session 2). 5. (Optional) Arrange for access to a computer laboratory (Days 2–4) 6. Create a template to be used by each group for a front page if computers are to be used. It should contain an area for the newspaper title and multiple columns into which students can insert the articles that have been typed using a word processing program.	Student choice in this learning activity is constrained. The choice is restricted because students must choose among the elements or compounds they researched in the previous lessons. Regardless of the limited nature of the current choice, it is essential that the teacher guide a student's choice for this newspaper article assignment. The critical aspect is the complexity of the element or compound. Some elements are more complex than others and have a more extensive and complicated history. Thus, guide students with greater background knowledge about science and history to those elements that will require a deeper understanding of both chemistry and history. Guide students with less background knowledge to those elements that have less complexity, yet will still provide an optimum level of challenge.

Unit Sequence—Curriculum of Connections	Teacher Reflections
Introduction (25 minutes)	
1. (Optional) Advise students that they can use Internet sites below if needed for their research on their element or compound (Days 1–4). See http://web.buddyproject. org/web017/web017/research.html. Click on the element "sodium" and then click on the words "sodium party" and browse though the pictures and videos accordingly. 2. Share with the students that they will be creating a newspaper front page in which they will feature a historical event associated with one of the elements or its important compounds that was already researched for the poster project by one of the current group members (Class Session 1). 3. In addition, inform students that they will have to do research and write about three other historical events that occurred during the same period of time as when their group's element or compound "made history" (Class Session 1). 4. Advise students that they are to work on this project at home (e.g., research, typing, and stenciling) each of the next three nights (Class Session 1). 5. Distribute examples of real newspaper front pages (Class Session 1). 6. Briefly discuss the nature of journalistic writing and how it varies from creative and short story writing: Distribute and review **Tips for Journalistic Writing** (Class Session 1) 7. Discuss some of the vocabulary such as "copy," "byline," and "editorial" (Class Session 1). 8. Circulate and review **Instructions for the Worthy Elements of News Project** with students (Class Session 1). 9. Distribute and review the **Newspaper Front Page Self-Assessment Rubric** and the **Newspaper Front Page Teacher-Assessment Rubric** (Class Session 1).	This project will provide students an opportunity to link the information regarding the properties and behaviors of the element they have previously studied to the historical and social contexts of its discovery or use. As a result of this activity, students will better understand that scientists and their discoveries are inexorably linked to the world in which they exist. Students will develop an appreciation for the process of scientific discovery that includes understanding that scientific exploration does not occur in isolation. The context in which scientific discovery and innovation take place is intertwined with the political and social landscape of the time in which the science understandings are evolving. By examining the connections between science and other historical events, students can see that scientific innovation is always affected by the cultural and political environment in which it is rooted. The interdisciplinary nature of these lessons makes it an illustrative example of the Curriculum of Connections parallel. Specifically, the big idea in these sessions is "system." This big idea helps students to see the whole world in a "grain of sand." The elements in the periodic table are a system. Further, the discovery of each element occurred within a social, historical, and political system. The notion of system serves as a bridge as students create real-world connections across disciplines, time periods, and cultures. Within this set of lessons, students will find themselves answering the following questions:

(Continued)

(Continued)

Unit Sequence—Curriculum of Connections	Teacher Reflections
10. Break the students into groups of two or three. Advise them that each student is to research and type at least one article. Instruct them that they will be asked to document their contributions to the project at a later time (Class Session 1). 11. Distribute the **Element and Compound List for Featured Article** sheet to the groups of students (Class Session 1). 12. Advise students to use the list to select an element or compound to use for the basis of the featured article and report this information to you. No two groups can feature the same element or compound (Class Session 1).	• How does looking at the periodic table reinforce my understanding of the word "system"? • How does my current understanding of "system" help me understand other systems? • What connections do I see between what I am studying and my own life and times? The integration of writing instruction into all disciplines is receiving more attention. Teaching literacy skills is increasingly seen as every teacher's responsibility—not just that of English teachers. Asking students to explore the type of writing used in newspaper journalism and coupling this with the use of technology, if possible, should prove to be more engaging for students. It is important to ensure that each student contributes to the newspaper front page product. The student self-assessment rubric, which must be signed by all partners of a student's group, will serve to document each student's contributions to the project. The rubric will necessitate that students reflect on what they learned as they examine their specific contributions to the project. This, in turn, reinforces students' responsibilities for their learning. Point out to students that the key features on the self-assessment rubric carry different weights. Review the rubric carefully with them. Share the rationale for the weighting. Specifically the comprehensiveness, significance, and accuracy of the scientific and historical content are more important than the mechanics and supplementary features, for example.
Teaching Strategies and Learning Experiences	
1. Distribute the resources to each group as appropriate to begin the research process (Class Session 2). 2. Take students to the library to complete their research (Class Session 2).	The teacher's role during the next few days is critical. Rather than preparing other lessons, the teacher must actively rove from group to group. Ask each group questions, such as: "What are you learning?" "How is your element used?" "Why was your element

Unit Sequence—Curriculum of Connections	Teacher Reflections
3. If possible, have students use the computer lab to begin the writing process for their feature article (Class Session 2).	needed at that particular time?" Then, listen thoughtfully while students verbalize. Be attentive to misunderstandings and misconceptions. Use questions to guide and shape their thinking so that they dispel their misconceptions.
4. Instruct students to write and type on the computer one more article for homework.	Also, pay careful attention to the connections they are making between science content and scientific and historical context. Specifically, scientific advances are affected—positively and negatively—by their historical context. This principal operates today. Understanding this connection will help students see that they play a significant role in scientific discoveries. For example, students have access to freeze-dried food and disposable diapers because of the space exploration in the 1960s. Across their lifetime, students will have the opportunity, as taxpayers and voters, to influence the course of scientific discoveries and history.
5. Collect the two articles, review them, give students feedback regarding the accuracy of the content and the grammar and have them make the edits (Days 2 and 3).	
6. Direct students to work on writing and typing the rest of the articles (Days 3 and 4).	
7. If publishing software is available, have student import the articles into pages. If not, have student create columns in the word processing software by using tables without borders or shading.	
8. Remind students to find appropriate graphics to use in their newspaper front page (Class Session 1).	
9. Instruct students to create a title for their newspaper (Class Session 1).	
10. Remind students to work on this project for homework and to make sure each member leaves each day knowing his/her responsibility for the evening's homework (Class Sessions 2, 3, and 4).	
Closure	
The students will view each other's work on a bulletin board display in the future.	It is important to share students' work and to use it as a subsequent tool for teaching as often as possible.

Unit 4 Appendixes

APPENDIX 4A: INSTRUCTIONS FOR THE POSTER PROJECT, WHAT'S MY ELEMENT'S STORY?

1. Each student will create a poster on poster board that is sized within the following dimensions: width range 15"–22"; length range 22"–25"; poster should depict the information gathered during research.

2. No freehand writing will be permitted on the poster. The information must be **typed** or **written using stencils**.

3. The following information must be included on the poster:

   a. The name and symbol of the element
   b. Two to three physical properties
   c. One to two chemical properties
   d. Discovery of the element (at minimum of three historical facts, who, when, and where)
   e. Occurrence in nature of the element
   f. Extraction or production method
   g. Use(s) and compounds of the element
   h. Health effects for animals or plants, if information is available

4. The research notes will be turned in with the poster.

5. Pictures, drawings, diagrams, or graphs should be included if possible as they add visual appeal and deepen understanding.

6. A bibliography of resources must be included using proper MLA format.

7. The poster will be assessed using a rubric that evaluates the quality of the content, the fact that all required components on the poster are included, thoroughness of research notes, neatness, visual appeal, spelling accuracy, and a complete and correctly formatted bibliography.

APPENDIX 4B: POSTER RUBRIC

Criterion	1	2	3	4	Your Score
Quality of Science Content	Information is cursory or incorrect. Little understanding of content is evident from presentation.	Some solid information presented; however, some information is incorrect or cursory.	Information is clear and correct throughout most of presentation.	Information is well presented, clear, and correct throughout.	1 2 3 4
Criteria	Much of the required criteria required are missing or contain insufficient information.	Some of the criteria are missing, and the lack of sufficient research is evident in some of the required areas.	Although the eight criteria were addressed, they could have been addressed more thoroughly as a result of more extensive research.	All of the eight criteria were completely and thoroughly addressed.	1 2 3 4
Graphics	Images do not connect to text and/or are not relevant and do not deepen understanding of the "element's story."	Images are not always relevant and thus do not provide additional insight as to the "element's story." Text citations are not always present.	Images are mostly relevant and add to the understanding of the "element's story." Text citations are usually present and identify the images.	Images are relevant, and complement the text. Each image is cited in the text and identified. The number of images is appropriate, and they enhance the understanding of the "element's story."	1 2 3 4
Mechanics	Text contains many spelling/grammar errors. Sentences seem disconnected, and there is carelessness throughout.	Text contains some spelling/grammar errors. Little logical structure or flow to sentences. Evidence of carelessness in writing.	Grammar and spelling are nearly flawless. Logical sequence apparent. Some wording is careless. Inconsistency in style.	Grammar and spelling are flawless, and the flow provides a logical pathway of ideas. Consistent and engaging style throughout.	1 2 3 4

(Continued)

(Continued)

Criterion	1	2	3	4	Your Score
Following Directions	Many of the directions such as poster size, keeping complete research notes, attaching research notes, no hand writing on the poster, etc., were not followed and only some deadlines were met.	Many of the directions such as poster size, keeping complete research notes, attaching research notes, no hand writing on the poster, etc., were not followed or deadlines were not met.	One or more of the directions such as poster size, keeping complete research notes, attaching research notes, no hand writing on the poster, etc., or deadlines were not followed or met.	All of the directions such as poster size, keeping complete research notes, attaching research notes, no hand writing on the poster, etc., were followed, and deadlines were met.	1 2 3 4
Poster Design	The poster is either cluttered or too empty. There is no text/image balance. No attention paid to variation in design.	Some parts of the poster are either cluttered or empty. Inconsistent attention paid to sizing of graphics, placement of graphics and text, and text wrapping.	Most of the poster contains well-placed objects, with thoughtful text/image balance and logical text wrapping.	Objects and text on the poster are well placed and sized. Poster is not cluttered or too empty. Logical text wrapping.	1 2 3 4
Quality of Bibliography	The bibliography is incomplete and contains errors in format.	The bibliography is incomplete or contains errors in format.	The bibliography is complete but contains a few errors in format.	The bibliography is complete and contains no errors in format.	1 2 3 4

APPENDIX 4C: LESSON 2 EXIT SLIP

Name _____

3 important facts I have learned from these posters:

2 connections I made with these posters:

APPENDIX 4D: INSTRUCTIONS FOR REACTIVITY OF SUBSTANCES LAB

1. Each student will wear safety glasses throughout this lab.

2. Each group will go to the stations around the room and carry out the reactions as instructed at the site.

3. Each student will identify the states of matter included in the reaction and record and discuss his or her observations. Each station is equipped with a thermometer except for the match and soda stations.

4. Each student will think and discuss whether what he or she saw was a chemical or physical change and why.

5. The lab partners will discuss all the questions at the end of the lab sheet, and then each partner will answer the questions on his or her own lab sheet.

APPENDIX 4E: DATA COLLECTION TABLE

Name _____   Date _____

Reactants	Observations/Experience	Evidence of a Reaction? Y or N
1. Copper penny and vinegar (leave overnight)	Today:	Today:
	Next day:	Next day:
2. Carbon graphite in vinegar (leave overnight)	Today:	Today:
	Next day:	Next day:
3. Iron nail in vinegar (leave overnight)	Today:	Today:
	Next day:	Next day:
4. From your experience, what will happen to an iron nail that sits in air for an extended period of time?		
5. From your experience, what will happen to a piece of pencil tip (graphite, which is a form of carbon) that sits in air for an extended period of time?		
6. From your experience, what will happen to a diamond (which is another form of carbon) that sits in air for an extended period of time?		
7. From your experience what happens when silver is exposed to air for an extended period of time?		

APPENDIX 4F: QUESTIONS FOR REACTIVITY OF SUBSTANCES LAB

Name _____ Date _____

1. Which substances react relatively with air and which do not?

2. Which substances reacted with vinegar easily and which did not?

3. Based on the data above, put the four elements into two categories and give the categories names.

APPENDIX 4G: LESSON 3 EXIT SLIP

Three new understandings about elements and/or the periodic table.

1. _____

2. _____

3. _____

Two questions you still have:

1. _____

2. _____

One resource that you need to understand the content better (e.g., pictures, time to discuss my learning with a partner, extra help, a video):

1. _____

APPENDIX 4H: ELEMENTS OF HEROISM INSTRUCTIONS

1. Using the properties, history, uses, and source of an element that you researched, write a story in which the element is personified as either a tragic or romantic hero.

2. The story should be written from the element's point of view, incorporating the chemical and historical aspects of the element as "he" or "she" proceeds through the adventure.

3. Remember to address the important aspects of heroism and its tragic or romantic aspects.

4. The story must be typed and be a minimum of two pages.

5. The story will be evaluated using the **Elements of Heroism Rubric**.

Name _____ Date _____

APPENDIX 4I: ELEMENTS OF HEROISM RUBRIC

Criteria	1	2	3	4	Your Score
Focus	The story addresses the topic of tragic or romantic "hero elements" but loses focus by including irrelevant ideas.	The story is focused on the topic and includes a few loosely related ideas.	The story is focused on the topic and includes relevant ideas.	The story is focused, purposeful, and reflects clear insight and ideas.	1 2 3 4
Quality of Science Content	The science content is incomplete or contains misunderstandings or inaccuracies.	The science content is briefly explained and contains some misunderstandings or inaccuracies.	The science content is explained sufficiently with few or no inaccuracies.	The science content is complete, accurate, and explained thoroughly. It is elaborated in such a way that conceptual understanding on the part of the reader is ensured.	1 2 3 4
Understanding of Literature Content	Apparent misunderstanding of material on heroes.	Limited understanding of material displayed by vague, unclear language or ideas.	Fairly clear understanding of material as evidenced by adequate expression of ideas.	Clear understanding of material displayed by clear, concrete language and complex ideas.	1 2 3 4
Mechanics	Frequent errors in spelling, grammar, and punctuation.	Grammar or punctuation errors, but the spelling is accurate.	Occasional grammatical errors and questionable word choice.	Nearly error-free, which reflects clear understanding and thorough proofreading.	1 2 3 4
Structural Organization	Story lacks logical progression of ideas.	Story includes brief skeleton (introduction, body, and conclusion) but lacks transitions.	Story includes logical progression of ideas aided by clear transitions.	Story is powerfully organized and fully developed.	1 2 3 4
Support	Few to no solid supporting ideas or evidence for the story content.	Story lacks sufficient support details and is loosely developed.	Story includes some supporting ideas and/or evidence for the story content.	Story includes developed details and provides superior support for the story content.	1 2 3 4

APPENDIX 4J: ELEMENT AND COMPOUND LIST FOR FEATURED ARTICLE

- Sodium (sodium hydroxide, sodium citrate, sodium nitrite)
- Potassium (e.g., potassium nitrate)
- Magnesium
- Calcium (e.g., calcium chloride)
- Copper
- Silver (e.g., silver chloride)
- Gold
- Boron (e.g., sodium metaborate)
- Aluminum (e.g., aluminum sulfate)
- Gallium
- Silicon (e.g., silicon dioxide)
- Nitrogen (e.g., nitrous oxide, nitric oxide)
- Phosphorous (e.g., sodium tripolyphosphate)
- Arsenic
- Sulfur (e.g., sulfuric acid, hydrogen sulfide)
- Bromine (e.g., potassium bromide)
- Fluorine (e.g., hydrogen fluoride)
- Chlorine (e.g., potassium chloride)
- Helium
- Hydrogen (e.g., hydrogen peroxide, potassium hydroxide)

APPENDIX 4K: INSTRUCTIONS FOR
THE WORTHY ELEMENTS OF NEWS PROJECT

Name _____ Date _____

In an effort to provide you with a better understanding of the context in which science takes place, you will be researching the historical and social context of the discovery or significant use(s) of an element or a compound. Each group will create a newspaper front page with the featured story being about the discovery or importance of an element or compound. Students will use word-processing or preferably publishing software, if available, to produce the articles for the newspaper front page.

General Project Requirements

- Each group of students will create a title for their newspaper and follow proper journalistic format for the items on a newspaper's front page, using the examples supplied by the teacher.
- Each newspaper front page must contain a feature article about the element or compound. It must include information about its discovery *or* importance. The previous research done by one of your group members on an element may assist you with this feature article.
- Each group will research *three other historical events* that occurred during the year of the element's or compound's discovery.
- Each of the other *three nonscience articles* must come from a different subject area, such as politics, economics, health, environment, sports, or entertainment. Each of these will be included on the front page of the newspaper.
- Each group will include supplementary features (e.g., graphs, letters, classified ads, print ads) in their newspaper front page.
- Each student will be required to complete the self-assessment that gauges his contributions to the group project. Each member of the group must validate the other group members' contributions by signing the bottom of each other's rubrics.

Specific Project Requirements

- The newspaper itself must be titled in large print, so that the title covers a significant portion of the total front-page width, as it does in a real newspaper.
- No free-hand writing will be permitted on the poster, including the title. The information must be *typed or written using stencils.*
- The articles (**six** in total) will be laid out on poster board that is sized within the following dimensions: width range: 15"–22"; length range: 22"–25."
- There will be *four* columns to the newspaper and no more than ½" between columns or between articles. The title of each of the articles must be bigger than the print used in the article itself.
- The article fonts should be easy to read (e.g., Times Roman) and the size should vary, as it does in real newspapers, but not be too small, so it is not too difficult to read.
- The newspaper must contain three or four pictures.
- Appropriate newspaper format, such as bylines, is to be followed (use real newspapers as your model).
- A typed bibliography is required.
- The project is due _____.
- Each student in the group must attach a **Newspaper Front Page Self-Assessment Rubric** to the back of the poster board.

Parent or Guardian's Signature _____

Date _____

APPENDIX 4L: TIPS FOR JOURNALISTIC WRITING

- Use third person point of view (avoid "you" or "I").
- Determine which of the 5 Ws and 1 H (who, what, where, when, why, and how) need to be included in the lead (which are essential).
- Select the key thought and put it first; emphasize this thought in the first five or six words by using a few colorful words that will spark the reader's interest.
- Use the inverted pyramid style (key facts first, followed by the less important ones).
- Limit a newspaper paragraph to one topic or one aspect of a topic.
- Keep paragraphs short. They make stories visually attractive due to narrow newspaper columns.
- Make the appearance of a story more appealing by using white space within and around it.
- Limit paragraphs to 75 words.
- Start paragraphs with significant words.
- Enliven stories with direct quotations. Quotations should be well chosen and should enhance a report. Quotations draw readers into a story, and, consequently, readers feel as if they are being directly spoken to (quotes typically are used in alternate paragraphs).
- Do not add any kind of editorializing. Stick to the facts and avoid giving opinions.
- The following contains tips on how to write effective headlines

Headline Dos

- Limit the number of words—6 to 10, generally.
- Use a smaller point size as you work down the page (the most important stories are highest on the page and have the largest headlines).
- Make sure the headline touches the byline, or first paragraph, of its article (don't put a photo between them).
- Give the most general, overall focus/summary of the story.
- Remember that the headline may be the only reason the reader decides to read the story.
- Avoid headlines that can have more than one interpretation.
- Use strong, active verbs ("to be" verbs are generally understood, but not written out).
- Use present tense verbs.
- Express a complete thought. Headlines usually read like simple sentences.
- Use a secondary headline—or subhead—to convey an additional idea of a story.
- Substitute a comma for the word "and."
- Capitalize only the first word and proper nouns and adjectives.
- Write a headline that is grammatically correct. Make sure a headline has a subject and verb.

Headline Don'ts

- Mislead the reader about the content of the article.
- Downplay, exaggerate, or sensationalize.
- Use the name of the school unless it's absolutely necessary.
- Use the verbs "participate" or "experience."
- Use labels or phrases for headlines.
- Put a period at the end of a headline.
- Use names, unless very well recognized. Use grades or positions instead.
- Use abbreviations or slang.
- Trivialize a serious story with the inappropriate use of puns or other word play.
- Separate words that belong together in a phrase. (All words in infinitives and prepositional phrases should be on one line.)
- Capitalize every word or every important word.
- Use "a," "an," or "the."

APPENDIX 4M: NEWSPAPER FRONT PAGE SELF-ASSESSMENT RUBRIC

Name _____   Date _____

Reactions and Interactions

Criteria	1	2	3	4	Your Score
Quality of Content in Featured Article	The science content of the featured science article is incomplete or contains misunderstandings or inaccuracies.	The science content of the featured science article is briefly explained, and contains some misunderstandings or inaccuracies.	The content of the featured science article addresses the scientific discovery or innovation in a thorough manner. The science content is explained sufficiently and with few or no inaccuracies.	The content of the featured science article is complete, accurate, and explained thoroughly. It is elaborated in such a way that conceptual understanding on the part of the reader is ensured.	1 2 3 4
Quality of Content of Three Additional Articles	The content of the three other articles is incomplete, inaccurate, or insignificant.	The content of the three other articles is either incomplete or has some inaccuracies.	The content of the three other articles is historically accurate and significant.	The content of the three other articles is historically accurate, thorough, interesting, and significant.	1 2 3 4
Significance of the Featured Article	The article does not focus on a significant scientific event or innovation in history.	The significance of the scientific event or innovation in history is questionable.	The scientific event or innovation has historical significance.	The scientific event or innovation has great historical significance, and the article is interesting to read.	1 2 3 4
Journalistic Quality of Articles	Articles are inappropriately informal and confusing to read. No attempt has been made to engage the reader with a good lead or a clear and logical presentation of facts or concepts.	Articles lack some necessary elements of a newspaper article: a good lead, clear presentation of facts, and/or an appropriately formal writing style.	Articles have good leads, logical and clear presentation of facts, and formal writing style.	Articles have good leads, logical and clear presentation of facts, and an appropriately formal writing style. Articles are interesting to read and hold reader's attention.	1 2 3 4

(Continued)

(Continued)

Criteria	1	2	3	4	Your Score
Graphics	Graphics do not clearly support or relate to the text.	Graphics sometimes support and/or relate to the text.	Graphics usually support and/ or relate to the text.	Graphics consistently support and/or relate to the text.	1 2 3 4
Layout	Design is messy and unattractive. It does not make good use of available space. There is poor balance of text and graphics.	Design is inconsistent. Some parts are attractive and space-efficient, but other parts are not. Inconsistent or poor balance between text and graphics is evident.	Design is mostly attractive and space efficient. Good balance of text and graphics exists, for the most part.	Design is attractive and space-efficient. Excellent balance of text and graphics exists throughout.	1 2 3 4
Mechanics	Text contains many spelling/grammar errors. Sentences seem disconnected, and there is carelessness throughout.	Text contains some spelling/grammar errors. There is little logical structure or flow to sentences, and evidence of carelessness in writing.	Grammar and spelling are nearly flawless. Logical sequence apparent. Some wording is careless and style is inconsistent.	Grammar and spelling are flawless and the flow provides a logical pathway of ideas. There is consistent and engaging style throughout.	1 2 3 4
Supplementary Features (e.g., graphs, letters, classified ads, print ads)	No supplementary features are included	A few supplementary features are included.	Many supplementary features are included.	Many outstanding supplementary features are included.	1 2 3 4

APPENDIX 4N: NEWSPAPER FRONT PAGE TEACHER ASSESSMENT RUBRIC

Criterion	1	2	3	4	Your Score
Quality of Content of Featured Article	The science content of the featured science article is incomplete or contains misunderstandings or inaccuracies.	The science content of the featured science article is briefly explained and contains some misunderstandings or inaccuracies.	The content of the featured science article addresses the scientific discovery or innovation in a thorough manner. The science content is explained sufficiently and with few or no inaccuracies.	The content of the featured science article is complete, accurate, and explained thoroughly. It is elaborated in such a way that conceptual understanding on the part of the reader is ensured.	1 2 3 4
Quality of Content of 3 Additional Articles	The content of the 3 other articles was, incomplete, inaccurate, or insignificant.	The content of the 3 other articles is either incomplete or has some inaccuracies.	The content of the 3 other articles was historically accurate and significant.	The content of the articles was historically accurate, thorough, interesting, and significant.	1 2 3 4
Significance of the Featured Article	The article does not focus on a significant scientific event or innovation in history.	The significance of the scientific event or innovation in history is questionable.	The scientific event or innovation has historical significance.	The scientific event or innovation has great historical significance and the article was interesting to read.	1 2 3 4
Journalistic Quality of Articles	Articles are inappropriately informal and confusing to read. No attempt has been made to engage the reader with a good lead or a clear and logical presentation of facts or concepts.	Article lacks some necessary elements of a newspaper article: a good lead, clear presentation of facts, and/or an appropriately formal writing style.	Articles have good leads, logical and clear presentation of facts, and formal writing style.	Articles have good leads, logical, and clear presentation of facts, and an appropriately formal writing style. Articles are interesting to read and hold reader's attention.	1 2 3 4

(Continued)

(Continued)

Criterion	1	2	3	4	Your Score
Graphics	Graphics do not clearly support or relate to the text.	Graphics sometimes support and/or relate to the text.	Graphics usually support and/or relate to the text.	Graphics consistently support and/or relate to the text.	1 2 3 4
Layout	Design is messy and unattractive. Does not make good use of available space. Poor balance of text and graphics.	Design is inconsistent. Some parts are attractive and space-efficient, but other parts are not. Inconsistent or poor balance between text and graphics.	Design is mostly attractive and space efficient. Good balance of text and graphics, for the most part.	Design is attractive and space-efficient. Excellent balance of text and graphics throughout.	1 2 3 4
Mechanics	Text contains many spelling/grammar errors. Sentences seem disconnected, and there is carelessness throughout.	Text contains some spelling/grammar errors. Little logical structure or flow to sentences. Evidence of carelessness in writing.	Grammar and spelling are nearly flawless. Logical sequence apparent. Some wording is careless. Inconsistent in style.	Grammar and spelling are flawless, and the flow provides a logical pathway of ideas. Consistent and engaging style throughout.	1 2 3 4
Supplementary Features (e.g., graphs, letters, classified ads, print ads)	No supplementary features are included.	A few supplementary features are included.	Many supplementary features are included.	Many outstanding supplementary features are included.	1 2 3 4

224

APPENDIX 4O: GRADE EVALUATION FORMAT

Name _____

Date _____

The first three criteria have a weighting factor of five. The last five criteria have a weighting factor of two. Your final score is calculated as follows.

Criterion	*Score*	
1. Quality of Content of Featured Article	_____	× 5 = _____
2. Quality of Content of 3 Additional Articles	_____	× 5 = _____
3. Significance of the Featured Article	_____	× 5 = _____
4. Journalistic Quality of Articles	_____	× 2 = _____
5. Graphics	_____	× 2 = _____
6. Layout	_____	× 2 = _____
7. Mechanics	_____	× 2 = _____
8. Supplementary Features (e.g., graphs, letters, classified ads, print ads)	_____	× 2 = _____
	Total Score	_____

Index

Ascending intellectual demand (AID), 2, 3, 4, 5

Burns, D. E., 1

Cause-effect relationship in systems lesson,
  69–72
Cause/effect T-chart, 90 (figure)
Cell building blocks preassessment, 153–156
Cell structure introduction lesson, 129–134
Cell structure/function preassessment, 157–161
Cellular function lesson, 140–145, 166–167
Chemistry unit. See Periodic table unit
Coaching, 7
Core curriculum, 4–5, 8 (figure)
  ascending intellectual demand and, 4
  assessment tools and, 4
  content-assessment alignment and, 4
  differentiated instruction and, 4
  extension activities and, 4
  inductive teaching approach and, 4
  powerful understanding, support of, 4
  resource materials for, 4
  state frameworks and, 4
  student grouping arrangements and, 5
  student products and, 5
  See also Parallel curriculum model (PCM)
Cornell note-taking format, 92–93 (figure)
Crime lab investigations, 30–32
Curriculum of connections, 5–6, 8 (figure)
  ascending intellectual demand and, 5
  assessment prompts/accompanying rubrics
    and, 5
  graphic organizers and, 5
  interdisciplinary teaching and, 5
  learning activities, analytic thinking and, 5
  resource materials for, 5
  scaffolded learning and, 5
  student expertise, development of, 5–6
  teaching strategies in, 5
  thematic continuity in, 5
  See also Parallel curriculum model (PCM)
Curriculum of identity, 6–7, 8 (figure)
  extension activities and, 7
  fit concept and, 7
  individual student learning profile and, 7
  learning activities, analytic thinking and, 7

self-actualization and, 7
student products and, 7
student surveys and, 7
teaching strategies in, 7
See also Parallel curriculum model (PCM)
Curriculum model/basic components, 3
Curriculum of practice, 6, 8 (figure)
  assessment rubric and, 6
  indirect teaching strategies and, 6
  learning contracts and, 6
  methodologies, student use of, 6
  primary source materials, deeper
    understanding and, 6
  scaffolded learning and, 6
  Socratic questioning and, 6
  state/national standards and, 6
  student expertise, development of, 6
  student grouping, fluidity in, 6
  student products and, 6
  teaching skills of practice and, 6
  See also Parallel curriculum model (PCM)

Data collection form, 95 (figure), 213
Data summary matrix, 96 (figure)
Debriefing strategy, 5
Decision-making matrix, 98–99 (figure)
Decision-making rubric, 100 (figure)
Deep understanding, 6, 7
Differentiated curriculum, 2–3, 4
Disasters. See Science-society convergence unit
DNA extraction lab, 27–30, 49–50 (figure)
DNA fingerprinting lesson, 30–32
DNA introductory lesson, 24–27
Dominant/recessive genes lesson, 15–19,
  42–46 (figures)

Elements. See Periodic table unit
Elements of Heroism rubric, 216–217
English instruction. See Integrated
  English-science unit
European genetic history lesson, 33–36
Exit slip form, 211, 215
Expertise, 3, 5–6
Extension activities, 4, 7
Exxon Valdez oil spill. See Science-society
  convergence unit

Genetics unit, 11
advanced study resources, 61–62
appendixes for, 42–62
assessment instrument, 60
background for, 11–12
content framework for, 12–14
DNA extraction lab, 27–30, 49–50 (figure)
DNA fingerprinting/crime lab investigations
lesson, 30–32
DNA introductory lesson, 24–27
dominant/recessive genes lesson, 15–19,
42–46 (figures)
European genetic history lesson, 33–36
graphic organizer for, 47 (figure)
introduction/preassessment, 15–19,
47–48 (figures)
organizing concepts for, 12
pedigree studies lab experience, 51–54
practicing genetics lesson, 36–39, 55–60 (figures)
principles for, 12
Punnett squares/heredity prediction lesson,
19–24
researcher skill rubric, 59 (figure)
scientific argument worksheet, 57–58 (figures)
skill development in, 12–13
standards for, 13–14
unit components/rationale, 14–15
Graphic organizers, 5
cause/effect T-chart, 90 (figure)
data collection form, 95 (figure)
data summary matrix, 96 (figure)
decision-making matrix, 98–99 (figure)
decision-making rubric, 100 (figure)
Exxon Valdez event map, 91 (figure)
note-taking format, 92–93 (figure), 164
persuasive essay organizer, 101–102 (figure)
persuasive essay rubric, 103 (figure)
questions for inquiry and, 94 (figure)
researcher skill rubric, 59 (figure)
scientific argument worksheets, 57–58 (figures)
structured academic controversy discussion
web, 165 (figure)
thinking quality evaluation chart, 97 (figure)

Heredity prediction lesson, 19–24

Identity. *See* Curriculum of identity
Integrated curriculum. *See* Curriculum of
connections; Integrated English-science
unit; Periodic table unit; Science-society
convergence unit
Integrated English-science unit, 107–109
advanced study resources, 172
appendixes for, 148–172
assessments for, 112–114, 148–161, 168–171
background for, 109
cell building blocks preassessment, 153–156
cell structure introduction lesson, 129–134
cell structure/function preassessment, 157–161
content framework for, 109–111

graphic organizers for, 164–165
intracellular movement lesson, 140–145, 166–167
introduction/preassessment for, 114
note-taking form and, 164
organizing concepts for, 109–110
parallel curriculum components and, 107
The Pearl/part 1 lesson, 122–128
The Pearl/part 2 lesson, 134–140
postassessment essay, 168–171
resource materials for, 109
skill development in, 111
standards for, 110–111
story elements preassessment, 148–152
structured academic controversy and, 162–163
structured academic controversy discussion
web form, 165 (figure)
systems introduction lesson, 114–122
See also Periodic table unit
Interdisciplinary teaching, 5–6
See also Integrated English-science unit;
Periodic table unit; Science-society
convergence unit

Journalistic writing guidelines, 220–224

Kaplan, S. N., 1

Language arts. *See* Integrated English-science
unit; Periodic table unit
Learning contracts, 6
Leppien, J. H., 1, 43, 46, 58, 90, 93, 94, 95, 96, 97,
99, 102, 149, 164, 165, 167, 171, 211, 213, 214,
215, 225

Metaphoric thinking, 5, 7
Methodologic skills, 7

Newspaper front page self-assessment rubric,
221–222
Newspaper front page teacher assessment
rubric, 223–224
Note-taking format, 92–93 (figure), 164

Parallel curriculum model (PCM), 1, 8 (figure)
ascending intellectual demand and, 2, 3
basic curriculum model and, 3
components of, 3, 4–8
core curriculum and, 4–5, 8 (figure)
curriculum of connections and,
5–6, 8 (figure)
curriculum of identity and, 6–7, 8 (figure)
curriculum of practice and, 6, 8 (figure)
four parallels, application of, 8
historical background of, 1–2
holistic approach of, 8
overview of, 2–3
qualitatively differentiated curriculum and, 2–3
student expertise and, 3
The Pearl/part 1 lesson, 122–128
The Pearl/part 2 lesson, 134–140

Pedigree studies lab experience, 51–54
Periodic table unit:
   appendixes for, 208–225
   assessments for, 177
   background for, 173–174
   compound properties lesson, 194–199
   content framework for, 174–177
   data collection table, 213
   element groupings/reactivity lesson, 186–194
   Elements of Heroism rubric and, 216–217
   exit slip form, 211, 215
   featured article, element/compound list for, 218
   grade evaluation format and, 225
   integrated curriculum and, 174
   introduction lesson, 178–181
   journalistic writing, guidelines for, 220
   matter: technology/social and historical
      context lesson, 200–205
   newspaper front page self-assessment rubric,
      221–222
   newspaper front page teacher assessment
      rubric, 223–224
   organizing concepts for, 174–175
   overview of, 177–178
   parallel curriculum components and, 173–174
   physical/chemical properties of elements
      lesson, 182–186
   poster project instructions and, 208
   poster project rubric, 209–210
   principles for, 175–176
   reactivity of substances lab, 212, 214
   skill development for, 176–177
   standards for, 177
   worthy elements of news project instructions
      and, 219
Persuasive essay organizer form, 101–102 (figure)
Persuasive essay rubric, 103 (figure)
Poster projects, 208, 209–210
Practice. *See* Curriculum of practice
Problem-based learning, 7
   See also Science-society convergence unit
Products. *See* Student products
Punnet squares lesson, 19–24
Purcell, J. H., 1, 43, 46, 58, 90, 93, 94, 95, 96, 97,
      99, 102, 149, 164, 165, 167, 171, 211, 225

Questions for inquiry chart, 94 (figure)

Ranzulli, J. S., 1
Reactivity of substances lab, 212, 214
Researcher skill rubric, 59 (figure)

Scaffolded learning, 5, 6
Science-society convergence unit, 63–64
   advanced study resources, 104–105
   appendixes for, 90–105
   assessments for, 69
   background for, 64
   cause-effect relationship in systems lesson,
      69–72

   cause/effect T-chart and, 90 (figure)
   content framework for, 65–68
   data collection form and, 95 (figure)
   data summary matrix form and, 96 (figure)
   decision-making matrix form and,
      98–99 (figure)
   decision-making rubric form and, 100 (figure)
   Exxon Valdez problem introduction lesson,
      72–75, 91 (figure)
   graphic organizers for, 90–103 (figures)
   introduction/preassessment for, 69–72
   note-taking format and, 92–93 (figure)
   organizing concepts for, 65
   parallel curriculum components and,
      67–68 (table)
   persuasive essay organizer form and,
      101–102 (figure)
   persuasive essay rubric and, 103 (figure)
   principles/generalizations for, 65
   questions for inquiry chart and, 94 (figure)
   scientific vs. personal perspectives and, 64
   site prioritization/persuasive argument
      construction lesson, 82–88
   skill development in, 66
   stakeholders' research activities lesson, 76–82
   standards for, 66–67
   thinking quality evaluation chart and,
      97 (figure)
   See also Integrated English-science unit
Scientific argument worksheets, 57–58 (figures)
Self-actualization, 7
Simulations, 7
Societal issues. *See* Periodic table;
   Science-society convergence unit
Socratic questioning, 6
Stakeholders' research activities lesson, 76–82
Standards:
   life science/grades 9–12, 14
   life science/grades 5–8, 13–14
   national science standards, 66–67, 110–111, 177
   state standards for English instruction, 111
Story elements preassessment, 148–152
Structured academic controversy, 162–163,
      165 (figure)
Student expertise, 3, 5–6
Student products, 5, 6
Synetics, 5
Systems study. *See* Integrated English-science
      unit; Science-society convergence unit

Thinking quality evaluation chart, 97 (figure)
Tomlinson, C. A., 1

Valdez oil spill. *See* Science-society
   convergence unit
Visualization, 7

Worthy elements of news project, 219

Zaremba, C., 53

CORWIN

A SAGE Company

The Corwin logo—a raven striding across an open book—represents the union of courage and learning. Corwin is committed to improving education for all learners by publishing books and other professional development resources for those serving the field of PreK–12 education. By providing practical, hands-on materials, Corwin continues to carry out the promise of its motto: **"Helping Educators Do Their Work Better."**